D0768291

MATERIALS
FOR
ARCHITECTURAL
DESIGN

VICTORIA BALLARD BELL
WITH PATRICK RAND

MATERIALS
FOR
ARCHITECTURAL
DESIGN

LAURENCE KING PUBLISHING

For Bryan and Sky

Published in 2006 by Laurence King Publishing Ltd
71 Great Russell Street
London WC1B 3BP
United Kingdom
Tel: + 44 20 7430 8850
Fax: + 44 20 7430 8880
e-mail: enquiries@laurenceking.co.uk
www.laurenceking.co.uk

First published in the U.S. by
Princeton Architectural Press
37 East Seventh Street
New York, New York 10003
www.papress.com

© 2006 Victoria Ballard Bell

All rights reserved. No part of this publication
may be reproduced or transmitted in any form or
by any means, electronic or mechanical, including
photocopy, recording or any information storage
and retrieval system, without prior permission in
writing from the publisher.

A catalogue record for this book is available
from the British Library

Every reasonable attempt has been made to identify owners of
copyright. Errors or omissions will be corrected in subsequent editions.

Editing: Scott Tennent
Editorial Assistance: Dorothy Ball, Sara Hart, Lauren Nelson,
and Tiffany Wey

Design: Paul Wagner

Front and back cover photographs: Luuk Kramer Fotographie

Special thanks to: Nettie Aljian, Nicola Bednarek, Janet Behning,
Penny (Yuen Pik) Chu, Russell Fernandez, Jan Haux, Clare Jacobson,
John King, Mark Lamster, Nancy Eklund Later, Linda Lee,
Katharine Myers, Jennifer Thompson, Joseph Weston, and Deb Wood
of Princeton Architectural Press —Kevin C. Lippert, Publisher

Printed in China

Acknowledgments

This book could not have happened without the help and support of many people. Many thanks for the endless hours and wise advice I received from Katie Wakeford. Her organizational skills, talent, and focused energy made this book a reality. Without her this book would not have reached completion. Also thank you to Pat Rand for his great generosity in sharing his abundant knowledge and advice. His time, expertise, and dedication raised this book to a higher level. This publication is as much the work of Katie's and Pat's as it is of mine.

Many thanks to the readers I have asked to help: Richard Kaydos-Daniels, David Hinson, Scott Wing, George Elvin, and Shannon Turlington. Thanks to Princeton Architectural Press, Scott Tennent, Paul Wagner, and especially to Clare Jacobson, who has nursed this book along from the beginning. Thank you also to Molly Guinan and Andrea Dietz for their early research aid. This book has been made possible through the generous support of the Graham Foundation for Advanced Studies in the Fine Arts and the AIA/AAF. Thank you also to Jonathan Rose, Stephen Goldsmith, and the Enterprise Foundation for their support through the Rose Fellowship Program. Most of all thank you to my parents, Val and Dick, for their love and support. Finally, this book would never have happened without the love, encouragement, wise guidance, and endless support of my husband, Bryan.

Table of Contents

Introduction

Architecture schools typically separate the required Materials and Methods course and the design studio, creating the impression that the two have little or nothing to do with each other. This misconception goes well beyond the academic realm, as the erroneous distinction between the "what" and the "how" of architecture is seen all too frequently in professional practice. Materials are often chosen at the end of the design process or even during the generation of construction documents for a building design, as if they are a mere afterthought, a color of paint applied to the building after the design has been formulated. Whether in the classroom or in practice, to consider design without regard to material can only result in a less successful building project.

The need exists to reintegrate these components of architectural education. The rise of design/build programs in the United States such as the Rural Studio at Auburn University, Studio 804 at the University of Kansas, and the Basic Initiative Program at the University of Washington have demonstrated the effectiveness of a holistic learning pedagogy that combines design, materials, construction methods, programming, and even community service. In Europe, the ETSAM in Madrid has a program in which students go to Central America, South America, or Africa to build houses for those in need; the Bartlett School and Oxford Brooks University in the United Kingdom also offer similar programs. All of these programs teach students decision-making skills and the understanding that what they design is critical to a project's success. Design/build students learn immediately that their choice of materials can be a powerful and didactic tool to this end.

The argument for an education that reconnects these subjects is effectively made by Ernest Boyer and Lee Mitgang in *Building Community: A New Future for Architecture Education and Practice*. They present seven essential goals for the education of an architect based on their research of accredited programs. One goal, "a connected curriculum," criticizes the separation of design from other, more technical coursework. To effectively teach young designers the practical and technical as well as the theoretical and artistic, these must be learned hand in hand.

This book offers just such an alternative by showcasing projects that marry an architect's design intention with the qualities of a material, a synthesis called *materiality*. Chosen to form a cohesive approach, sixty case studies presented here inspire, encourage, and push the use of materials in the design process.

That such a marriage between material and design is only now being made explicit is not surprising. Materials have been used to express statements for years, but it is only recently in our history that *how* we use them—not to mention the onset of an entirely new palette of material options—has begun to advance and revolutionize architecture. Prior to the twentieth century, materiality spoke more to place, to locale, and in a way was more purely definitive as to what a building should look like: architects tended to use materials that were available and plentiful in their location and thus uniquely representative of that place, such as the indigenous woods used for the saltboxes and meeting houses of New England in the 1700s, or Thomas Jefferson's use of the red clay of Virginia to make the distinctive bricks that defined his buildings in the early 1800s. In the northeastern United States in the 1870s and '80s, Henry Hobson Richardson used stone to convey an idea of monumentality and permanence.

In Europe, bold statements of materiality were being made by the mid-nineteenth century. Henri Labrouste used iron, a material new to large public buildings, in his Bibliotech Ste. Genevieve in Paris (1850). The use of iron at that time was a proclamation that this was a building of high technology. Joseph Paxton's Crystal Palace, an exposition hall in London built just one year later, was a modular cast iron and glass building that used its materials to symbolize industrial, technological, and economic superiority. The large areas of glass and cast iron were an expression of materials and intention and were a precursor to the glass curtain wall.

The twentieth century saw the rapid development of these early seeds of materials and design intentions integrating together as one. The early purveyors of modernism used materiality in this way to help support their ideals. Auguste Perret began using reinforced concrete throughout France in the early 1900s as a representation of a new architectural style, not just a new material to replace stone. He designed a garage for Renault in 1905 and the Theatre des Champs-Elysees in 1913, both in Paris, as well as many other public and industrial buildings in France. Erik Gunnar Asplund's Stockholm Library (1918) also exemplified a new monolithic and clean-lined look of concrete. In the United States, Frank Lloyd Wright used unprecedented poured-in-place concrete for the Unity Temple in Oak Park, Illinois (1906), as well as for the more notorious Fallingwater in Bear Run, Pennsylvania (1934). Le Corbusier, a pupil of Perret's, used concrete to achieve the monolithic and sculptural qualities he strived for at a time when concrete was not considered a common building material. Through his villas and religious and civic buildings erected in America, Europe, Asia, and Africa, he reached a new level of sculptural architecture utilizing the properties of this single material, when no other would have achieved the desired effect.

Likewise, Mies van der Rohe was able to push the use of glass and steel to provide a level of purity in construction and a minimalist quality in space. As modernism was refined, materiality continued to support the design intentions of those willing to look at materials in novel ways. One can think of Pierre Chareau's use of glass at Maison de Verre (1932), or more generally of Alvar Aalto's love of wood or Eero Saarinen's obsession with concrete.

Postmodernists of the 1980s promoted an alternative approach to materiality: they chose to deny it as a part of architecture. The use of faux veneers and imitation materials expressed a style that showed little regard for an ethic of truth to material. As these materials flooded the construction market, the distinction between what is real and what is false became harder than ever to identify. Architecture's approach to materiality had spun 180 degrees since that of the early modernists.

Today, materiality is an exciting and quickly expanding concept in the construction process. Global corporations like DuPont and Weyerhauser are continually generating new materials and new uses for existing materials. Industries that once serviced a small segment of products are now engaged in much more in-depth research and development of new materials that are more effective, more efficient, and more environmentally sensitive. Once merely a tool for architects and largely confined to the realm of engineering, materiality has now become an instrumental methodology for a clear and bold design statement.

The wealth of innovations in this realm has made materials an enormous field of study in itself. The use of plastics, for instance, has exploded with every technological advance, while the more traditional materials have stayed in demand as well. The wide range of colors and sizes of concrete block, for example, offers an exponential increase in selection. "Green" materials— those that are sustainable and sensitive to our environment—have also become mainstream. In some ways it is almost impossible to write a comprehensive book on materials today with the ever-changing and ever-growing advancements taking place across the board. It is almost impossible to keep pace with the latest and newest types of materials being introduced to the construction field.

Materials have also entered into a new realm of distinction with this onset of advancement in engineering and technology. We are at a point in history when technology allows for the "design" of specific materials to fit the unique needs of a building. Frank Gehry's signature metal panels are a great example: each is individually engineered for its precise position in the building. Such technology has introduced a period of new expressionism in the glory of materials and their qualities. Materiality has now become a mature philosophy in the field of architecture: How are materials expressed in a building—are they surface or structural, modern or vernacular? What kind of materials are appropriate? How does the structural material relate to the enclosure materials, or are they same?

This book is organized to serve as a basic reference and examination of five materials that have pushed this philosophy—glass, concrete, wood, metal, and plastic. These materials, unlike traditional masonry, have properties that are still being discovered and exploited in new ways. Each chapter begins with a basic material primer, a brief history, design considerations, and a summary of the various types and/or production methods. The content has been selected to give the reader a basic understanding of the material.

These introductions are followed by case study projects offering examples of some of the best and most inspired uses made by architects from around the world in the past few years. The case studies have been selected by a survey of contemporary practices for whom design intention and materials have been successfully joined. Projects range from small to moderate in scale, allowing a focus and clarity of expression to yield an understanding of the building in its entirety and as a didactic prototype for the young designer. These architects love materials and are not concerned about deviating from the norm. There are examples of a material being pushed to new and experimental heights, such as the Aluminum Forest by Micha de Haas, a building made almost completely of aluminum. There are examples of a mundane material being used in a new or different way, such as the Springtecture H project by Shuhei Endo, where corrugated metal is curved and looped to create spaces. There are the more modest projects where experimentation meant creativity, such as the Rural Studio's Masons Bend Chapel, which used car windows as glazing. These projects make an expression not only with the types of materials used but also in how they are put together. The construction detail drawings for all of these projects have been highlighted because this is where we learn most about the designers' ideas in putting their buildings together as well as their unique philosophies regarding materials. This is where we begin to understand how a material is connected, how it needs to be treated, and how it relates to the other materials in the building.

When a material is used in new and unexpected ways, or where its characteristics are presented in an unconventional condition, the level of design is raised. ARO's use of glass in its Soho loft is mesmerizing, as it is utilized structurally, counterintuitive to what we are accustomed to seeing but furthering the design's intention toward open space; the properties of glass were used in a creative manner in order to achieve a design solution. The result is an engaging and innovative stair that appears to float in space. Likewise the use of precast concrete in the Retirement Home built in Basel, Switzerland, by Steinmann & Schmid Architekten exemplifies the way in which thoughtful design and a proficient understanding of a material creates a practical and beautiful building. O'Connor & Houle Architecture uses a white polycarbonate to skin their 50 Argo Street house to give the owners varying levels of translucency and privacy. Elsewhere, Despang Architekten is always sensitive to the synthesis of materials and design, such as their use of a prefabricated structural wood system designed for the ILMASI School in Garbsen, Germany. *Materials for Architectural Design* aims to inspire designers to think of materials as a palette from which to imagine how an idea or concept can be crystallized and realized with the use of a material. This book is dedicated to all of us who love materials and to all of us who love to design. The two belong together.

GLASS

THE BASICS

At its most simplified understanding, glass is a hard, brittle, usually transparent material composed of earthen elements that have been transformed by fire. The manufacturing process heats the raw materials until they are completely fused; they are then cooled quickly, becoming rigid without fully crystallizing. The resulting material contains properties of both crystals (mechanical rigidity) and liquids (random, disordered molecular arrangement) but actually is different from either state. Glass can be formed in many ways, the most common being cast, blown, rolled, extruded, and pressed. On a cellular level, glass fibers can be made into a wool, which can be used for acoustical and thermal insulation. Glass can also be used in electrical circuitry and highly specialized equipment components.

Because glass has the inherent qualities of transmitting and filtering light, it is often used for poetic metaphor and spiritual symbolism. Its ability to transform the appearance of light and intensify colors gives it an atmospheric value like no other material. Although glass is used in a vast array of industries and common objects, its presence in architecture is perhaps both profound and practical. It is an endlessly fascinating and versatile material, and is also desirable because it is 100% recyclable and has an unmatched resistance to deterioration.

Architectural glass can be defined as glazing in a building's openings and, in some situations, as its walls and roof. This glazing can be of many types, colors, and forms. Understanding the basic qualities and many different types of glass available to architects will allow a larger, more creative palette from which to design buildings.

Glass can be manipulated in a surprising number of ways. Molten glass can be blown, poured into a mold, or pressed into a form. Cold glass can be slowly heated to a pliable state, then manipulated to create other shapes, or it can be adhered to other pieces of glass or laminated with other materials through industrial adhesives.

The process of slowly cooling a molten material until it is solid is called *annealing*. The annealing of glass is very slow compared to molten steel or silver, but it is an integral step in the creation of glass as a material. If molten glass cools too quickly, it may be stressed at room temperature and break easily. This stress or strain can be critical for a large sheet of glass. Highly strained glass breaks easily if subjected to mechanical or thermal shock.

HISTORY

Glass is an ancient material, dating back more than 5,000 years. It is believed that the material originated around 3500–3000 BC in Egypt and eastern Mesopotamia (present-day Iraq) with the creation of beadlike forms that were valued as highly as precious stones. Around 1700–1600 BC, during Egypt's eighteenth dynasty, artisans developed the skill of creating translucent bottles, jars, and the first window panes for buildings. This process used heat to transform sand, seaweed, brushwood, and lime into a range of forms and colors.

The earliest glass was most commonly cast in formwork, but a major breakthrough occurred some time between 27 BC and AD 14 with the discovery of glassblowing, attributed to Syrian craftsmen from the Sidon-Babylon area. The Romans began blowing glass inside molds in the last century BC, allowing for a larger variety of hollow shapes. A bubble of molten glass was placed on a blowing iron and then manipulated by blowing it into a desired shape. Mouth-blown glass revolutionized the art form, allowing for a thinner, more translucent, light-transmitting material.

This revolutionary technique eventually led to the development in the sixth century AD of transparent glass windows, which replaced the thin, nearly opaque stonelike sheets of alabaster or marble used in buildings. The Romans, often credited with being the first to make glass large enough for windows, used colored glass sheets set in a frame of wood or bronze for a more translucent pane. In the Middle Ages, under the direction of the Catholic Church, glass began to be used not only as a means to create spiritual environments with vast arrays of colors and glistening light but also as a method of telling the story of the Christian faith in Medieval and Gothic cathedrals. The explosion of stained glass in European architecture resulted in a proliferation of inspirational spaces decorated with colored reflections of light, producing structures like no others in the world.

Glass did not take on a significant structural capacity until many centuries later. In the mid-nineteenth century, the French artisan Gustave Falconnier mass-produced hand-blown glass bricks in oval and hexagonal forms, which became extremely popular—Le Corbusier and Auguste Perret enjoyed using them—despite their limited load-bearing capacity and problems due to condensation development. The French architect Joachim built the first structural dome of concrete and glass in 1904. In 1907 Friedrich Keppler, a German engineer, invented and patented interlocking solid glass blocks that could be placed into reinforced concrete structures, allowing for load-bearing capacity as well as light transmission. In the 1930s the Owens Illinois Glass Corporation produced the hollow glass block, which is commonly used today.

Laminated glass was invented in 1910 by Edouard Benedictus, a French scientist who patented the process of strengthening flat glass by inserting a celluloid material layer between two sheets of glass. It was marketed as a safety glass under the name Triplex.

In the 1950s, the British inventor Alastair Pilkington completely transformed the way in which glass was used in architecture through his development of float glass—the process used to produce 90 percent of architectural glass today. In this process, molten glass floats on a bed of denser molten tin, mass-producing large sheets of flat, optically superior transparent glass at an affordable cost, thereby revolutionizing the way in which glass could be used in building design. Larger sheets of glass—and hence larger windows—were available with greater uniformity and fewer surface imperfections. Pilkington's invention, along with the developments of sealants, contributed to the onset of glazed office towers, as the glass curtain wall was quickly regarded as a status symbol for buildings representing progress and style. Mies van der Rohe's use of glass and steel at the Illinois Institute of Technology in Chicago in 1940 represents an early example, as does his Seagram Building in New York (1958). Other landmarks of architectural glass include Skidmore Owings and Merrill's Lever House in New York (1952) and Eero Saarinen's General Motors Technical Center in Detroit (1955). In the 1960s and '70s, advancements in reflective, tinted, coated, and insulating glass exploded, giving designers the ability to control the amount of heat and solar gain in curtain wall buildings. The ensuing decades of the twentieth century ushered further advancements of the glass industry into three distinct areas: environmental control, structural uses, and a vast array of surface and color treatments.

DESIGN CONSIDERATIONS

When selecting the type and use of glass in a project, one looks for an optimal balance between aesthetics and function. The wide variety of architectural glass commercially available coupled with the versatility and creativity one can explore with the material makes the design process exciting and challenging. Understanding the basic properties and terminology used in the vast glass industry will allow a designer a useful palette from which to design.

Glass is an inherently strong material and is weakened only by surface imperfections. *Tempered*, or heat-treated glass, is stronger and more resistant to thermal stress and impact than annealed glass. Glass also possesses a hard surface, resisting scratches and abrasions. When stressed, it will rebound to its original shape until it reaches its breaking point, which is again much higher if glass has been tempered. Glass is chemical- and corrosion-resistant and is impervious to most industrial and food acids. It is also shock-resistant and can withstand intense heat or cold as well as sudden temperature changes.

Thermal conductivity is the measure of a material's ability to transmit heat through its body. Glass is thermally a poor insulator. When two or more sheets of glass are combined together with an airspace, however, heat loss can be reduced significantly. Two- and three-paned windows that have hermetically sealed airspaces between them are good insulating windows, especially for cold climates. Further, the thermal insulating qualities of glass can be improved by using a low-emissivity (low-e) coating on the glass.

The transparency and translucency of glass has historically given an aesthetic quality to architecture like no other material. It gives a building the ability to change, to move, and to create certain environments. The way in which light transmits through a piece of glass in a building can be a powerful design tool for an architect. How light changes through the day and how it appears within the space is a frequently overlooked factor. Designers often think about the quantitative considerations of light entering a building rather than the qualitative. The color or texture of a light beam or how it hits a surface can all be controlled and manipulated with specific intent. Glass can reflect, bend, transmit, and absorb light, all with great accuracy. When light hits a piece of glass, some is reflected from the surface, some passes through, and some is absorbed in the glass. The measurement of these three properties are called *reflectance* (R), *transmittance* (T), and *absorbency* (A). Each of these are expressed as a fraction of the total amount of light falling on a piece of glass: Light = R + T + A. Most architectural glass is partially transparent with little reflectance and absorbency. This equation is important in understanding the wide range of types of glass from which a designer has to choose, as certain types may better fit a project than others. There are hundreds of glass compositions as well as different coatings, colors, thick-nesses, and laminates, all of which affect the way light passes through the material.

When designing with glass, there are three types of forces to consider: *tensile* forces, which exert a pull on glass; *compressive* forces, which squeeze glass; *shear* forces, the combination of tension and compression, which pull glass in two directions. Tensile forces are the most critical to understand, because glass is much weaker in tension than in compression. The strength of glass is highly dependent on the condition of its surface rather than its molecular composition. When it fails, it begins with a small fissure or crack that grows until breakage.

Glass can be strengthened through *prestressing*, *chemical coating*, or *lamination* in order to help it resist break-age. Prestressing is often done by a thermal tempering process in which glass is heated to the point of malleability and then is quickly cooled, creating a drastic clash in temperature between the cooler surface and the hotter interior of the glass. This differential eventually dissipates but forces the surface into a state of compression and the interior into a state of tension. Though it increases the strength of glass, when it does fail the stresses in the glass are released as it fractures favorably into many small pieces.

Glass can also be strengthened by a chemical process in which it is immersed in a molten salt bath, coating the surface with large ions of salt and displacing smaller ions. This coating produces compression on the surface, which strengthens the glass.

The lamination process simply sandwiches sheets of glass together with heat with a transparent vinyl inter-layer between the glass. When this occurs, the inner sheets of glass shrink more when cooled, causing the outer sheets of glass to be put into compression. If laminated glass breaks, the vinyl interlayer holds the glass shards in place, making it a good glass for skylights or safety applications.

TYPES

There are six basic types of commercial glass made today, which are differentiated by composition and use:

→ **Soda-lime glass** is the least expensive type of glass and, not surprisingly, is also the most common, accounting for 90 percent of all glass made, most typically seen in the production of bottles, jars, and common consumer items. Nearly all architectural glass is some type of soda-lime glass. It is usually composed of 60–75 percent silica, 12–18 percent soda, and 5–12 percent lime. It is not resistant to sudden temperature changes or high temperatures.

→ **Lead glass** is a relatively soft glass with a high percentage of lead oxide, used for electrical applications as well as some art glass. It is slightly more expensive than soda-lime glass and also does not withstand sudden changes in temperature or very high temperatures.

→ **Borosilicate glass** is a silicate glass with at least 5 percent boric oxide. It has a high resistance to temperature changes and chemical corrosions, properties that lend well to its use in products such as light bulbs, headlights, pipes, laboratory glassware, and bakeware.

→ **Aluminosilicate glass**, commonly used for electronic circuitry, contains aluminum oxide and is similar to borosilicate glass but has a greater resistance to high temperatures and better chemical durability.

→ **96% silica glass** is a borosilicate glass which has been melted to remove almost all of the non-silicate elements. It is a very unyielding glass to heat, resisting heat shock up to 1,652 degrees F (900 degrees C). This glass contains 7–15 percent boron oxide and has a low coefficient of thermal expansion. Since its thermal fatigue resistance is high it is usually used where fire protection is needed.

→ **Fused silica glass** is a pure silicon dioxide in a non-crystalline (liquidlike) state. It is very rarely used, as it is a very expensive and difficult glass to fabricate. Its purposes are usually highly specialized, such as specific components for medical and chemical equipment.

The technological evolution of architectural glass rapidly increased toward the end of the twentieth century with the development of new coatings and different laminates. The glass industry is vast and diverse, making it difficult to enumerate every type and variation of glass available. Additionally, there are a number of ways to manufacture glass. For architectural purposes, flat glass is the most common type produced, of which there are three basic varieties: plate, sheet, and float, all of which are still made today, though float glass is predominant.

→ **Plate glass** was the first large-scale production process of smooth, clear glass, devised in France in the late seventeenth century. Glass was cast and polished on a flat surface and then rolled, ground, and polished for a relatively undistorted, clear transparency. Joseph Paxton's Crystal Palace in London in 1851 used mostly plate glass.

→ **Sheet glass**, or **drawn glass**, was first developed in Belgium in the early twentieth century. Large sheets of transparent glass are produced by drawing molten glass onto a flat surface, smoothing it out with a roller, then grinding and polishing it on both sides. Sheet glass has inherent distortions, which increase as the size of the sheet increases. This was a work-intensive process but was the only known way to produce sheets of glass until the invention of float glass a half-century later. Sheet glass is still used today in small window lites.

→ **Float glass** revolutionized the way glass was used in architecture. It is created by floating molten glass on a surface of molten tin, then annealing it slowly to produce a flat, transparent sheet. It is often produced in continuous ribbons. Its surface is smooth and heat-polished and does not require any grinding or polishing as sheet or plate glass do. Different patterns, textures, thicknesses, and colors can also be produced this way.

→ **Crown glass**, perfected in the Middle Ages, is a process in which molten glass is mouth-blown through a long, hollow iron stick, creating a large bubble that opens at one end in a bowlike shape. This is spun and reheated until it flares out to a flat disk. The molten glass is then cracked off and placed in a kiln (or lehr) to cool slowly to prevent cracking. Once cooled, sheets or panes are cut from the flat areas in the glass. The center of the sheet, where the iron was attached, is much thicker and more irregular than the outer edges. This is called the *bull-eye* or *bullion glass*, and in the seventeenth and eighteenth centuries was considered inferior, to be used as window panes in the homes of the lower class. Crown glass can be clear or artistically swirled with colors. Many artisans in the Middle Ages used crown glass for stained-glass windows. Today, only artists who specialize in the craft of historic glass still use this process.

→ **Cast glass** is made by pouring molten or liquid glass in a mold to form a particular shape before it is cooled and released. Cast glass is one of the oldest methods in glass history, with early vessels dating back to Egypt and Mesopotamia as early as the fifteenth century BC. The method of casting glass is typically used today mostly by artisans or for ornamental and design-specific purposes. Architecturally, cast glass is used in the forms of channel glass products, glass block, patterned (textured) glass, or in a custom-designed glass system. The thickness, shape, and surface texture can vary according to the mold that is made to hold the glass.

The following are additional types of glass that are made with different qualities to enhance their performance. These are more specialized glass, each with highly developed capacities.

→ **Tempered glass**, often called **toughened glass**, is considered a type of safety glass. It is four to five times stronger than "normal" annealed glass, and when shattered, it breaks into many small, cubed fragments rather than dangerous shards. It is float or plate glass that has been heated and rapidly cooled, increasing its inherent strength and ductility. It is used for windows that are exposed to high wind pressure or extreme heat or cold, as well as for windows and doors where there is a chance people could bump or fall into them. Almost all large sheets of architectural glass are tempered, thereby reducing the required thickness of the glass. It is more expensive than annealed glass and can have some distortions from the tempering process.

→ **Laminated glass** involves sandwiching a transparent sheet of polymer, such as polyvinyl butryal, between two or more layers of flat glass using an adhesive. This is a durable and versatile glass, and can be used in a variety of environments. Among other uses, laminated glass can be used to diffract sunlight in a skylight, insulate sound in a recording studio, or be used by security facilities in need of bulletproof or fire-retardant windows. It is useful in skylights or in storefronts because the product remains in place even if the surface glass is broken.

→ **Glass blocks** are massive glass units that are available in a wide range of sizes, shapes, textures, and colors. Installed like unit masonry, these blocks are produced by melting glass and then casting it into shells; two shells are fused together to make one block, sometimes with a void in the center. Some glass-block walls can meet fire resistance codes.

→ **Channel glass** is a self-supporting, U-shaped glass system with a textured, translucent surface. It is produced by casting and is usually set vertically in an aluminum framing system. This glass system provides a wall that can support itself while also providing large areas of light transmission. It can be used for almost all applications, eliminating the need for vertical and horizontal frame members and only requiring a perimeter frame.

→ **Insulating glass** is two or more sheets of glass separated by a hermetically sealed space for thermal insulation and condensation control. The airspace between the sheets of glass can be filled during the manufacturing process with either dry air or a low-conductivity gas, such as sulfur hexafluoride. This gas can enhance thermal efficiency approximately 12 to 18 percent and can also help with sound insulation. The thermal performance of double-glazed or triple-glazed windows can be further improved by the addition of a low-emissivity coating on one or all of the layers of glass.

→ **Wire glass** involves steel wires rolled into sheets of glass. A wire mesh is inserted during the manufacturing of plate glass, allowing the glass to adhere together when cracked. It can qualify as safety glass for some applications and can be used as a fire-resistant glazing in doors and windows. Although it is no stronger than glass without wire mesh, when cracked or broken the wire holds the glass together.

Church of the Sacred Heart

MUNICH, GERMANY // ALLMANN SATTLER WAPPNER ARCHITEKTEN
LAMINATED GLASS, VARIED TRANSLUCENCY

DESIGN INTENTION

The Herz-Jesu-Kirche Church (Church of the Sacred Heart) is an adaptable and flexible space of worship for the city of Munich. Through its extraordinary enclosure system, the church altar and nave can be modified for different services and uses. Large glass doors on either side of the rectangular plan open outward to the churchyard, signifying a welcoming gesture to the city. At night, the church becomes a beacon of light amidst the city life.

A central gathering place and center of worship, the Church of the Sacred Heart uses glass to metaphorically represent its role in the city, symbolizing an open, bright, and nonrestrictive relationship with the outside world. Its floor plan and use of an adaptable space reinforce this idea of versatility and inclusiveness.

MATERIALITY

Since the advent of stained glass in Germany and France in the tenth century, the relationship between glass and light has been a significant element in liturgical architecture. The qualities of light can be perceived as a spiritual design tool, thus making a glass church a rational decision. In this project glass not only transmits and filters light but also acts as structure and space-defining feature.

The church is designed as two shells with contrasting material properties. The exterior shell materials consist chiefly of glass and stainless steel, both very durable and requiring minimal maintenance. These protect the relatively vulnerable inner shell, made up of maple laminate and fabric, forming the apse and sanctuary. It is as if the outer envelope is a glass cabinet whose portals can be opened to reveal the precious interior. Like the glass outer assemblies, the interior finishes are layered, providing highly varied degrees and types of connections between interior and exterior. The outer shell appears to be pure glass, as the steel-frame structure is stepped back from the glass walls to minimize its presence. The bold appearance is further enhanced as the glass box changes in translucency progressively from entrance to nave, filtering the light into the various parts of the church through changes in intensity, color, and refraction. The adjoining stainless steel surfaces are made to be sympathetic with translucent glass elements by blasting the stainless steel with small ceramic beads, reducing the gloss of the metal surface to a softer satin finish. The broad east elevation is composed of a gradual transition from transparent cladding elements (glass) on one end to opaque elements (stainless steel) on the other.

The rational custom-designed frame and skin system is responsive to issues of scale, structure, and environmental control. Structurally, horizontal glass fins attach to the glass wall and act as beams by transferring lateral wind loads to the suspended steel-post structure. The glass fins act in tension on the edge away from the wind load and in compression on the edge closest to the wind load. The use of glass as a load-bearing component withstanding wind pressure permits a filigree steel construction and maximum transparency of the shell. The requirements placed on the optic function of the building shell are met by the complex system of facade glazing.

The varied translucency of the glass is achieved through three techniques. First, on the main facade, an external etching imprints the surface and varies in transparency with the height and length of the building. The glazing becomes more opaque closer to the altar end of the church and more transparent at the entrance. Second, in the structure of the portal facade, artistic patterns on the float glass exterior were applied and then processed by heat in the conversion of the float glass into single-pane safety glass. Third, in the roof glazing, a white silkscreen-printed surface and .63 in. (16 mm) spaces between panes moderates direct sun exposure and provides thermal insulation qualities. Thermal control is achieved by using insulated glass with argon gas in the cavity and by applying a coating to manage heat loss. The treated glass diffuses the sunlight and provides a uniform level of interior illumination.

TECHNICAL

The strength of the structural glass members is achieved through lamination. The horizontal glass strips are 1.54 in. (39 mm) in thickness, consisting of three layers of low-content iron oxide safety glass. The outer and inner layers are each .39 in. (10 mm) thick, and the middle layer is .59 in. (15 mm). Between each pane is a .06 in. (1.5 mm) sheet of polyvinyl butyral (PVB). The glass and plastic are bonded together under heat and pressure, achieving a significantly stronger and more ductile assemblage than glass alone. The resulting sandwich is also safer in case of breaking as the PVB would hold the glass fragments together. The vertical glass fins are comprised of three strips of float glass, each .47 in. (12 mm) in thickness, with PVB resin as intermediate "glue."

The outer surface is insulated glass consisting of an outer layer of .11 in. (2.8 mm) single-pane laminated safety glass, with .06 in. (1.5 mm) PVB intermediate layer with neutral solar protection. A .63 in. (16 mm) space between layers is filled with argon gas, and a neutral heat protection coating is applied between the panes. The inner surface is .39 in. (10 mm) low-content iron oxide glass; its profiled surface is made with crystal granulate and varies according to the courses of the facade.

A Thiokol-sealed metal frame supports the glass using custom joinery details. Wind bracing is provided at each joint in primary glass panels horizontally and vertically. Wind suction of glass panels out of the frame is prevented by aluminum plates at the center of each edge, which become ornament in the elevation.

The two large portals each weigh 24 tons (21.8 metric tons) and measure 64 ft. tall x 48 ft.wide (19.5 x 14.6 m) . Glass panels in the portal are 35 x 35 in. (.9 x .9 m) insulated (5 x 20 x 5 mm) safety glass panels with artistically patterned profiled surface.

Glass in the roof consists of an outer layer of .47 in. (12 mm) laminated glass with white silkscreen printed surface and neutral solar-protection layer in inter-pane space. The inner layer is also of laminated glass (6 x .75 x 6 mm).

01 View from the southeast
   with closed facade
02 East elevation

01

02

03   Glass assembly axon
04   Open facade
05   Glass wall section
06   Horizontal glass detail
07   Interior circulation

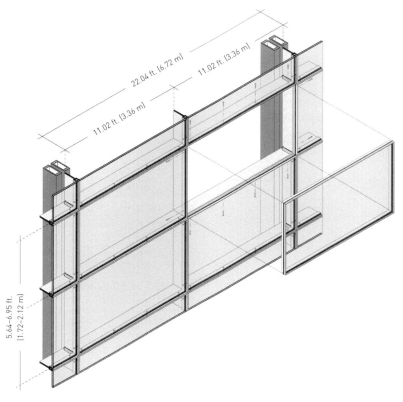

22.04 ft. (6.72 m)

11.02 ft. (3.36 m)

11.02 ft. (3.36 m)

5.64–6.95 ft. (1.72–2.12 m)

03

04

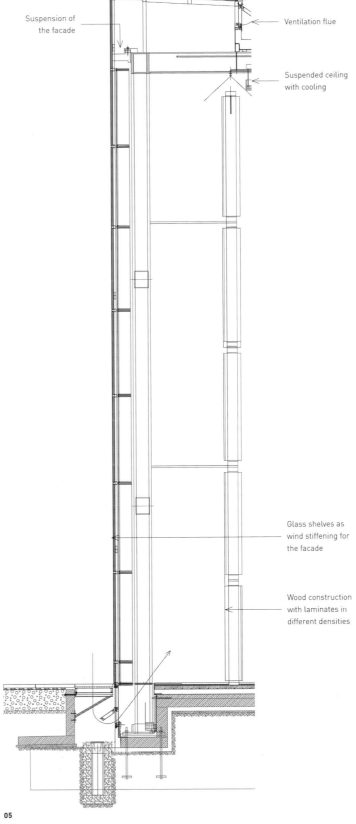

Suspension of
the facade

Ventilation flue

Suspended ceiling
with cooling

Glass shelves as
wind stiffening for
the facade

Wood construction
with laminates in
different densities

05

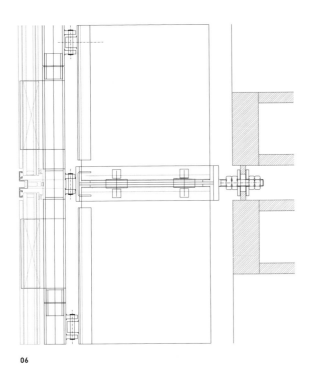

06

07

Laminata Glass House

LEERDAM, THE NETHERLANDS // KRUUNENBERG VAN DER ERVE ARCHITECTEN
SODA-LIME GLASS, LAMINATED ASSEMBLY

DESIGN INTENTION

This research-driven design—a winning entry in a competition organized by a local housing corporation—redefines the use of glass as a building material and attempts to alter preconceived notions about how this material can be used. The project required more than four and a half years to research, design, and document, and fourteen months for actual construction. The house is full of deliberate conceptual juxtapositions: closed and open, robust and fragile, brittle and flexible, serene and dynamic, rough and refined. The underlying scheme is best described by visualizing a rectangular block formed by gluing 2,000 sheets of plate glass together. Within this block, spaces are carved out to create living areas with varying levels of privacy and lightness. The refraction of light viewed from the edges of stacked glass presents an undulating and compelling quality of light throughout the house. This house has dual design concepts: one goal is to use glass in a new and experimental application, and the other is to design a beautiful and functional home. By using a common material in an uncommon and counterintuitive manner, a striking alternative appearance results that exploits the material's inherent physical strength and visual properties.

MATERIALITY

The construction of the house involved pre-cutting more than 10,000 sheets of .39 in. (10 mm) thick float glass to size, then gluing each piece into its place on site. The sheets were adhered in sets of ten using a two-component silicon compound. This was performed in a temporary steel building erected over the construction site to control the temperature and moisture while the laminations dried and silicon set under pressure.

The massive walls of laminated glass rest on the concrete foundation walls that form the basement. Although glass itself is naturally brittle, this inflexibility is countered by the use of a particular silicon compound that, according to its manufacturer, is UV-resistant and flexible. A certain amount of movement is allowed between each sheet of glass to allow flexibility as a whole. Although a single sheet of unlaminated glass is easily shattered, taken together the laminated glass is as strong as concrete, according to the designer.

The glass walls support the roof, which is composed of a plywood structure held in place by aluminum ties. The walls provide thermal mass, heating slowly from the sun during the day and retaining the energy to warm the space after dark. Radiant cooling and heating is provided by running tempered water through tubes cast into the concrete slab, which serves as the main floor. All services in the main (upper) floor, are dis- tributed via the floor or roof assemblies. The massive glass walls, combined with the central floor-heating system, are capable of economically maintaining a constant temperature in winter, and are thick enough to absorb and dissipate the summer heat without transferring excessive amounts into the interior.

Viewed from the sides, the glass sheets refract the light in such a way that provides sufficient privacy while still flooding the interior with natural illumination. Even brilliant, clear float glass is translucent but not transparent when viewed edgewise; this provides sufficient visual privacy for domestic living. Where clear vision glass is required for views, the conventional insulated float glass is set in minimal frames.

Glass is used to provide structure, enclosure, and luminance. Very few materials can perform all three of these functions simultaneously in a building. Because of its normally high cost per volume, glass is typically used as gossamer cladding over a structural frame. Here it is striking in that it is a heavy mass, comparable to historic masonry structures. This is exploited both structurally and for its thermal properties. Because the glass layers are laminated using flexible glue, each piece behaves as a planar column with continuous lateral bracing.

Typically, out-of-plane (lateral) loads are the primary threat to glass. In this building the plane of the glass is aligned with the direction of applied loads (vertically and perpendicular to the wall), thereby minimizing exposure of its thin dimension to the most threatening loads. Though glass is an excellent compressive material, the bearing capacities of the walls are determined by the resilient material that isolates the glass from the concrete foundation and slab.

Daylight not only illuminates interior spaces on the upper floor, but also those on the lower floor. Numerous circular holes in the concrete slab directly below the glass walls allow light to be transmitted vertically between levels.

TECHNICAL

Soda-lime glass is relatively inexpensive and is the most common commercial glass, ideal for most windows made today. Through massive laminations of this single material, an inherent strength results, as well as a new appearance by exposing the green-hued edges. The walls are also made of .39 in. (10 mm) thick float glass. Each piece was fabricated for a specific location in the building. The glass is not anchored to the foundation; it simply sits on the concrete below.

By making the glass walls thick—on average 13 in. (33 cm) thick—the tensile and compressive forces are distributed harmlessly over larger dimensions. Glass acting in compression is effective because bending is prevented by lamination. Here, lamination is achieved using layers of glass that are sandwiched together with a silicon inner layer. Sheets of glass were placed on a specially made steel table, where they were cleaned by hand and coated with a permanent, flexible silicon adhesive. The glass and silicon were bonded together under heat and pressure, producing a thicker, stronger, acoustically superior, and safer glass product. If broken, the glass will tend to adhere to the silicon, qualifying it as a safety glazing material.

The roof is anchored using aluminum extrusions that are glued to a 1.2 in. (30 mm) sandwich of three .39 in. (10 mm) thick layers of laminated float glass. This laminated assembly serves as a planar column that spans vertically up to 21.8 in. (55.4 cm) above the ceiling, meeting the underside of the stressed-skin plywood roof structure. In this zone above the ceiling, enclosure is provided by conventional insulated glass that is adhered to minimal metal frames.

01　Ground-floor plan
02　Exterior view at night

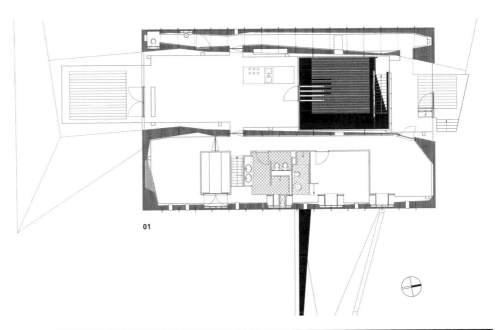

01

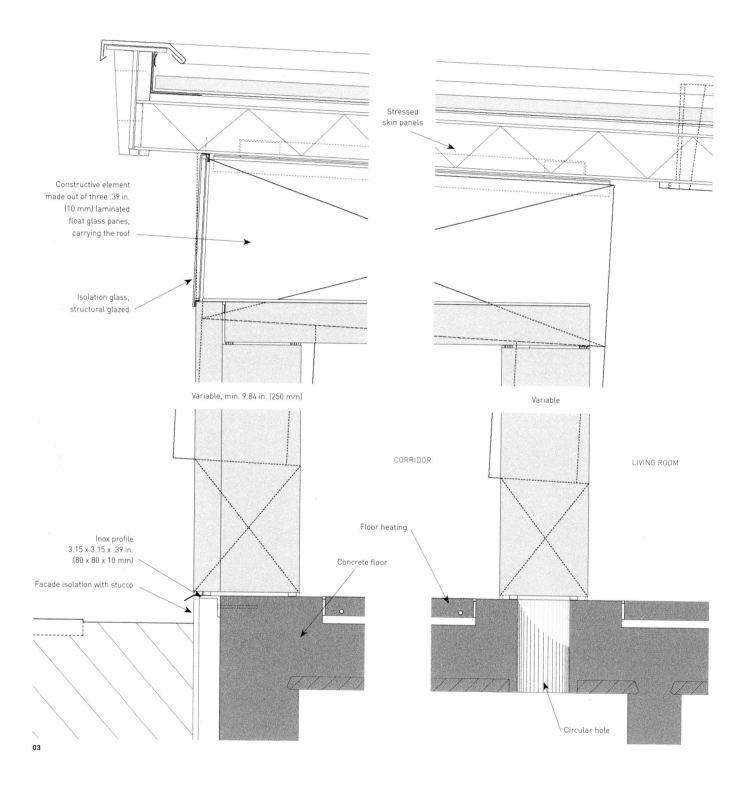

Stressed
skin panels

Constructive element
made out of three .39 in.
(10 mm) laminated
float glass panes,
carrying the roof

Isolation glass,
structural glazed

Variable, min. 9.84 in. (250 mm)

Variable

CORRIDOR

LIVING ROOM

Floor heating

Concrete floor

Inox profile
3.15 x 3.15 x .39 in.
(80 x 80 x 10 mm)

Facade isolation with stucco

Circular hole

03

03　Wall section
04　East elevation
05　Interior glass wall
06　Interior glass wall and window

04

05

06

Masons Bend Community Center

MASONS BEND, ALABAMA, USA // AUBURN UNIVERSITY SCHOOL OF ARCHITECTURE: RURAL STUDIO (FORREST FULTON, ADAM GERNDT, DALE RUSH, JON SCHUMAN; SUPERVISED BY PROFESSOR SAMUEL MOCKBEE AND BRYAN BELL)
TEMPERED GLASS

DESIGN INTENTION

Masons Bend, Alabama, is a rural, African-American community in the Blackbelt region of Hale County. The area is near the Black Warrior River and is historically a cotton farming landscape. It has recently gained some renown for the work by Auburn University's Rural Studio to help the community by building houses and structures for the residents. This triangular patch of land, adjacent to the red dirt road that leads to a small cluster of houses, contains a rammed earth community center. The structure was built for $20,000 by four fifth-year architecture students, as their thesis project.

This low-income community has a tradition of reusing and salvaging materials. Due to their tight budget, the designers followed this cultural precedent by using the local earth and salvaged glass to create both a contextually relevant and bold solution.

MATERIALITY

The local red dirt was the primary material used to construct the walls, while sheets of aluminum and panes of glass roof the building with an asymmetrical barnlike shape. To bring light into the space from the east, the students used ninety Chevrolet Caprice Classic car windows from a Chicago salvage yard. They bought all of these windows for a total of $90 and reused them as the glazing system for the center. The windows were placed on a light steel frame and bolted with rubber gaskets to allow movement. Bolts passed through the existing holes in the car glass, originally used for the mechanism that raises or lowers the windows; no additional holes or cuts were needed in the glass to assemble the windows, which cannot be altered after tempering.

Laminated glass was used in vehicular windshields long before it became common in building applications. In this example, technology transfer literally applies the auto industry's products to architectural uses. This project demonstrates the opportunistic use of found objects (the windows) that differ from conventional architectural glass. They are irregular in shape, convex, with two holes near one edge—all features which became integral to this scheme's solution. The lapped assembly of pieces, like scales of a fish, make it unnecessary for edges to be sealed in the open-air structure. The glass skin is separated from the primary structural frame by an intermediate frame of steel tubes, whose delicate scale permits maximum benefit from the skin's transparency. Layered glass gives the enclosure system visual complexity; as light passes through one, two, or three layers, degrees of green tint are increased. The glass skin is made of many elements explicitly fastened to a frame; this contrasts profoundly with the rammed earth walls, which are monolithic and jointless. The cool blue-green hue of the glass also complements the warm orange-red hues of the rammed earth walls.

TECHNICAL

Tempered glass is a type of safety glass that is heat-treated for increased strength and resistance to impact stresses. It is made by a process of heating annealed glass to 1,200 degrees F (649 degrees C) and then quickly cooling it. This process creates permanent compressive stress on the edges and face and tensile stress in the core of the glass, resulting in a product that is three to five times stronger than regular annealed plate glass, but which is more expensive. If broken, it fractures into small granules rather than jagged shards. Tempered glass cannot be cut, drilled, or altered after it is manufactured.

01 Steel structure prior to installation of car windows
02 Installing car windows
03 Section detail of window connection
04 Installed windows from interior
05 Installed windows from exterior

01

02

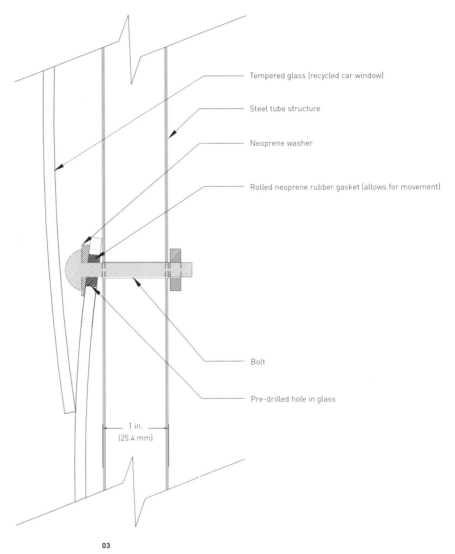

Tempered glass (recycled car window)

Steel tube structure

Neoprene washer

Rolled neoprene rubber gasket (allows for movement)

Bolt

Pre-drilled hole in glass

1 in.
(25.4 mm)

03

04

05

Glass Stair

NEW YORK, NEW YORK, USA // ARCHITECTURE RESEARCH OFFICE (ARO) WITH GUY NORDENSON
TEMPERED LAMINATED GLASS, STRUCTURAL CAPABILITY

DESIGN INTENTION

This 7,000-square-foot (650 sq. m) residence in New York City's Soho neighborhood occupies the sixth and seventh floor of a former warehouse with large open spaces and natural light from several exposures. The former industrial space was reprogrammed as residential while preserving the openness of its original function. The design for this residence treats the space as an open landscape and considers the angles of the sun as it moves across the living areas. The sun's daily course inspired the selection of materials, which were chosen for their texture, color, reflectivity, and transparency in relation to the light animating these different surfaces. A glass-supported stair provides access to the roof garden and acts as the main sculptural element. This stair defies traditional beliefs about the structural capability of glass while retaining the openness and lightness of the overall loft design.

MATERIALITY

This project challenges observers to think of this typically brittle, fragile material as strong and reliable. Steel is supported by glass—the reverse of what is expected.

The structural plane of the glass initially seems nonexistent, but then draws attention to itself as it challenges preconceptions about what glass can do. Floor-to-ceiling sheets of laminated glass provide the structural stability for the stair. The risers are attached to these sheets with milled aluminum u-brackets and delrin wedges. The risers are stainless steel tubes connected by milled aluminum sub-treads, which are then overlaid with oak treads to provide the stair's walking surface.

The glass appears to carry more load than it actually does. Its structural basis is the cantilevered stair first designed by Andrea Palladio in Venice in 1560. While this stair is not a pure cantilever, but rather is described by the architects as "structurally cascading," the principles are similar. Each riser rests on the back edge of the tread below it so the load cascades down the steps and to the floor. This counteracts torsion (rotational stress) in the plane of glass. It appears that the glass sheet is not strong enough for the task, but in reality the chief role the glass sheet plays is to resist the twisting of the stainless steel tubes.

TECHNICAL

The load "cascades" from riser to tread down the staircase, with torsion accumulating so that the last riser carries the largest load. In a computer model used to analyze the design, the unanchored lowest riser twisted in the opposite direction of the risers above it, causing the virtual glass wall to break. To solve this, the next-to-last riser projects unsecured beyond the glass edge, which gives an even more unstable appearance yet solves the torsion problem.

Large pieces of vertical structural glass are made up of three layers: a center layer of .75 in. (19 mm) tempered glass, with a .37 in. (9.5 mm) layer of annealed glass on both sides, for a total of 1.5 in. (38 mm). These elements chiefly resist torsion of the stainless steel tube sections that serve as risers in the stair.

Holes in the glass for receiving the steel risers were cut with a water jet before the glass was tempered. The riser tube sections are joined to the glass with milled aluminum u-brackets, with Delrin wedges as the material that actually engages the glass. Metal treads and risers are connected in series to form a structural unit that behaves like a zig-zagged cascading slab.

01

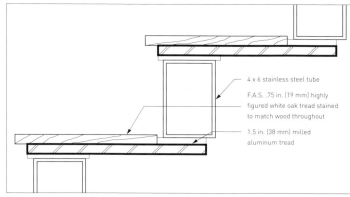

4 x 6 stainless steel tube

F.A.S. .75 in. (19 mm) highly figured white oak tread stained to match wood throughout

1.5 in. (38 mm) milled aluminum tread

02

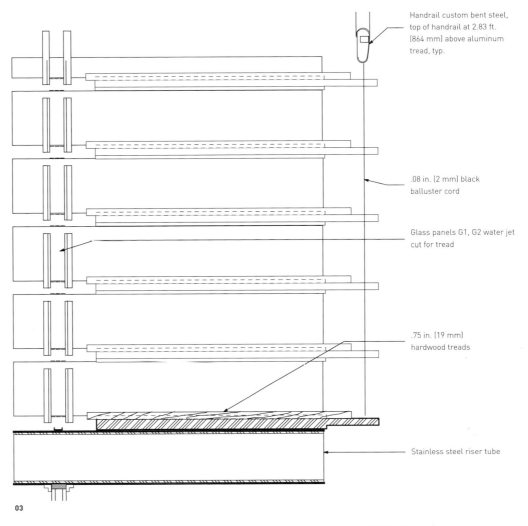

Handrail custom bent steel, top of handrail at 2.83 ft. (864 mm) above aluminum tread, typ.

.08 in. (2 mm) black baluster cord

Glass panels G1, G2 water jet cut for tread

.75 in. (19 mm) hardwood treads

Stainless steel riser tube

03

04

05

01 Glass stair
02 Detail of tread
03 Lateral section of stair
04 Tread detail
05 Stainless steel tube detail at glass connection

R128

STUTTGART, GERMANY // WERNER SOBEK
INSULATED GLASS, ENERGY EFFICIENCY

DESIGN INTENTION

This glass-and-steel house is located on a steeply sloped site with panoramic views of Stuttgart. Although this house seems sterile and completely transparent, it is a home where comfort and privacy issues for the inhabitants have been met. It is a completely recyclable, emission-free, energy self-sufficient building. The house has no interior doors, switches, or interior walls. All appliances and environmental systems are controlled by motion sensors and voice commands, while aluminum ceiling panels hide the lighting fixtures and air vents. Electric power comes from the solar photovoltaic panels on the roof.

This is an experimental house designed by a professor of engineering and architecture at the University of Stuttgart, who is also the head of the Institute for Lightweight Structures and Conceptual Design in Stuttgart, as well as the owner and principal of an engineering company. The design resulted from his desire to have an all-glass house with unencumbered views of the surrounding city and countryside that would also employ contemporary engineering concepts for sustainable buildings.

MATERIALITY

This project demonstrates the value of integrating the choice of cladding material with all other design decisions. In this building, structure, enclosure, mechanical, and electrical designs are all interdependent. The glass panels that envelop the house are triple-glazed with inert argon gas-filled cavities that provide insulation performance comparable to a 3.94 in. (10 cm) slab of rock wool. The efficiency of these glass panels allows room temperatures to remain comfortable all year round. All primary construction materials, which include twenty tons of glass and twelve tons of steel, are recyclable and emission free; no organic compounds are present in the primary structure or enclosure systems.

The building, which took only eleven weeks to construct due to its modular assembly of standardized elements, is an elegant, minimal prismatic solid. It is an archetypal frame, clad with skin that is not visible. The building is environmentally aware, but the orientation of the building on the site is not critical. The building proportions, design, and details are not adapted to a particular solar orientation.

TECHNICAL

Argon is an efficient insulator because of its density and poor heat conductivity. It is an odorless, colorless, tasteless, non-toxic gas, six times denser than air; it is used to replace air between glass panes, thereby reducing temperature transfer. This greatly effects the glass's *R-value*—the value of a material's resistance to heat flow. The R-value is expressed as the temperature difference that is required to cause heat to flow through a unit of area of material at the rate of one heat unit per hour. In this case, argon gas in triple glazing increases the R-value by approximately 58 percent compared to double glazing.

Another strategy to improve glass insulation is to use low-e glass, a material with a transparent metallic oxide coating applied to the inner glass surface. The coating allows shortwave energy such as light to pass through, but reflects longwave infrared energy such as heat, which improves its thermal resistance.

The interior is open except for a vertical shaft that houses "sanitary installations" that are veiled in translucent glass and aluminum (a movable tub for bathing and relaxing is not within this subspace). The modular accessible floor and ceiling accommodate all horizontal services. During the summer, heat radiated into the building is absorbed by water-filled ceiling panels and transferred to a heat store. In winter, the heat exchanging system is reversed and hot water circulates through the ceiling system for space heating.

Several glass panels are operable sash, opening awning-style, providing for natural ventilation. Fixed triplex glass cladding panels are cradled in custom stainless steel "yokes" near each corner. This provides nodal connection to the glass without requiring penetrating bolts. An EPDM membrane bounds each piece of glass. Vision glass facades on all elevations offer views to the west over the scenic Stuttgart Basin and in other directions.

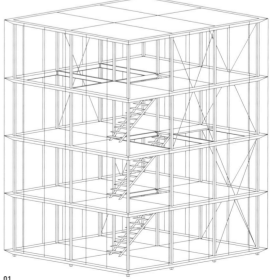

01 Steel structural system
02 Exterior view

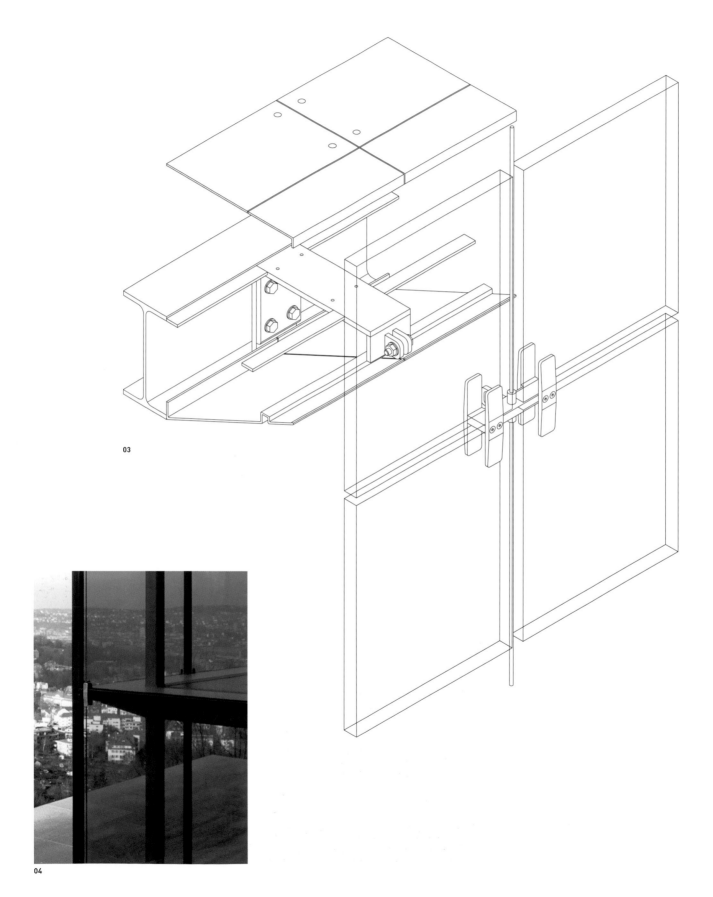

03

04

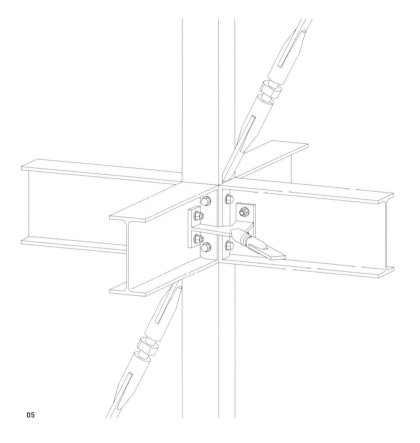

05

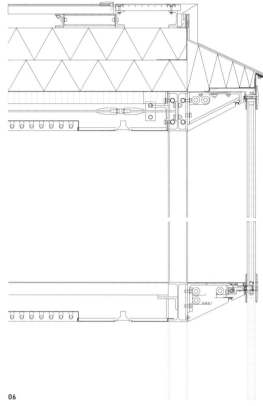

06

03   Glass connector assembly
04   Building corner
05   Steel-to-cable connection
06   Detail of wall section
07   Cross-bracing cables
08   Interior view of steel and glass

07

08

Crystal Unit III

HIROSHIMA, JAPAN // KATSUFUMI KUBOTA
GLASS CURTAIN WALL

DESIGN INTENTION

In a small town north of Hiroshima, the tradition of having a family living space located above the family business is a common urban architectural type. Situated on a busy street corner, the Crystal Unit III follows this traditional model but with a variation. The lower floor is used as a café, while the family lives in a more private, contained space within the larger "tube" on the two levels above. The design challenge was to create a very lightweight and transparent structure while separating the business from the privacy of the residential spaces on the upper floors.

MATERIALITY

Glass is used to minimize barriers between the café interior and the street. Detailing of the glass walls strives to appear flush and minimal to give the appearance that the building is one long glass tube. This glass volume is structured with a steel frame and a reinforced concrete foundation. The skin and structure are integrated to minimize the intrusion of structural elements and to free the interior space. There are no internal columns or beams; the steel frame acts as a single rigid structural system. The result is a large yet seemingly hollowed-out glass structure. The open orthogonal geometry of the metal skeleton dominates the retail shop portion, compared to more compartmented volumes of the residential portion.

Hiroshima averages 61 in. (1.55 m) of rain per year, and temperatures range from 40 degrees F (4 degrees C) in the winter to 90 degrees F (32 degrees C) in the summer. It is also a seismically active area. Single glazing is not prone to condensation in this climate, however the architect reports that overheating is a problem in summer, and heat loss is a problem in winter. Some sash are operable for ventilation, and air conditioning is provided, while radiant heating (water) in the floor slab is used in winter.

TECHNICAL

A curtain wall is a non-structural exterior cladding system supported at each building story by the frame, rather than bearing its load to the foundation. The main advantage of the curtain wall is that since it bears no imposed vertical load, it can be thin and lightweight regardless of the height of the building. The idea is that of a thin wall that hangs like a curtain on the structural frame. Curtain walls can be prefabricated or constructed on site.

This project appears to use the curtain wall strategy because of the minimal sizes of columns and beams—but in fact, the mullions here are structural, carrying the loads of the roof. The primary structure is integrated with the horizontal and vertical mullion system. This is a rigid frame, thus no shear walls nor diagonal bracing are required. All steel members are field welded.

Bent-formed stainless steel plates serve as secondary support for each piece of fixed glass at the top and bottom edges. Waterproof silicon sealant prevents moisture intrusion at all butt joints, and flush glass sheets are bonded by silicon structural sealant to the frame. Exterior glazing is tempered single .31 in. (8 mm) float glass.

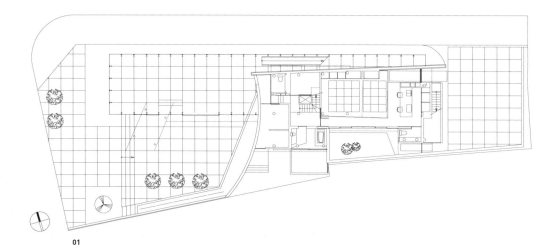

01 Ground-floor plan
02 Café interior
03 North facade
04 Southwest corner

01

02

03

04

05

05 Stainless steel supports and silicon joint
06 Operable sash
07 Steel frame
08 Roof/wall/floor connection details

06

07

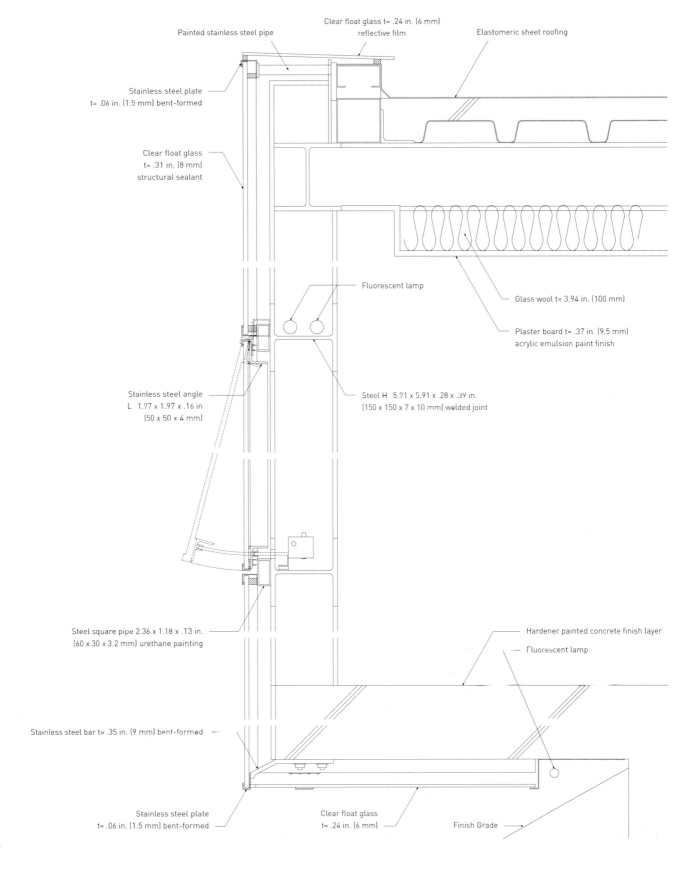

Painted stainless steel pipe

Clear float glass t= .24 in. (6 mm) reflective film

Elastomeric sheet roofing

Stainless steel plate t= .06 in. (1.5 mm) bent-formed

Clear float glass t= .31 in. (8 mm) structural sealant

Glass wool t= 3.94 in. (100 mm)

Plaster board t= .37 in. (9.5 mm) acrylic emulsion paint finish

Fluorescent lamp

Stainless steel angle L 1.97 x 1.97 x .16 in (50 x 50 x 4 mm)

Steel H 5.91 x 5.91 x .28 x .39 in. (150 x 150 x 7 x 10 mm) welded joint

Steel square pipe 2.36 x 1.18 x .13 in. (60 x 30 x 3.2 mm) urethane painting

Hardener painted concrete finish layer

Fluorescent lamp

Stainless steel bar t= .35 in. (9 mm) bent-formed

Stainless steel plate t= .06 in. (1.5 mm) bent-formed

Clear float glass t= .24 in. (6 mm)

Finish Grade

The German Foreign Ministry, Lichthof facade and roof

BERLIN, GERMANY // JAMES CARPENTER DESIGN ASSOCIATES
GLASS COATINGS, CABLE-NET STRUCTURES

DESIGN INTENTION

The Lichthof is the interior public space of the German Foreign Ministry office building, designed by Mueller Reimann Architekten. The facade of the Lichthof is a critical urban and cultural boundary for the revitalization of the ancient center of Berlin. This boundary shapes how the public views the Foreign Ministry Office, how the civil servants view the city, and how ever-changing reflections are created on both sides of the wall. Using a conventional material such as concrete or masonry, this north-facing wall would leave the back of the interior courtyard in shadow for most of the year. The glass-and-steel facade effectively provides the required structural properties with minimum visual obstruction, resulting instead in a light and delicate enclosure. The properties of glass were exploited to make light levels more balanced while concurrently heightening the occupants' awareness of the changing levels of light throughout the year.

MATERIALITY

Two cable nets in parallel planes stretch across the glazed opening of the Lichthof, which is braced and stiffened by this net. One set of cables is oriented vertically and is close to the outer glass skin, while the second set is oriented horizontally and is held away from the skin, allowing the assembly to act as a three-dimensional frame. Horizontal shelves of glass are attached to stainless steel struts that span from the vertical cables to the horizontal cables. The structure relies upon the thickness of this assembly in order to resist wind loads. This is done through the horizontal glass shelves, which act in compression, and through the cables, which act in tension. The structural loads are transferred to the primary steel structure that borders the glazed opening, giving maximum lightness to the elevation.

The delicate members of the wall, combined with the reflectivity of the glass, give a sense of fragility to the membrane. The horizontal glass shelves not only act structurally but also reflect light up into the interior. These glass bands have a special coating that divides sunlight into two halves, transmitting and reflecting opposite halves of the spectrum.

To reduce the mass and presence of the literal enclosure system, several strategies were employed. The glass enclosure layer was placed out of the plane of the primary structure, while the stout tube columns occur within the interior space. The only opaque materials in the elevation are the horizontal and vertical tension cables, the elegant strut/patch plate connections, and the slender beads of silicon caulk between the glass panels. There are no diagonal members nor lateral bracing elements. The result is an elevation surface that is more than 98 percent vision glass. As the design evolved, the number of elements in the facade and the complexity of their assembly were significantly reduced in order to maximize the transparency of the enclosure system.

TECHNICAL

Cable-net structures are one variation of lightweight tensile structures, consisting of continuous tension and discontinuous compression systems. The cables are woven steel, much like rope, and are prestressed. In cable-net structures, the spaces between the network of cables can be covered with conventional materials such as glass, plastic, or metal sheets.

The properties of clear glass can be altered significantly using sophisticated coatings. In this facade, three coatings were applied to the glass. The primary enclosure glazing is single-glazed water-clear laminated vision glass, and has an external heat-reflective coating to resist condensation formation during cold weather. Glass panels in a central portion of the facade received an additional colorless semi-reflective coating to create the impression of a semitransparent mirror floating within the facade.

The slender "blades" of glass floating on the inner layer of cables are also single-glazed laminated vision glass, but received a special coating that reflects half of the light spectrum upward while permitting the other half to pass through. The coatings modulate the reflectivity of heat, sunlight, and color. This produces a constantly changing field of color on either side of the glass wall. The result is a facade and roof that balance functional illumination but also animate the spaces with subtle changes in the level and color of light.

Cast stainless steel struts link the two sets of cables, serve as patch plates to secure the primary plane of glass, and also hold the slender "blades" of selectively reflective glass.

The luminous roof uses tinted ("solar shading") insulated glass panels, supported by lenticular cable trusses that effortlessly span more than 26 feet (7.92 m).

Bands of reflective glass that were to be applied to beams as shown in the schematic drawings (fig. 03) were not included in construction.

01 Glass facade
02 View from interior

01

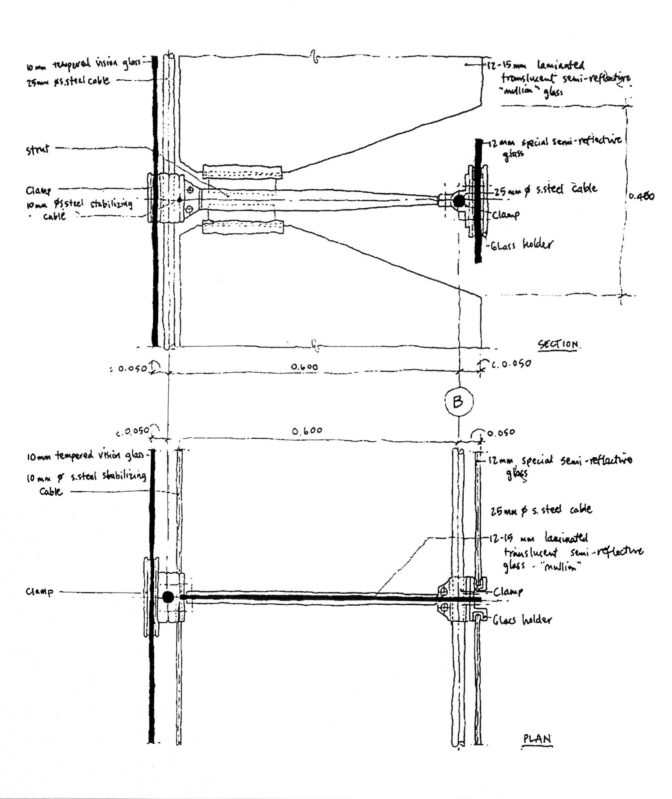

10 mm tempered vision glass
25 mm ø s.steel cable

strut

Clamp
10 mm ø s.steel stabilizing
cable

12-15 mm laminated translucent semi-reflective "mullion" glass

12 mm special semi-reflective glass

25 mm ø s.steel cable

Clamp

Glass holder

0.480

SECTION.

±0.050   0.600   c.0.050

B

c.0.050   0.600   0.050

10 mm tempered vision glass
10 mm ø s.steel stabilizing cable

12 mm special semi-reflective glass

25 mm ø s.steel cable

12-15 mm laminated translucent semi-reflective glass - "mullion"

Clamp

Clamp

Glass holder

PLAN

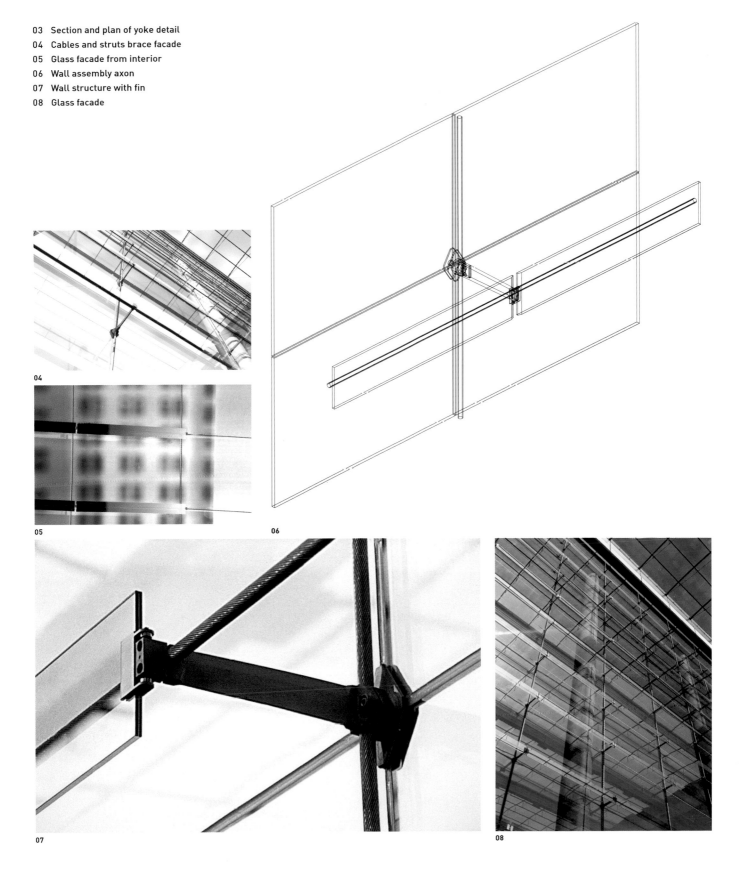

04

05

06

07

08

440 House

PALO ALTO, CALIFORNIA, USA // FOUGERON ARCHITECTURE
CAST GLASS

DESIGN INTENTION

This 5,000-square-foot (465 sq. m) house represents a clear example of a modernist aesthetic, employing an open plan and expressing current building technologies. New uses of existing glass products and structural systems as well as a rich selection of exceptional materials are used. With glass as the primary element, other materials such as limestone, steel, cedar, granite, pear wood, and other local woods come together to create a carefully orchestrated series of spaces that relate to the outside as well as interior adjacent spaces. Even materials as commonplace as plaster are manipulated to suggest a unique quality of finish and the intervention of the human hand.

The architects set out to create a domestic environment that, while simple, is full of visual surprises and tactile fulfillment. The clients requested that all surfaces and details be considered for their tactility, color, luster, and translucency. The result is a rich palette of materials and a glass structural system that is well-suited for the domestic scale and program.

MATERIALITY

Materials in this house are used to express its programmatic elements and to enhance the overall spatial experience. A steel frame governs the building configuration, while the glass cladding controls views to and from the exterior. Planes of vision glass or channel glass are used between spaces to make boundaries ambiguous, allowing light to pass through walls, ceilings, and floors to activate three-dimensional awareness. Glass is used to identify the primary circulation spine, serving as a transparent link between the living spaces and exterior gardens. This glass spine organizes the relatively open living spaces on one side of the plan, standing in opposition to the thick, linear wall treatment on the other side, which contains the closed, private rooms.

Translucent channel glass is positioned in the building to soften the sunlight from the front and rear gardens, creating a veil-like screen for privacy. It also imparts an intrinsic pale green hue to the light passing through it into the living spaces.

The construction details demand very close tolerances between the steel frame and the channel glazing elements. This displays the architect's confidence in her ability to coordinate alignment and the sizes of frame and cladding elements. The channel glass segments were cut to length in the field to meet the steel frame, including oblique cuts to align with the stair stringer.

TECHNICAL

Because glass is a liquid material during manufacturing, it can be cast in a great variety of shapes to meet structural, visual, and lighting needs. In this case, a standardized glass channel has been cast to create a self-bracing glazing product contained within a custom-designed aluminum perimeter frame. This glazing system requires a flexible sealant to weatherproof the spaces between the glass channels. This system is advantageous because there is no need to incorporate vertical or horizontal metal members within the wall. Curves can be created easily in plan, and the system provides a relatively efficient thermal- and sound-insulating wall system.

Two other factors had considerable influence on the form and details of this house. The building footprint was prescribed by the previous building; it is legally considered an addition because it rests on the remnant foundation of the earlier house. Also, the building is located in a seismically active area. The steel frame has moment connections; details for glass accommodate the anticipated movement.

In this contemporary application, self-supporting C-shaped channels in lengths up to 15 feet (4.57 m) are held in aluminum peripheral clips at the upper and lower edges. The channels are overlapped to create a double-walled glass construction, adding depth to the wall and allowing for a higher insulation value. The outermost layer of glass was cast with a surface texture to give a slightly milky effect. Glass floor panels and stair treads in the circulation zone are sandblasted to further enrich the sense of layered glass.

01 Sectional perspective looking south
02 Sectional perspective looking east
03 Rear elevation
04 Rear entry and circulation spine

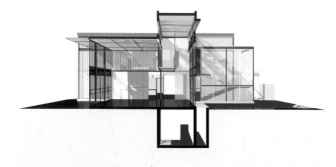

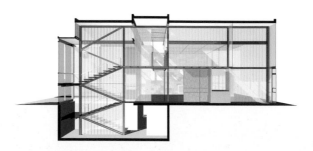

03

04

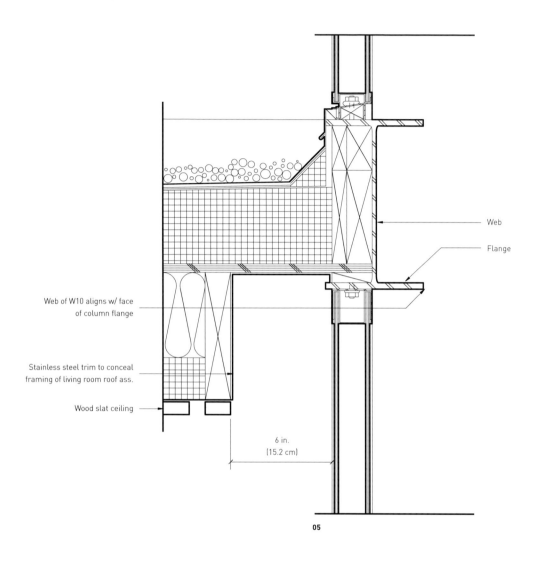

Web

Flange

Web of W10 aligns w/ face
of column flange

Stainless steel trim to conceal
framing of living room roof ass.

Wood slat ceiling

6 in.
(15.2 cm)

05

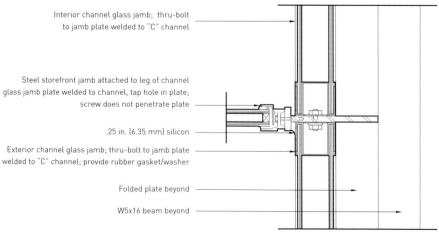

Interior channel glass jamb; thru-bolt
to jamb plate welded to "C" channel

Steel storefront jamb attached to leg of channel
glass jamb plate welded to channel, tap hole in plate;
screw does not penetrate plate

.25 in. (6.35 mm) silicon

Exterior channel glass jamb; thru-bolt to jamb plate
welded to "C" channel; provide rubber gasket/washer

Folded plate beyond

W5x16 beam beyond

06

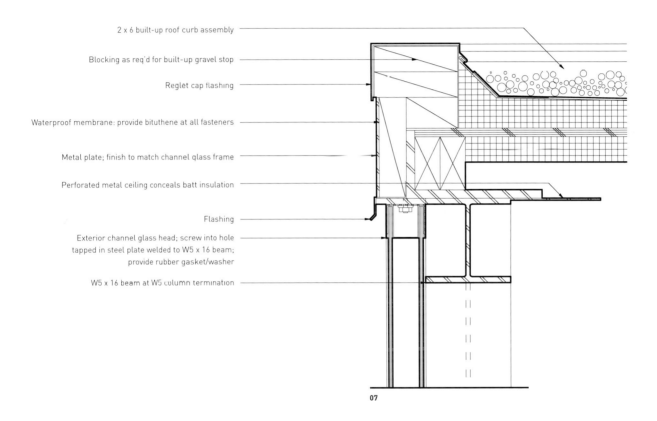

2 x 6 built-up roof curb assembly

Blocking as req'd for built-up gravel stop

Reglet cap flashing

Waterproof membrane: provide bituthene at all fasteners

Metal plate; finish to match channel glass frame

Perforated metal ceiling conceals batt insulation

Flashing

Exterior channel glass head; screw into hole
tapped in steel plate welded to W5 x 16 beam;
provide rubber gasket/washer

W5 x 16 beam at W5 column termination

07

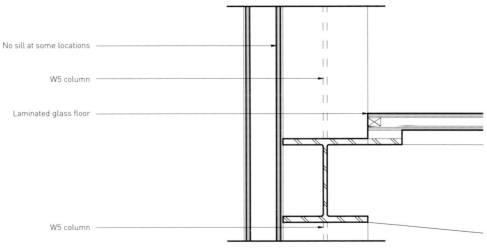

No sill at some locations

W5 column

Laminated glass floor

W5 column

08

Architecture Pavilion at the Technical University of Braunschweig

BRAUNSCHWEIG, GERMANY // VON GERKAN, MARG AND PARTNERS
CHANNEL GLASS SYSTEM, DIFFUSED LIGHT

DESIGN INTENTION

This exhibition pavilion for an adjacent architecture school was built on the campus of the Technical University of Braunschweig in Germany, sited in an axial alignment to the existing university complex and courtyard. The architect's goal was to design a flexible exhibit space for the architecture school that is compatible with the existing fabric of the campus and which becomes the focus of the courtyard where it is sited. The design intent was to create an image that projected out to the campus while providing a state-of-the-art exhibit venue. The pavilion's entrance is from a footbridge that leads directly into the upper gallery at the mezzanine level. A ceremonial stair leads down to the lower level where large doors open up into the courtyard, expanding the pavilion's space and allowing for a relationship to the outdoor court. A simple square floor plan allows for a wide degree of flexibility for different exhibition layouts, while an interior wall system of panels suspended from sliding bars allows for reconfigurable exhibit plans.

MATERIALITY

A double skin of translucent channel glass allows for a level of diffused light for exhibitions while projecting function and refinement within the existing courtyard. The use of glass and the abstraction caused by the diffusing surface gives this building a pure quality in contrast to the surrounding opaque, historic buildings. Daylight enters through central skylights and via the double-skin facade. The glass panels that make up the facades provide some degree of thermal insulation. Glass is used as a light diffuser but also as way to give the building an airy feeling amidst the density of the existing campus. The result is an ambiguous form that seems to hover over the courtyard.

An abstract quality results from the wall system, a self-supporting glass shell that is separate from the steel structure. By removing specific references such as doors, windows, and story indications, the system provides an abstract purity. At the same time, the interior light is even and diffused, well-suited for viewing exhibits.

TECHNICAL

This channel glazing system was first manufactured in Germany in the 1920s. This product, Profilit from Bauglas Industries in Germany, is comprised of C-shaped cast glass channels available in lengths of up to approximately 23 feet (7 m). It provides weather and moderate thermal protection when doubled and installed in metal channels at the top and bottom, as in this case. A double skin of identical cast translucent panels provides a high level of uniform illumination while still providing the gallery with needed visual and acoustic privacy from the surrounding courtyard.

This glazing system requires a second material such as caulk to seal or weatherproof the spaces between the glass channels. Joints between adjoining glass elements and aluminum channels are sealed with one-part moisture curing silicon sealant. It was developed as an industrial glazing system and is an economical alternative to common glazing options. Aerogel insulation and low-e coatings can be used in channel glass systems to enhance thermal performance.

The channel glass is self-supporting in this application. No frame or bracing system is typically required, though in this case it is braced at approximately 10 ft. (3.05 m) intervals vertically. As detailed, the channel glass must be in place before or concurrent with the placement of some steel elements at the cap. The choice of this glazing strategy has a distinct impact on construction sequence and many details.

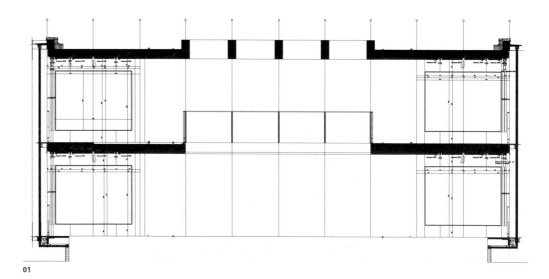

01 Building section
02 West facade
03 Northeast corner

01

02

03

04   Section detail at wall-to-floor
      connection
05   Plan detail at wall-to-floor
      connection
06   Section detail at wall-to-roof
      connection
07   Pavilion interior
08   Space between glass wall and
      wall panel

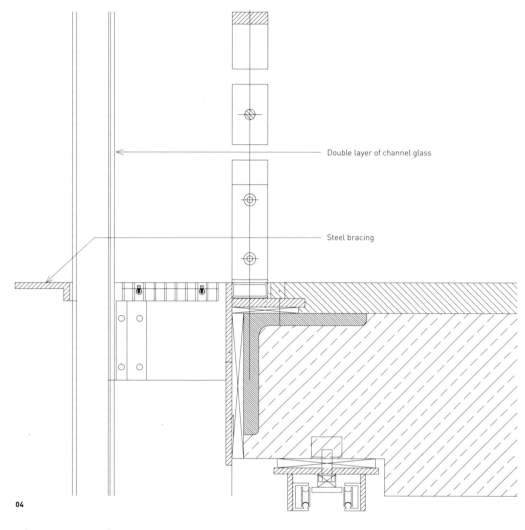

Double layer of channel glass

Steel bracing

04

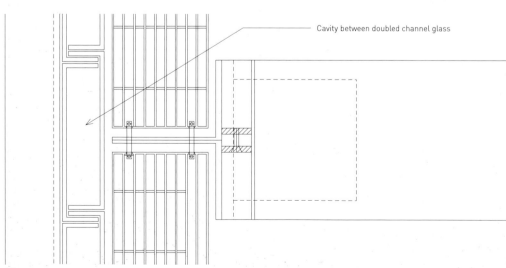

Cavity between doubled channel glass

05

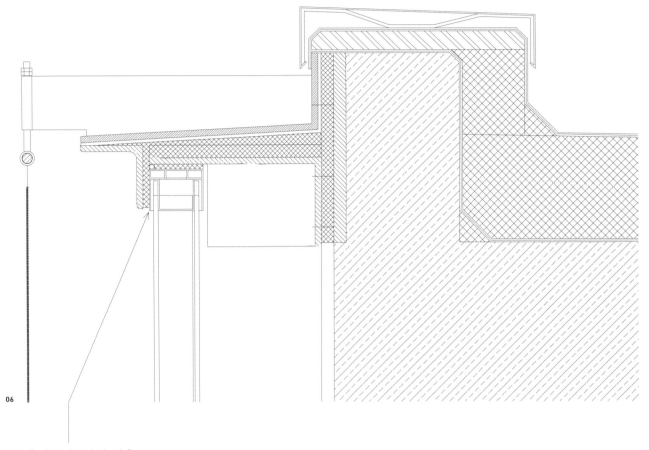

06

Aluminum channel at head of
channel glass with one-part
moisture curing silicon sealant

07

08

New 42 Studios

NEW YORK, NEW YORK, USA // PLATT BYARD DOVELL WHITE ARCHITECTS
DICHROIC GLASS, FACADE LIGHTING

DESIGN INTENTION

This ten-story building on 42nd Street and Broadway in New York City holds rehearsal studio space for performing arts groups, administrative offices, and a ninety-nine-seat black-box theater. It is located in the heart of the Theater District, where LED and neon signs pulsate all day and night. Lighting designer Anne Militello worked with the architects to give the facade a colorful and textured presentation that works suitably with the structure of the building and within the vibrant urban landscape. The design concept works with the rhythms and pace of this lively district by creating a building that changes throughout the day and night with color, light, and energy. The combined effect of various light sources and systems results in a seemingly infinite variety of lighting patterns.

MATERIALITY

This building has one primary facade, which is animated through form and proportion by day and through light and reflection by night. This project demonstrates that conventional glass can be transparent, translucent, mirrorlike, or opaque, depending on its luminous context. Further, it also reveals the special qualities of dichroic (two-color) glass, which transforms full-spectrum natural light into either magenta, blue, or yellow hues, depending on the light's angle of intersection with the glass. Dichroic glass is a manufactured product that can cast a range of colors depending on the position from which it is viewed. A piece of dichroic glass has a dielectric coating or thin layers of metal oxides, which produces these prismatic colors. Static glass elements yield dynamic lighting displays as the source light either moves, as sunlight during the day, or is dimmed or pigmented via lighting fixtures at night.

This building's glass curtain-wall system is synchronized to work with light, color, and metal louvers to create a remarkably dynamic facade. In front of the glass curtain wall, painted steel fins extend from the building's floor slabs. These fins hold an even lighter layer of perforated stainless steel louvers, which act as brise-soleil and as a light monitor for the facade. The reflections from the metal fins, attached to the armature, constitute most of the facade's visual content by day. The glass creating the enclosure is in a separate plane 4 ft. (1.22 m) away from the array of louvers. The glass and perforated metal are exploited for their ability to simultaneously reflect and transmit light.

Additionally, light is projected from a battery of over three hundred artificial lighting fixtures (five in each bay) set on the catwalks. Some have dichroic glass lenses, others have colored gels. These lights can be "played" as if notes from a musical instrument. They are programmed for a seven-day composition, although theoretically a new composition can be programmed at any time.

The lower left portion of the front facade is composed of acid-etched glass with an arrangement of dichroic glass pieces placed vertically, horizontally, and perpendicular to the plane of the facade. From every direction, pedestrians will see an interesting visual display.

The transparent glass skin is a water-repellant backdrop to the externally animated lighting displays. Translucent studio curtains are drawn at night, providing a neutral backdrop for the visual display outside. Glass and the mediating fenestration system convey the rigorous order of the underlying architectural form, and even the "ghost" of the Selwyn Theater, which formerly occupied this part of the site. The layered elevation permits the visual qualities of glass and non-glass elements to form a complex, dynamic collage using elements that are actually static. Thus, the architectural skin is shown to be easily manipulable to convey specific meaning, or can simply stimulate the senses.

TECHNICAL

A wide variety of glass and non-glass products with differing physical properties can be made as laminates applied to the surface of glass. Dichroic glass is a manufactured product made of polymer sheets sandwiched between panes of glass, which produces prismatic properties. When sunlight passes through at various angles, magenta, blue, or yellow colors are emitted. Artificial light produces no colors in this glass unless the light is designed to provide a full spectrum source.

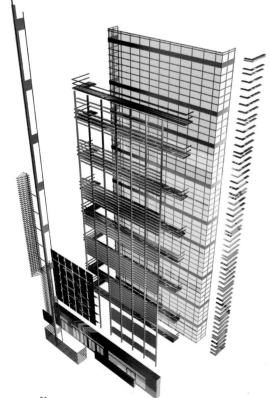

01 Facade assembly
02 South elevation
03 Dichroic glass fins
04 Wall section

02

03

Clevis and end
threaded rod
guardrail, typ.

Firestopping and spandrel insulation

Painted steel vertical strut

Perforated, ground, and
formed stainless steel blades

Scrim lighting fixture

Aluminum and glass
curtain wall assembly
with zero sightline inset
vert. units

Pedestal mounted fin tube
radiator with formed metal
enclosure

Raised dance floor

Formed aluminum
ceiling reveal

A

04

CONCRETE

THE BASICS

Concrete's massive and monolithic quality results from a mixture of Portland cement, water, and aggregate (usually made up of crushed stone or gravel and a fine sand). As a material it is strong in compression, and when enhanced by steel reinforcement it can also have great tensile strength. Concrete can take any shape or form through casting, and can have a variety of surface textures, finishes, and colors.

Concrete's uses in architecture are numerous and diverse. It can be used for structural members including columns, beams, roofs, floor slabs, footings, and foundations, as well as for cladding and paving. It is a fireproof construction material, as it neither burns nor rots. It is also relatively low in cost. Perhaps its most advantageous quality is its sculptural malleability; it is a shapeless material in which form, size, and texture must be designed.

Concrete varies in quality according to the proportions and characteristics of the cement, water, and aggregate from which it is made. Its strength is determined by its water/cement ratio: generally, the less water, the more strength. This ratio also affects the material's water-resistance and durability. *Admixtures*—materials added to the base of water, cement, and aggregate—can be mixed into the concrete to improve its workability or to change its characteristics, such as increasing its strength, speeding or slowing its curing time, or changing its color or texture (see pp. 57–58).

Aggregate makes up approximately three-quarters of concrete's total material volume, giving the material its main structural capability. Therefore the strength of a concrete mix also depends heavily on its aggregate. In most applications, the ideal is an evenly graded mix of fine and coarse aggregate. Portland cement is a fine, gray powder, and is manufactured from a number of raw materials, including lime (derived from limestone, marble, or seashells), iron, silica, and alumina (all derived from clay or shale). As water is combined with the cement and a chemical bond is formed with the aggregate, heat is given off—known as the *heat of hydration*, or *curing*, which is a byproduct of the setting and hardening of the concrete. Concrete's specified compressive strength is generally developed within twenty-eight days after placement, but its strength continues to increase as the hydration process evolves.

HISTORY

The ancient Romans discovered concrete while quarrying limestone for mortar. They unearthed a silica- and alumina-bearing mineral that, when mixed with limestone and burned, produced a cement. This cement—which we now know was an early version of Portland cement—was much more adhesive and cured quicker than any material they had seen, and it utterly transformed their construction technology. This early version of concrete can be seen in the unreinforced dome of Hadrian's Villa, a palace built near Rome between 125–135 AD. With the fall of the Roman Empire, the knowledge of concrete technology was lost, not to be rediscovered until 1756, when a British engineer, John Smeaton, performed the first scientific investigations of cements. In 1824, Joseph Aspdin patented what he named Portland cement, after the English Portland limestone. Portland cement has remained the dominant cement used in concrete production ever since.

Reinforced concrete was invented and developed simultaneously by a group of engineers in different countries during the 1850s. In Paris in 1854, J. L. Lambot built reinforced concrete boats with iron bars, wire, and mesh. This technique of reinforcing concrete with steel did not become widespread, however, until after a French gardener, Joseph Monier, registered for a patent for reinforcing concrete flowerpots with iron mesh in 1867. He then developed his process into building concrete water tanks, bridges, and eventually beams and columns. Also in 1854, William Wilkinson from Newcastle, England, began to use reinforced concrete in house construction, applying for a patent for the construction of "fireproof dwellings, warehouses, other buildings and parts of the same." A French builder named Francois Coignet built concrete houses using iron-reinforcing rods in France and the United Kingdom from 1850 to 1880. In the 1870s, Thaddeus Hyatt, an American, made and tested reinforced concrete beams. Hyatt's research is generally now credited as the basic principals of how we use reinforced concrete today. In 1875, a house with reinforced concrete walls, beams, floors, and stairs was built in Port Chester, New York, by W. E. Ward, and is considered the first reinforced concrete building in the United States. Also in the 1870s a French builder named Francois Hennebique applied for a patent for a reinforced concrete system to build concrete houses. He established a franchising empire to build concrete houses in many countries, including France, Belgium, Italy, and South America. By the end of the nineteenth century major structures were being built of reinforced concrete, and engineering design methods were established for its use. In the 1920s, the French engineer

Eugene Freyssinet created a scientific basis for prestressed concrete, an invention that allowed concrete to be used in large-scale structures. Freyssinet's research and design led to roads, bridges, and large harbor construction, as well as airplane hangars at Orly Airport in Paris.

As the twentieth century progressed, concrete's material qualities were employed in such remarkable structures as Frank Lloyd Wright's Unity Temple in Oak Park, Illinois (1905), the roof of Le Corbusier's Ronchamp Chapel in France (1955), and Eero Saarinen's Dulles Airport in Virginia (1962) and TWA Terminal at JFK Airport in New York (1962). In each of these projects, the architect used the material to achieve a very specific design goal by exploiting the inherent properties of concrete.

DESIGN CONSIDERATIONS

The biggest advantage to using concrete for designers is its range of possible forms and shapes, limited only by its formwork. Concrete's sculptural qualities and variety of surface textures, in addition to its structural capabilities, makes it a versatile design tool. It can take on linear forms in the shape of beams and columns, just as steel and wood; it can mimic the dense, wall-like forms of stone or masonry. Uniquely, concrete can also take on a planar form, such as a floor slab. It is a material that has such vast possibilities that magnificent designs can result—though magnificent failures can result as well. Craftsmanship and forethought are critical in concrete design in order to avoid the mundane character the material is also capable of.

Executing a desired appearance takes a great deal of knowledge and foresight. Detailed specifications, drawings, and discussions between the architect and the contractor are necessary to achieve the desired quality, and material mock-ups and site visits may be required for a very specific appearance and outcome. For foundations and other purely functional purposes, where the concrete's appearance does not matter, detailed specifications are still vital to ensure the correct densities and ratios of concrete in order to perform its function in the building.

However sculptural and moldable concrete is, minor imperfections in its surface are typical. Though part of the material's inherent character, it is difficult to get a perfectly smooth surface of uniform color. Using smooth, nonporous materials such as metal to line the formwork helps, but there are many factors to consider to achieve a desired surface texture. The concrete mix itself, the aggregate size within the mix, admixtures, the casting and finishing techniques, environmental conditions, and even the scheduling of the concrete trucks—all affect the material's ultimate appearance.

Concrete surfaces can have an wide array of textures or colors. Surfaces can be sandblasted to expose aggregates for a specific aesthetic; dyes and mineral pigments can be added to concrete to achieve almost any color, as in many concrete floors; polishers and coatings can also be applied after curing to achieve a smooth or coated surface. When still freshly mixed, concrete can be manipulated to achieve a preferred texture, or objects can even be cast into the concrete.

Concrete can fail as an architectural material if any component of its mixing, placement, or curing is incorrect. Other disadvantages include its weight and the complexities involved in the forming process. There are some recent advances in concrete technology, however, in which admixtures can improve its disadvantages as a material. Admixtures can lighten concrete's weight without compromising its strength. For instance, *high-performance concrete* is an ultra-light concrete containing fibers that make the material self-reinforcing, eliminating the need for any steel reinforcement. This allows for thin concrete members to be manufactured without losing any structural capability. *Self-consolidating concrete* has admixtures that allow the concrete to stay extremely fluid during the pour without compromising the strength of the material. It does not require vibration after pouring and allows for pouring into difficult molds or constrained areas. There is also new technology in a *transparent concrete*, which contains glass fibers that allow for a level of light transmission. These are just three of the many advances and research in concrete technology being investigated. The desired appearance of the material is arguably limited only to the extent which a designer is educated about the material and the limits of that designer's imagination.

TYPES
REINFORCED CONCRETE
Reinforced concrete is the combination of steel and concrete to give the material added strength. This is an inspired marriage of materials since the steel is protected from corrosion by the concrete and the concrete gains tensile strength, a quality it does not possess on its own. Reinforced concrete is well-suited to situations where

both tensile and compressive strength is needed. Steel reinforcement bars, high-strength steel cables, or steel mesh are placed in the concrete in areas where there will be tension. *Prestressed* concrete applies a compressive stress to concrete by *pre-tensioning* it with steel strands. In pre-tensioned concrete, the concrete is cast around stretched, high-strength steel strands, allowing it to cure, then releasing the external tensioning force on the strands. Stress is then transferred to the concrete, taking advantage of its intrinsic strength in compression. Most precast concrete structural elements are prestressed. *Post-tensioned* concrete is made by stressing lubricated steel strands after the concrete is cured. Site-cast concrete spanning systems such as beams and floor decks are often post-tensioned. Both prestressed and post-tensioned concrete result in more slender, efficient assemblies than conventional reinforcement.

Reinforced concrete is most often used in structural beams, columns, wall panels, slabs, or any other structural construction such as bridges and roads. Designers of reinforced concrete buildings must take care to design and construct it well, or the steel can corrode and rust, and cracking can occur. In wet and freezing conditions, some building codes require epoxy-coated rebar and/or a sealer to keep water out and to prevent cracks and failure.

CAST-IN-PLACE CONCRETE

Cast-in-place concrete, also called *poured-in-place* and *site-cast*, is defined as concrete that is poured directly on site. An advantage to this site-specific method is that the concrete is cast specifically for one job, allowing for an unlimited sculptural quality with no restrictions on size or shape since it is cast exactly where it will remain. However, the construction process can be slow since more time is needed to build or set the formwork at the site. Additionally, the costs can be higher since the formwork is made on site and in some cases is not used again. This cost can be defrayed if pre-made, reusable formwork is used. Cast-in-place can be risky since environmental conditions can affect the pour, and controlling temperature and moisture can add cost and difficulty.

The formwork into which the concrete is cast acts as a mold that holds the shape of the concrete until it has hardened and has developed sufficient strength to support its own weight. Formwork can be a major cost consideration. It can be specially constructed for each project or can be reusable, prefabricated units of standard lumber, plywood, metal, fiberboard, or reinforced synthetics. The key to typical formwork is that it be strong and stiff enough to support the large weight and fluid pressure of wet concrete. Forms must also be tight to prevent loss of liquid or cement paste. Generally, the higher the quality of formwork, then the better the resulting concrete. Formwork is usually coated with a suitable release agent or other material before the concrete is cast to prevent water absorption or unwanted bonding between the form and the concrete. *Form ties* are metal devices that are used to prevent the formwork from spreading as the lateral load of plastic concrete is imposed. When the formwork is removed, the wires or rods remain in place and are usually twisted, broken, screwed, or pulled off, depending on the type of form tie. The configuration of the form panels and the location of the form ties are important design considerations in wall appearance.

PRECAST CONCRETE

Precast concrete is generally made at a factory before being moved to and installed at the site. It uses an automated system of mixing and casting in a controlled environment, which yields consistency in craft and materials. It can be cast as panels, slabs, and beams, as well as complex shapes for structural or enclosure elements, or any other form in the building construction. Precast building systems are a booming industry; their use can accelerate the construction process and can also be a time-saving and cost-effective method for projects that utilize a number of uniform or large-scale members such as airports, parking structures, or stadiums. Precast concrete cladding panels that are attractively finished and which contain insulation and some building services are becoming more viable.

The formwork in which precast concrete is cast is usually made of high-quality steel, coated plastic, or wood, and can be used many times, yielding a more consistent and controlled concrete member. Since the formwork is not made on site or used only once, this reduces the unit cost of the concrete products. Time is also saved since there is no formwork to fabricate or remove from the site. Precast units are usually cured with steam to create the ideal amount of moisture and heat for the concrete to cure quickly. Precast concrete products can be cast, cured, and removed from forms in twenty-four-hour cycles, with a high-quality result. On the construction site, precast members can be erected very quickly, much like steel. They can also be erected in poor weather conditions without having to wait for concrete to cure properly, in contrast to cast-in-place concrete.

Because precast concrete must be transported to the site, there are a number of practical limitations to consider. The concrete units can often be extremely heavy and large, making transportation to the construction site difficult, as the size of the units are prescribed by the legal highway or rail line capacities between the factory and the building site. The infinite sculptural qualities of concrete can similarly be constrained by these transportation restrictions. Some portions of a building cannot practically be precast due to the size or shape of the piece, or the logistics of transportation and erection. Foundations, slabs on grade, or other large elements cannot be precast. Repetitive, consistent, and manageably sized elements are more viable for precasting.

Precast concrete can also be cast at the site and then moved into its final location. One of the most common of these practices is called *tilt-up* concrete. This method eliminates the constraints of transporting precast members over roadways to the site, but issues of climate and creating proper formwork need to be addressed, as with cast-in-place concrete.

CONCRETE MASONRY UNITS

Concrete masonry units (CMUs) are technically considered a type of unit masonry, but are made using special concrete that is precast into formwork. CMUs are typically manufactured as hollow-core 8 x 8 x 16 inch (203 x 203 x 406 mm) blocks. They are usually cast in metal molds, released immediately, and then steam-cured to a specific moisture content. The blocks can be made with different densities of concrete dependent on their intended use. They are often employed as back-up walls for brick or stone, but are increasingly used alone as an economical structural wall construction. Their hollow cores allow for reinforcing steel and grout to make the wall load-bearing.

The American Society for Testing and Materials (ASTM), which establishes standards for materials of construction, governs CMU use for load-bearing construction. C90 is the common, hollow load-bearing unit, and is the most economical masonry wall one can construct. Among others, the C129 is a hollow, non-load-bearing unit, the C145 is a solid load-bearing unit and the C55 is cast in a common brick dimension. The ASTM also specifies different grades, types, and weights for each block. CMUs are an economical way to build a load-bearing wall relatively quickly and easily. One can also achieve an insulated wall with CMUs when the hollow cores are filled or when a cavity wall is constructed. Strength can be increased by filling the CMU cells with concrete and steel. CMUs are available in an almost endless array of colors, textures, and sizes, giving a designer much to select. Disadvantages to CMUs include the weight of the units and the dependence on skilled workmanship at the construction site. Unless a CMU wall is built well, it can be unattractive, leak, or have structural problems.

AUTOCLAVED CELLULAR CONCRETE

Autoclaved cellular concrete, or ACC (also called *autoclaved aerated concrete*, or *AAC*), is a lightweight, ther-mally efficient, and structural concrete that has been in use in construction in European countries since the mid-twentieth century. Its use in the United States is still much less prevalent, primarily due to the large financial investment in acquiring the manufacturing equipment. It is a silica-rich material that contains sand or fly ash (a byproduct of coal combustion), lime, Portland cement, aluminum powder, and water. ACC is often not made with fly ash due to availability and its quality control. The aluminum powder reacts chemically with the other materials and creates tiny hydrogen bubbles, causing the concrete to expand to approximately twice its original volume. The mix is then moved into an autoclave, a chamber that is airtight and filled with pressurized steam, where the porous material gains strength, durability, and rigidity by a chemical reaction over a twelve-hour period. ACC can be used in load-bearing walls for shorter buildings and as curtain walls in taller buildings. It has a very high air content, causing it to weigh about two-thirds less than typical concrete. It also has nearly twice the amount of thermal insulation values than conventional concrete. It has a density approximately one-fifth of standard concrete and one-tenth the compressive strength. ACC can be manufactured with different densities; higher densities result in higher compressive strength but lower insulation values. Unlike normal concrete, which usually needs additional insulation, ACC can function as a structural insulating wall by itself. The overall insulation value varies, depending on the climate, *R-value*, and the thermal mass effect. It can be formed into blocks, panels, lintels, or floor slabs, and has been utilized as an alternative to wood, as it can be shaped by conventional carpentry tools, is relatively lightweight, does not rot or burn, has fairly good sound absorbing qualities, and resists insects. Some of the disadvantages of using ACC are that it has a high embodied energy due to the high energy demands of the autoclave. It also might not perform as well as more conventional types of construction in warmer climates. ACC needs to be protected from the environ-ment and surface abrasion with either siding, plaster, stucco, or other suitable finishes.

RAMMED EARTH

Rammed Earth construction is the forceful tamping to compact a mixture of earth and cement into a formwork system to create a dense and structurally stable wall. Professionally constructed rammed earth involves using heavy mechanized pneumatic equipment with a rubber or steel tip to efficiently compact the soil. The mix is approximately 8 percent water, 3 percent cement, and 89 percent soil. Ideal soil contains both sand and clay, but should not contain organic materials such as peat or loam, which would decompose. Formwork must be heavily reinforced to withstand the force of the compactor. Formwork may be textured or smooth to give the final surface different qualities. Walls are typically made at least 1 foot (30.48 cm) thick to allow for the compacting equipment to reach each "lift" of earth of 4 to 12 inches (10.16 to 30.48 cm). Each lift can be differentiated if a striated final appearance is desired, or the appearance of each lift can be minimized for a monolithic effect. Rammed earth walls are a good thermal mass, energy efficient, fire resistant, and considered environmentally friendly. Disadvantages include the risk of not ensuring the correct earth mix, and the labor (and therefore the cost) could be higher than other construction types. Considerations for utilities and HVAC systems inte-grated into the walls must also be taken into account.

FIBER CEMENT

Fiber cement is a manufactured product increasingly used as a siding material. Fiber cement is a combination of cellulose fiber material, Portland cement, silica, sand, water, and other additives. This fiber material provides tensile strength and helps prevent cracking. It is made in sheets and autoclaved, a process of curing in which heat and steam dries the product under pressure. This process gives fiber cement a low moisture content, making it a stable product that has little warping or movement. It is a good product to use in place of wood where there is excessive moisture or a chance of termites. It can be made into boards for a horizontal lap siding or in a panel sheet, much like the proportions of standard plywood, for siding purposes. It can be applied in much the same way as wood siding, however its higher weight makes it more unwieldy to manage relative to a wood product. Fiber cement products are usually available with a smooth face surface or an embossed texture to mimic actual wood.

ADMIXTURES

Admixtures—materials other than water, aggregate, and cement that are added before or during the mixing pro-cess—can greatly improve the quality of concrete by increasing its strength, workability, and durability and help-ing it cure under poor environmental conditions. In addition to improving the performance of concrete, admixtures can also add color or change its final appearance.

→ **Air-entraining** admixtures increase concrete's workability and are considered one of the most common and beneficial admixtures. They also protect concrete from freeze-thaw damage by having thermal insulating properties. In high concentrations, concrete with these admixtures is lightweight and non-structural, given its proportion of air to mass. These admixtures reduce concrete's strength, so one should consult with engineers to ensure the concrete will meet the needs of the application.

→ **Accelerating** admixtures make concrete cure or harden more quickly, thereby reducing construction time and project costs. These admixtures allow for formwork to be removed sooner and, in colder climates, may give the concrete needed strength before the onset of freezing temperatures. However, they can also cause shrinkage and discoloration to the concrete as it cures. Calcium chloride, a common ingredient in accelerating admix-tures, can corrode any embedded ferrous metals in the concrete. Therefore use of this chemical must be care-fully monitored.

→ **Retarding** admixtures slow the curing or hardening process down, allowing more time to place and finish the concrete. Retarders are commonly used in massive engineering applications, especially in the construction of bridge decks, dams, and very large foundations. They offset the normally high temperatures given off during the hydration process and avoid complications when unavoidable delays between mixing and placing occur. Due to the longer timeframe for setting, concrete containing retarders may be vulnerable to environmental conditions during the curing period. It may also be more vulnerable to *creep*, a permanent deformation in a material caused by structural stress.

→ **Super plasticizers** are organic compound admixtures that transform a stiff concrete pour into a more fluid and workable mix. They also can permit a reduction of the water content to increase the concrete's strength. Slag cement, fly ash, and microsilica are some ingredients that can plasticize the concrete to make it more workable, keep the water content low, without sacrificing the concrete's compressive strength.

→ **Water-reducing** admixtures allow for a 5 to 10 percent reduction in the amount of mixing water needed while retaining the same amount of workability for the concrete. These different chemicals can produce a higher-strength concrete and aid plasticity, but may slow the hydration process and decrease the early strength of the concrete. Different types of chemicals added to concrete can be called water-reducing ad-mixtures; their advantages and disadvantages vary depending on the particular chemical used.

→ **Fly ash** admixtures are made from a powdered waste product of coal-fired power plants and can increase concrete's strength and decrease its permeability. They can also improve a mix's workability and reduce the required amount of mixing water.

→ **Pozzolans** admixtures are mineral admixtures that include cementitious materials and natural pozzolans such as volcanic ash, fly ash, and silica fume. These admixtures improve the workability of the concrete and reduce the internal temperature during the curing process. If the internal temperature of curing concrete gets too hot, the pour will not cure properly, possibly compromising its structural integrity and causing shrinkage or cracking.

→ **Pigmenting admixtures** can be added to concrete to achieve a desired color. There are three primary methods to color concrete. The *integral method* mixes the coloring agent throughout the concrete mix, usually done while the concrete is in the batching silo or mixing truck. The resulting colors are gener-ally muted but are uniform throughout. The *dry method* of coloring is applied to exposed surfaces after the concrete has been placed. The coloring agent is troweled into the surface and forms a thin veneer of color on the slab. These colors are generally more vibrant than the integral method because the concentration of pigment on the sur-face is typically greater. Finally, concrete can also be colored with a chemical stain that penetrates cured concrete surface, generally producing an uneven and variegated color effect due to varying absor-bencies of the concrete surface. Chemical stains react directly with the existing concrete's minerals and pore structure.

In addition to these admixtures there are many others, all of which have particular purposes. *Freeze-protection* admixtures allow concrete to cure at temperatures below 20 degrees F (11.1 degrees C). *Fibrous* admixtures— short fibers of glass, steel, or plastics—give the concrete added reinforcement at a micro-level. *Shrinkage-reduc-ing* admixtures (SRAs) decrease the effects of drying shrinkage by reducing the concrete's surface tension, and *corrosion-inhibiting* admixtures contain calcium nitrite to protect reinforcing steel, and any other ferrous metal within the concrete, against corrosion.

MOVEMENT JOINTS

Buildings move due to many factors, including thermal change and environmental stress. Movement is often accommodated by separating sections of a building to move independently within a prescribed range. Building movement joints are the flexible connections between these sections.

There are four basic types of concrete joints:

→ **Control joints** allow for controlled cracking along a formed, tooled, or cut joint. They allow for shrinkage of the sections of concrete.

→ **Construction joints** occur when successive concrete pours abut one another. Seams between successive pours, called *cold joints*, are often a point of weakness; reinforcement bar and interlocking keys may be used to tie the two concrete members together.

→ **Expansion joints** are engineered joints that allow two adjacent structural elements to move independently of each other when subjected to stresses. They allow for both contraction and expansion of the concrete sections.

→ **Isolation joints**, which are a type of expansion joint, are used to separate concrete into individual structural elements or to isolate the concrete from other construction materials.

The size and frequency of joints varies depending upon many factors, including thermal and moisture conditions, loading conditions, and strength of the materials.

Maryhill Museum of Art Overlook

GOLDENDALE, WASHINGTON, USA // ALLIED WORKS
REINFORCED CAST-IN-PLACE CONCRETE, SCULPTURAL QUALITY, PLACEMENT

DESIGN INTENTION

This project was constructed on a bluff above the Columbia River Gorge in Washington State, on the grounds of the Maryhill Museum of Art. A "ribbon" of concrete cascades down a gentle slope to create a seemingly continuous line in the landscape. A single concrete slab emerges from the ground and moves across the landscape, enfolding eight volumes that open and close to the sky through horizontal and vertical planes. Through the experimental spatial approach of this outdoor museum piece, the designers intended to enhance the qualities of the landscape without placing any references or social qualifiers in the composition. The various surfaces are marked with openings that establish specific references in the landscape. The intentionally ambiguous scale and program give a feeling of a sublime composition to match the site.

MATERIALITY

One of the prime advantages of cast-in-place concrete is its ability to take on almost any shape or form while maintaining high structural capacity. Here concrete is used to create the image of a continuous ribbon that dives up and down into the earth with a single monolithic piece. Subtractive manipulations of the concrete alter spatial conditions and frame views.

The use of cast-in-place concrete has allowed this structure to create a number of walls, planes, openings, and platforms that appear to unfold and engage the landscape using one continuous material. The effect is a material stretched beyond the intuitive sense of its physical limits. The uniform cloak of concrete conceals the complex and varied configuration of steel reinforcement within, which is the co-dependent material relied upon to make the formal manipulations possible. Few materials are as versatile as reinforced concrete, as demonstrated here by its capability to carry loads and face exterior conditions in such varied orientations.

The central achievement in this project is the dematerialization of cast-in-place concrete. Concrete typically records its environment at the time of its making, such as taking on the dimensions and surface textures dictated by formwork or by subtle reactions to the temperature and humidity of the air around the concrete during the first few days of its life. The concrete seen here minimizes these indices of its making in favor of an abstract purity. Concrete is a means here, not an end. Its material properties are not expressed but rather are repressed. The designers and craftspeople insightfully anticipated the normal tendencies of the material and sought to control them. This datumlike form will likely become a reference to observe the subtle actions of nature on a material. As time passes the surfaces may change slightly, in accordance with their exposure to the sun and to weather, and in relation to the ground plane.

TECHNICAL

Concrete is strong in compression but relatively weak in tension. When steel reinforcement is embedded into concrete it can resist tension and compression and becomes a versatile construction material. Deformed reinforcing bars made of mild steel are typically used to impart tensile strength to concrete. In this project, conventional steel reinforcement was used throughout, with post-tensioning cables added in the longer elevated spans.

Form surfaces were made of medium-density overlay (MDO) sheets coated with two layers of clear varnish—one applied before form assembly and one after, creating a watertight seal and giving the concrete a smooth, shiny surface. Joints in the formwork were biscuited and glued together to ensure dimensional accuracy and to help hold the formwork together at joints and corners during concrete placement.

The concrete mix design was a modified version of the Oregon Department of Transportation bridge mix specification. Plasticizer and high-range water reducer admixtures controlled curing time over the long interval after batching, and ensured that the mix would easily flow into all of the spaces within the formwork. All concrete was placed in one continuous pour to ensure uniformity of the mixture and to minimize cold joints. The ambient temperature on the day of placement averaged 55 degrees F (12.7 degrees C)—optimal for long-term strength development in concrete.

Areas where concrete flow would be difficult were given special attention by careful vibrating through access chases in the formwork. This was especially important in lengthy horizontal sections far below the exposed upper concrete surfaces. Vibrators in all locations were prohibited from contacting form surfaces in order to ensure uniformity of the final concrete appearance; this was very difficult due to the density of reinforcing bars in some locations.

The ribbon of concrete is a uniform 10 in. (25.4 cm) thick, 150 ft. (45.72 m) long, with horizontal spans reaching as far as 37 ft. (11.28 m). The corners of the concrete are not chamfered, and voids and cold joints are not evident, despite the absence of cosmetic treatments to the concrete surfaces after formwork was removed. Special trowelling techniques were developed to achieve a very hard and smooth top surface of the concrete to match the surfaces formed by contact with the formwork.

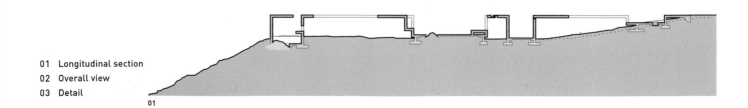

01 Longitudinal section
02 Overall view
03 Detail

01

02

03

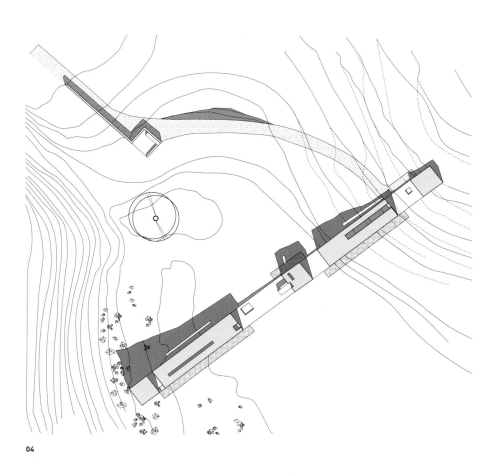

04

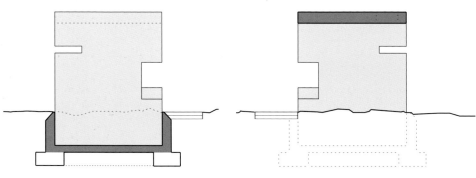

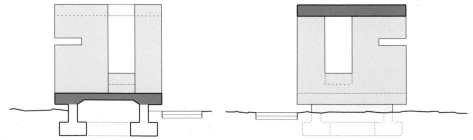

05

06

07

Hafengebaude Rohner

**LAKE CONSTANCE, AUSTRIA // BAUMSCHLAGER & EBERLE
REINFORCED CANTILEVER, MODULAR COORDINATION**

DESIGN INTENTION

Located on waterfront property overlooking a busy lake marina, this small office building was erected after a flood destroyed the original office space. The deceptively simple structure—construction was completed in only three months—is sophisticated in its sculptural and structural properties. The entire building is a cantilever and is aligned to focus on the waterfront beyond. This elevated structure not only creates a dramatic relationship with the site but also provides security if another flood were to occur. The client requested a sculpted office space that would allow for framed views of the surrounding land and water. Programmatically, the building is simply two spaces with mechanical services and a stair located in the "pedestal" entry structure. The elevated volume accommodates the program and avoids the threat of flooding. The architect sought to minimize the portion of the building that was anchored to the landscape in order to associate it more with the nearby sails, water, and wind.

MATERIALITY

Cast-in-place concrete is uniquely appropriate to achieve the bold profile of this building. The side walls of the building act like deep structural beams, constraining the number and size of windows so as not to compromise the overall structural system. Secondary building systems and insulation were housed between the interior faces of the concrete and the finished wood walls that sheath the interior. The result is the appearance of a wood box inserted within a concrete box. The aesthetic coolness of the concrete is balanced by the warmth of the interior wood. One appreciates each material more because of the presence of the other. The open ends of this prismatic shape present framed views to the land and water—the essential duality of the site.

The elevated volume is objectified by its unique position in space and by the unsettling juxtaposition of form and material. We know from previous experience that concrete is massive compared to its strength, yet here it curiously cantilevers in an unexpected dimension. This project startles the observer by juxtaposing our acquired sense of the material with a levitating form that is alien to that material.

The broad elevations are simple and bold: an ambitious cantilever, the enfronting plane, the single horizontal slot window. It is also complex and subtle, consisting of variations in concrete hue, and the rational pattern of form markings and ties. The concrete is significant at these two scales because the architect deliberately addressed both scales.

TECHNICAL

The ability of concrete to transfer loads through complex shapes is effectively demonstrated by this "C-clamp" structure. The load at the top end of the "C," which is suspended in air, is transferred and supported by a massive, 2.33 ft. deep x 8.66 ft. wide x 56.25 ft. long (.71 x 2.64 x 17.15 m) footing, which is anchored in soil. Vertical loads and rotational twisting are resisted by the mass of the soil that holds the structure. By hiding the lower portion of the "C" shape in the ground, the building appears to float in air. This ambitious cantilever exploits the capacity of conventionally reinforced cast-in-place concrete to carry significant compression and tension loads. It also demonstrates the high degree of structural continuity intrinsic to this construction system.

Cast-in-place concrete is typically cast episodically due to practical considerations, but performs structurally as a single, monolithic unit. Continuity is provided by the steel reinforcement, and by some degree of bonding between the concrete in abutting sections. Formwork size and placement are an important part of the design whenever cast-in-place concrete is exposed. The formwork used here for the elevated mass is of a different scale than that for the anchoring podium and is oriented horizontally. All concrete elements are based on a 1 x 3 x 12 volumetric ratio. The height of this elevated mass is exactly six form modules tall; the length is eight modules. A fractional increment of the module is used at each end to simplify conditions at the corners. The dimension between interior faces of the long walls is exactly seven form modules.

Load-bearing cast-in-place concrete does not readily receive secondary services such as conduit, pipes, or ducts. Even if cast into the concrete, they are unalterable thereafter. In this design, the architect provided a uniform 6.30 in. (16 cm) wood inner layer to accommodate these services with ease, and to dress the rooms with special finishes. The concrete walls, floor, and roof are all planar and of a uniform 7.87 in. (20 cm) thickness. The concrete used has an untreated, natural finish. It will acquire a patina as it responds to nature.

01 View from south
02 Longitudinal section
03 Transverse section in office
04 Transverse section in core
05 East elevation

01

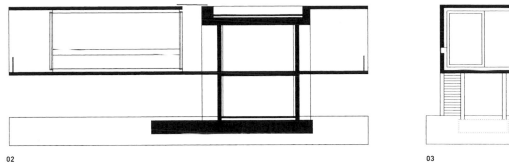

02

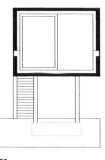

03

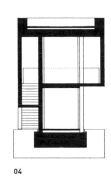

04

05

De Blas House

SEVILLA DE LA NUEVA, MADRID, SPAIN // ALBERTO CAMPO BAEZA
CAST-IN-PLACE CONCRETE

DESIGN INTENTION

This house is located on a north-facing hill in the mountains near Madrid, Spain. A large, solid concrete box serves as a platform upon which a smaller, skeletal steel frame rests, containing a delicate glass box. The concrete platform is nestled into the hillside, acting as a retaining wall and foundation for the lightweight structure above. All of the functional, domestic spaces—the kitchen, dining room, and bedrooms—are located in the lower level, within the concrete volume, while the upper glass box is used as a living room with views of the surrounding landscape. The design concept was to imbed a heavy, cavelike "podium" upon which a light, delicate structure would rest. Both lower and upper structures are engaged with the existing landscape in different ways—one integrated with the ground and the other as a place to look out upon the surrounding environment. The concrete mass stands in contrast with the lightness and linearity of the steel.

MATERIALITY

This project demonstrates the varying expressions possible with concrete, spanning from the very rough to the highly refined. Cast-in-place concrete forms the walls of the lower level of the house, or the anchoring "base." More refined precast prestressed hollow-core concrete elements are used for all floor and roof spans. This project deftly utilizes the inherent qualities of concrete: good compressive strength, conforms well to different site circumstances, and connects well with steel. Concrete's weight and mass meet the needs of retaining walls and serve as a foundation for another structure. The thick walls also have excellent thermal mass properties and give substantial structural strength to the house.

Nearly all buildings use reinforced cast-in-place concrete for their foundation material. Its strength and its capacity to conform to the often irregular shape of the excavation makes it a uniquely suitable foundation choice. In this project, the foundation becomes larger, emerging from the earth and accommodating a large part of the program; yet it remains subservient to the superstructure, in this case made of a contrasting system of construction.

The exposed board-formed concrete of the base is rustic on the exterior, similar in character to the surrounding landscape. This is in sharp contrast to the refinement of the templelike frame perched upon it. Openings through these concrete walls are few and small, consistent with the architect's intention to make these interior spaces feel cavelike. Even the door to the lower floor is finished with a matching concrete outer face and is set flush with the face of the concrete wall.

TECHNICAL

Native soils in this region are granular, and the climate is arid, thus basement spaces are not vulnerable to water intrusion nor expansive soils. Drainage media including drain tile, continuous drainage mat, and waterproofing protect the subgrade concrete walls. The 9.8 in. (25 cm) thick reinforced concrete walls retain the earth and carry gravity loads down to the foundations. Elevated slabs and ground slab are precast hollow core elements that are prestressed to increase their efficiency and reduce their mass. Precast floor spanning elements are 7.9 in. (20 cm) deep, and roof spanning elements are 5.9 in. (15 cm) deep; all are 47 in. (120 cm) wide.

The finish flooring, made of tile and concrete, is isolated from the structural slabs using thermal and moisture barriers. Concrete roof decks are topped with a thin cast-in-place concrete slab that can accept pedestrian traffic. Below it is rigid thermal insulation and a waterproof membrane.

The concrete slab that is the roof of the framed living space is also precast prestressed concrete, but has a painted steel-plate fascia and is finished with a painted plaster ceiling, concealing the concrete from direct observation.

01 Plan
02 View through roof pavilion
03 Roof view

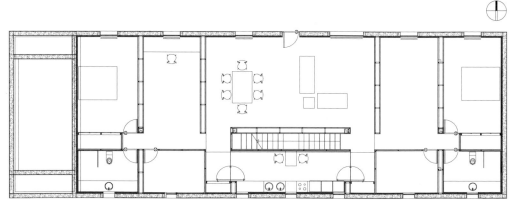

02

03

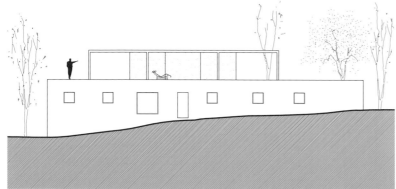

04

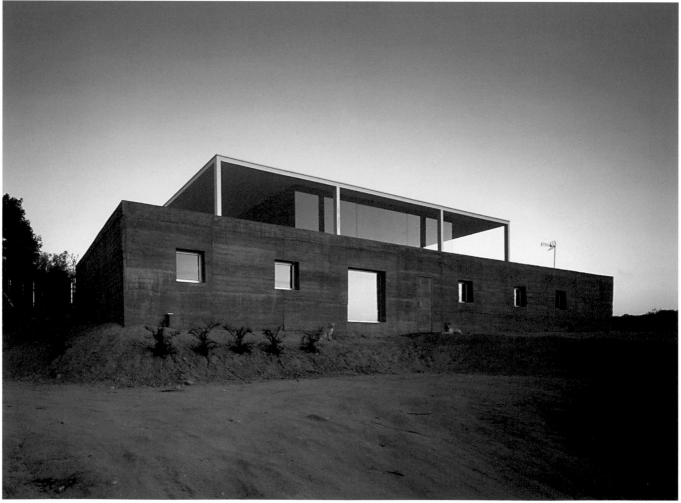

05

04 **North elevation**

05 **View from northwest**

06 **Wall section**

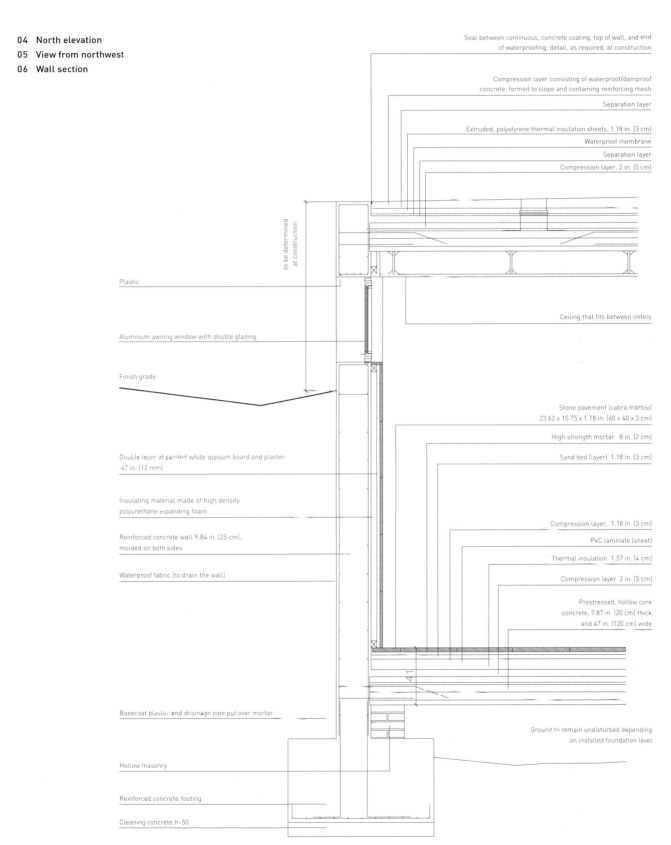

Seal between continuous, concrete coating, top of wall, and end of waterproofing; detail, as required, at construction

Compression layer consisting of waterproof/dampproof concrete, formed to slope and containing reinforcing mesh

Separation layer

Extruded, polystyrene thermal insulation sheets, 1.18 in. (3 cm)

Waterproof membrane

Separation layer

Compression layer, 2 in. (5 cm)

Ceiling that fits between lintels

to be determined at construction

Plastic

Aluminum awning window with double glazing

Finish grade

Stone pavement (cabra marble)
23.62 x 15.75 x 1.18 in. (60 x 40 x 3 cm)

High strength mortar .8 in. (2 cm)

Sand bed (layer) 1.18 in. (3 cm)

Double layer of painted white gypsum board and plaster .47 in. (12 mm)

Insulating material made of high density polyurethane expanding foam

Compression layer, 1.18 in. (3 cm)

PVC laminate (sheet)

Thermal insulation 1.57 in. (4 cm)

Reinforced concrete wall 9.84 in. (25 cm), molded on both sides

Compression layer 2 in. (5 cm)

Waterproof fabric (to drain the wall)

Prestressed, hollow core concrete, 7.87 in. (20 cm) thick and 47 in. (120 cm) wide

Basecoat plaster and drainage pipe put over mortar

Ground to remain undisturbed depending on installed foundation level

Hollow masonry

Reinforced concrete footing

Cleaning concrete h-50

Valdemaqueda Town Hall

VALDEMAQUEDA, SPAIN // PAREDES PEDROSA ARQUITECTOS
REINFORCED CAST-IN-PLACE CONCRETE, TEXTURED SURFACES

DESIGN INTENTION

This 5,666-square-foot (527 sq. m) public building is located in Valde-maqueda, Spain, between Madrid and the province of Avila. The small town is low in density and is set among a pine forest and a rolling mountain range to the north. The building completes one edge of the public plaza, a fundamental and vital feature of Spanish village life. Neighboring buildings are constructed of granite or painted masonry walls with slate or clay tile roofs.

This civic building is inspired by its natural site and its village context. A large concrete frame embraces the smaller spaces of this building and represents a cultural metaphor for the civic role of individuals within the larger community. The goal was to fit this building within the scale of the town while still retaining a prominent public presence and, most importantly, clearly defining the town square. Though small in size, this project required four years to complete. The slow, deliberate process became a catalyst for refinement of the design, purifying the design intentions to their most economical and potent resolution.

MATERIALITY

The general building configuration resolves urban objectives with project program. The result is two rectangular volumes of cast-in-place concrete linked at a skew by a glazed entrance hall. Wood accents warm the primary elevation toward the public square, while slate panels matching the formwork module accent the opposite elevation, facing an open landscape. The material palette is different than neighboring buildings, but is compatible through its color and texture. The town hall's stature as a public building is expressed through its formal and material uniqueness relative to the context.

Concrete is an appropriate choice for the town hall because it symbolizes civic strength and longevity through its material qualities. It was chosen as the primary material because it could easily integrate with the existing landscape and would complement the colors of the common local materials—iroko wood, gray slate, and aluminum—which were used throughout the interior and exterior of the building. Reinforced concrete serves as the structural material, creating 7 in. (18 cm) thick planar frames that these other materials occupy. All concrete was cast in place.

TECHNICAL

Reinforced concrete is used as the primary structure and enclosure system. Conventional reinforced concrete construction was used, with walls and spanning decks comprised of simple planar configurations. Textures on the structural concrete were purposefully controlled during the casting process. Two types of molds were used to contain the cast-in-place concrete: large metal panels created smooth surfaces while wood planks provided for textured areas which reduced the monolithic scale of the concrete and recalled the regional surface textures and materials. The natural concrete finish on the exterior will age gracefully in this climate. Maintenance obligations should be minimal. Some interior concrete surfaces were painted white to refine their expression.

The capacity for formwork to impart texture to cast-in-place concrete is evident. Simple geometric massing and fenestration patterns are made compatible with the vernacular context by subtle textural variations in the exterior concrete surfaces. The bold geometries of the masses are subdivided and are used to articulate the wall surfaces, producing panel treatments of varying orientation and refinement while adding little expense.

The climate in this area permits floor plates and some exterior walls to directly connect interior with exterior without any isolating thermal or moisture protection. The thermal mass of the basic structure assists in moderating interior temperatures. The south wall is an exception; it employs recessed openings, cavities, and thermal insulation to appropriately respond to this harsh exposure.

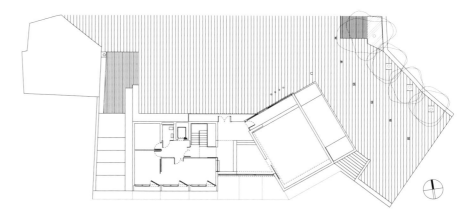

01 Plan
02 South elevation
03 North elevation

02

03

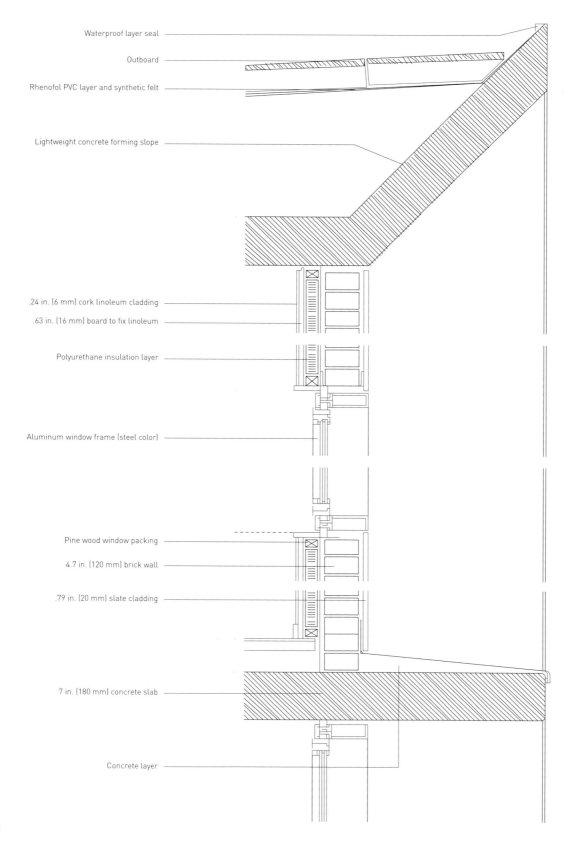

Waterproof layer seal

Outboard

Rhenofol PVC layer and synthetic felt

Lightweight concrete forming slope

.24 in. (6 mm) cork linoleum cladding

.63 in. (16 mm) board to fix linoleum

Polyurethane insulation layer

Aluminum window frame (steel color)

Pine wood window packing

4.7 in. (120 mm) brick wall

.79 in. (20 mm) slate cladding

7 in. (180 mm) concrete slab

Concrete layer

04 **Wall section, roof detail**
05 **North elevation**
06 **Wall section, window detail**

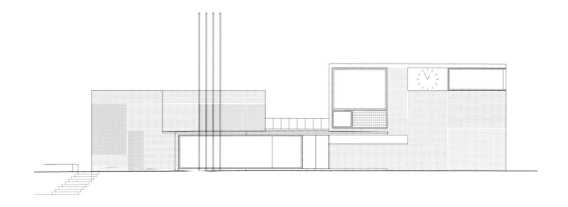

05

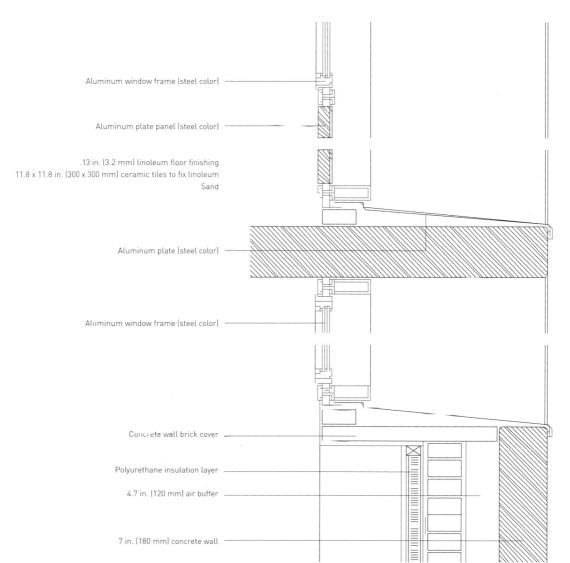

Aluminum window frame (steel color)

Aluminum plate panel (steel color)

.13 in. (3.2 mm) linoleum floor finishing
11.8 x 11.8 in. (300 x 300 mm) ceramic tiles to fix linoleum
Sand

Aluminum plate (steel color)

Aluminum window frame (steel color)

Concrete wall brick cover

Polyurethane insulation layer

4.7 in. (120 mm) air buffer

7 in. (180 mm) concrete wall

06

LOOK UP Office

GELSENKIRCHEN, GERMANY // ANIN JEROMIN FITILIDIS & PARTNER
CAST-IN-PLACE CONCRETE, INSULATING LAYER

DESIGN INTENTION

This three-story office building for LOOK UP, an international advertising and communication company, sought to be highly recognizable to the public and to be well-suited to the specific workings of the firm. The two upper floors are designed as the "creativity zones," and are expressed in a pure glass "box," where open and transparent administrative and conferencing areas are located. The ground floor is the "production zone," and is expressed in a heavy concrete base, where the realization of the final products is completed. The design concept was to delineate the different work zones in two distinct materials.

MATERIALITY

The intention was to express a purity of monolithic material using concrete. This is achieved by incorporating the insulation within the two layers of the concrete wall. Precast concrete louvers on the sunny elevation express a similar theme at a minor scale.

The west wall and all the interior walls, floors, and stairways are concrete that was cast in place with a smooth-faced finish. The walls are cast in a yellow pine, 6.56 ft. (2 m) modular formwork, used repetitively for a consistent finish throughout the building. Only the concrete blades on the southern side of the building are precast components. These comblike blades of concrete create a brise-soleil (sun-break louvers) for the southern face of the glass wall for optimum shading in the summer and sunlight in the winter.

Cast-in-place concrete is typically mixed near the construction site and requires a form to give it shape. Cast as a thick liquid, concrete will take the shape of the void created by the formwork. The exterior surfaces will retain the texture of the formwork's surface, which is typically made of wood, plastic, or metal. Release agents of wax, oil, chemicals, or plastic allow for separation between the concrete and the form, especially in more intricate surfaces. The predominant cost factor when considering cast-in-place concrete is the formwork, which must be carefully designed for both aesthetic and economic reasons, especially when the concrete is to be left exposed, as in this project. It is generally most economical to make formwork using elements of uniform size, shape, and thickness as is structurally possible in the construction process. Alternatively, cast-in-place concrete can be used to make irregular geometric shapes using formwork that is not of uniform or repetitive configuration.

Reinforced concrete is prone to *creep*, which is the minor deformation of materials under continuous loading. Details in this building anticipate this tendency by allowing a margin of safe movement wherever brittle materials adjoin the concrete. For example, large glass panels are installed into embedded stainless steel channels at their lower and upper edges; approximately .79 in. (2 cm) is provided at the top edge for movement, creep, and deflection.

Concrete is typically massive and volumetric in its embodiment. This is the case with the base of this building and with the solid volumes that contain servant elements on upper floors. However, this building also presents a contrasting character to this material, one of slenderness and almost machinelike crispness, seen in the brise-soleil.

TECHNICAL

The design of the exterior concrete walls involves two concrete planes that sandwich a 3.15 in. (8 cm) layer of insulation. This is a variation of a conventional multi-wythe masonry technique, in which the outer plane is restrained from buckling by anchoring it to the inner plane. The strategy for reinforcement to link the concrete layers is borrowed from masonry wall design, and the outer layer of concrete is detailed with thermal movement joints, as would be employed in a masonry veneer.

The load-bearing inner layer of concrete is a reinforced, 6.7 in. (17 cm) thick wall, while the exterior layer is 3.94 in. (10 cm) thick and contains reinforcement mesh. The two layers are connected by rebar or metal ties, which are doweled into the thicker load-bearing wall and anchored to the front wall. The casting of the concrete integrated the HVAC, electrical, and plumbing systems so that no pipes or wires would be seen on the concrete surfaces. Appropriate recesses were provided in the concrete for light switches, conduits, sockets, light fixtures, and other services.

This project was the first in Germany to use this particular multilayered method of construction. The outer layer achieves its unprecedented 3.94 in. (10 cm) slenderness by using mesh reinforcement rather than conventional reinforcement bars. The horizontal division in the two-story glass wall on the west elevation is a 7.5 in. (19 cm) square reinforced concrete beam, which seems to span a full 33 feet (10 m). It is actually supported at 6.5 foot (1.98 m) intervals by steel tension mullions suspended from the roof slab. This concrete element braces the glass wall against lateral loads and is a reference to the upper-floor slab.

Concrete is used as load-bearing structure, exterior and interior finish, thermal mass, and as daylight control system. Heating is provided by a steam system beneath the floor; there is no artificial cooling system. Heating costs are low due to the effectiveness of the direct gain and insulation strategies.

The horizontal brise-soleil are made of precast concrete, measuring 4 in. x 1.66 in. x 18.75 ft. (10 x 52 x 571 cm), arrayed vertically at 15 in. (38 cm) intervals. These are precise rectangular prisms without chamfers. They create a striking visual pattern of light and shadow on this south exposure.

01 Plan
02 Southwest corner

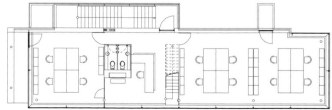

01

03

04

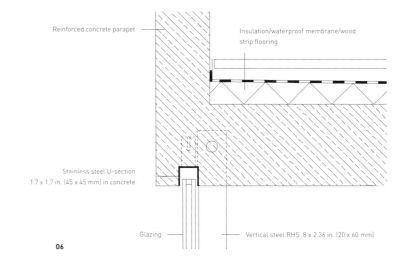

Reinforced concrete parapet

Insulation/waterproof membrane/wood strip flooring

Stainless steel U-section
1.7 x 1.7 in. (45 x 45 mm) in concrete

Glazing

Vertical steel RHS .8 x 2.36 in. (20 x 60 mm)

06

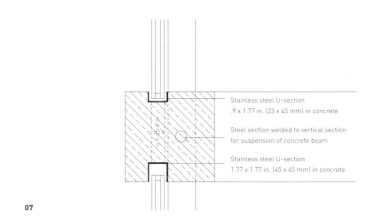

Stainless steel U-section
.9 x 1.77 in. (23 x 45 mm) in concrete

Steel section welded to vertical section
for suspension of concrete beam

Stainless steel U-section
1.77 x 1.77 in. (45 x 45 mm) in concrete

07

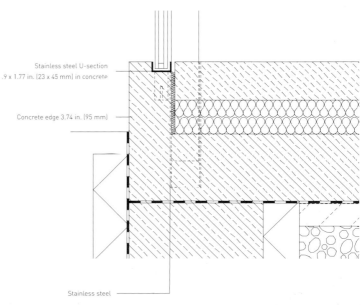

Stainless steel U-section
.9 x 1.77 in. (23 x 45 mm) in concrete

Concrete edge 3.74 in. (95 mm)

Stainless steel

05

08

Signal Box Switching Station

**ZURICH, SWITZERLAND // GIGON/GUYER ARCHITEKTEN
CAST-IN-PLACE CONCRETE, PIGMENTED CONCRETE**

DESIGN INTENTION

This building functions to supervise rail traffic in the Zurich urban area. It stands on the edge of the train tracks near the Gottlieb Duttweiler Bridge, the point at which the city's urban housing gives way to outlying industrial districts. The top floor is occupied with offices and workspaces, while the three lower floors contain technical equipment such as relays, computers, rotary converters, and power equipment for the rails. The lower floors also contain a generator room and ventilation facilities. Because this equipment gives off large amounts of heat, a climate-controlling envelope was needed that could store heat while also dispersing excessive heat to the surrounding environment. This building uses the materials and pigments of the local urban context to create a functional and unique building that reflects its site.

MATERIALITY

A patina-like discoloration caused by the dust produced by train brakes marks all of the objects and structures near the train tracks. This characteristic led the designers to use a brown-red iron oxide pigment admixture in the concrete to give the structure a contextual color from the outset. Oxidized particles of iron, which are the same chemical bases as the dust from the train's brakes, are used as the pigment. The color was added to the concrete via the integral method, in which the pigment was mixed into the cast-in-place concrete, resulting in a uniform color throughout. The use of cast-in-place concrete also allowed this building to be a seamless monolithic mass, free of the joints and elemental expression of precast concrete. This visual quality is well suited to this building, which is meant to be dense and secure when viewed from the outside.

Concrete is intrinsically porous to a limited degree. Over time it typically absorbs water-soluble constituents of its host environment, often in varying patterns dependant on the amount of exposure to soiling ingredients. This project anticipates this material attribute and turns it into an advantage. By introducing the constituents of the environment directly into the initial mix, the concrete is imparted with these qualities as it is made. Change in appearance after completion due to exposure should therefore be minimized and controlled through this planned pigmentation. Wear and tear, as might be expected on the outside of such a building, is camouflaged: chips or divots in the concrete are less noticeable because the color runs deeper than the walls' surface.

TECHNICAL

The exterior walls are in fact composed of two cast-in-place elements: an inner and an outer layer, separated by rigid insulation, which provides a thermal break between the inner and outer surfaces and permits the inner layer to serve as a moderating thermal mass. This double-layered concrete wall construction provides the thermal mass needed to store heat and insulate the building. Additional insulation is used in the administrative and office areas. The inner layer of concrete is of a different character than the exterior due to differences in color and formwork, reflecting the fact that the inner and outer are distinct conditions. The concrete mix for the exterior wall elements received iron oxide pigment to give it a rust-red/brown hue without adversely affecting other properties, while the concrete for the interior layer is of a standard gray mix. Conventional formwork was used for the exterior surfaces, and is oriented vertically, while interior formwork was of a smaller scale and was oriented horizontally.

The detailing of the exterior of the building minimizes horizontal surfaces that shed toward the exterior surfaces, as these may alter the uniform pigmentation of the building elevations. Wall surfaces are flush and unarticulated, with windows eliminated on the lower machine floors, while upper-floor window glazing is set flush with the concrete wall surface, minimizing soil-collecting sills. The total wall thickness is 20 in. (50 cm): on the top floor, the outer layer of concrete is 10 in. (25 cm), rigid insulation is 2 in. (5 cm), and the inner layer of concrete is 8 in. (20 cm), and bears the load of the floors and roof above. Reinforcing bars form a dense cage in order to carry loads and to protect the sensitive electronics inside the building from exterior disturbances.

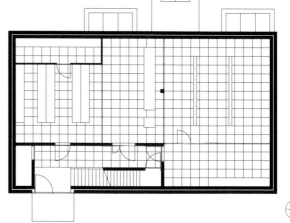

01 Ground-floor plan
02 Longitudinal section
03 Southeast corner

01

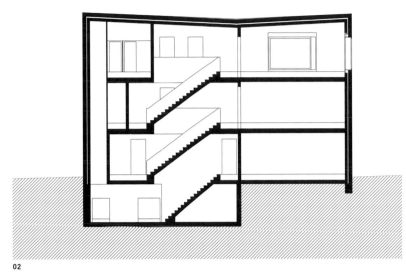

02

03

04   Interior concrete finish
05   Plan detail of wall at window opening
06   Adjacent railroad tie
07   South elevation

0   0.5   2

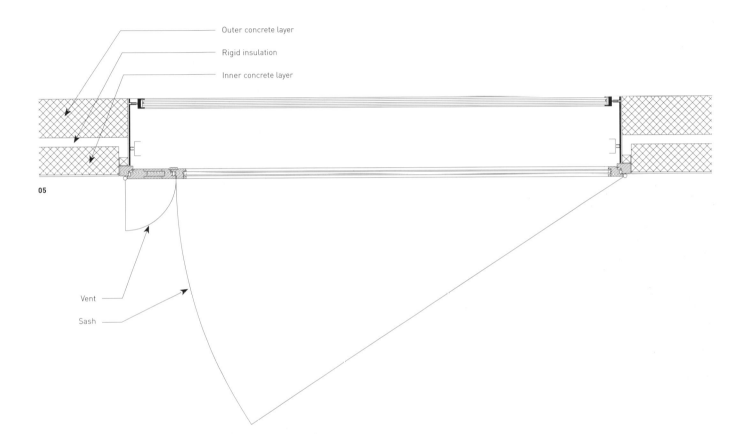

Outer concrete layer

Rigid insulation

Inner concrete layer

05

Vent

Sash

06

07

Crematorium

BAUMSCHULENWEG, BERLIN, GERMANY // AXEL SCHULTES AND CHARLOTTE FRANK
REINFORCED CONCRETE CONSTITUENTS, MONUMENTAL SCALE

DESIGN INTENTION

This crematorium is located in one of the largest cemeteries in old Berlin. The reinforced concrete building contains two ceremonial halls for fifty visitors and one larger hall for two hundred and fifty. The center hall contains a series of tall concrete columns, symbolizing trees in a forest and seemingly distributed randomly throughout the building. At the top of these columns, a round shaft of light pierces the roof, suggesting that the columns miraculously use light to hold up the structure. The design concept for this crematorium is to celebrate silence and light by creating ceremonial spaces through the use of monochromatic finishes. Concrete is used to craft a serene and quiet atmosphere. The proportions of the space and the use of a monumental concrete scale add to the overall spiritual and sacred quality.

MATERIALITY

Reinforced concrete is used here for the monolithic, smooth, and pure forms it can create. A light-colored cement was used in the concrete mix to achieve the monochromatic color that lends to the serene setting. All of the columns are structural in the main hall; some are under compression and others are under tension. A double-T steel member was cast into the concrete columns to add strength needed to support the roof. Cast-in-place concrete is used structurally and as the enclosure system, but its chief importance to the designers is its capability to render the intended scale and solemnity, especially in the ceremonial halls. Concrete is manipulated to convey symbolic content through its size, shape, configuration, and surface quality.

The architects had very ambitious expectations regarding the concrete finish, but the contractor had no previous experience in the required advanced techniques. Construction of the relatively unimportant lower-floor rooms became the testing grounds where expectations and abilities were brought to resolution. Unlike other construction materials, cast-in-place concrete becomes permanent before one has a chance to fully observe it inside the forms. Once forms are removed, the concrete can be accepted as is, altered by adding or subtracting from the surface, or else removed altogether. With this material, the architect's role therefore possibly goes beyond design and specification to include considerable involvement during the construction phase, as in this case study. The quality of this project demonstrates the rewards of a deliberate and active collaboration between architect and contractor.

TECHNICAL

After considerable research regarding the concrete mix, the architects specified a light gray blast furnace slag cement, yellow sand, and river-dredged coarse aggregates. The initial color was a pale ochre, but it lightened and cooled in hue as it carbonated over time.

To give the intended serene blue color to the concrete, the architect initially wanted to use cobalt pigments in the concrete mix, but this proved too expensive. The second option was to use a mineral stain to color the concrete after formwork was removed. Conventional form release agents were prohibited because the architect felt this would hinder the acceptance of the stain by the concrete. Instead, forms were prepared by shot-blasting the steel surfaces, then by lacquering them to give them a smooth, glassy finish, which would make removal easier. Formwork was typically left in place for three or four days (seven days maximum) before removal. The concrete was then promptly wrapped in polyethylene for seven more days to protect it from evaporation. The concrete developed light and dark gray patches on the surface, caused by air pockets under the polyethylene. Initially unwelcomed, this pattern was later considered a desirable marbled finish. Wall and column surfaces were rubbed down by hand, then were dry-brushed to remove minor surface blemishes.

It was only after all of the concrete had been cast that it was learned that the mineral staining strategy would also be prohibitively expensive. A cool, faintly blue hue was finally imparted to the monochromatic concrete interior surfaces by installing operable turquoise metallic varnished louvers near large windows. The light that enters the space reflects off of these louvers, conveying the hue from the louvers to the concrete.

The proportions and quality of the ingredients added to a concrete mix determines the strength, color, texture and general properties of the concrete member. As water is added, a chemical reaction called hydration takes place between the water and cement and creates heat that causes the concrete to eventually harden. The water-cement ratio is the most critical factor in determining the ultimate compressive strength of concrete; too much water can decrease the strength of cured concrete. This ratio also significantly affects concrete's workability during placement as well as its weathering properties. The *design strength* of concrete is the minimum compressive strength of cured concrete and is reached after curing for 28 days. A typical design strength is 3,000 psi (20.68 MPa). Since both strength and surface finish were critical in this crematorium, the water-cement ratio was optimized to produce a concrete mix that could readily be worked into formwork and would yield sufficient strength.

At 32.8 ft. (10 m) high, the concrete columns and walls were cast in three lifts; care was taken to avoid cold joints and to control mixes between successive lifts. The result is a uniform appearance with a velvety sheen. Additional steel reinforcement was used in the 230 ft. (70 m) long concrete walls so that no movement joints would be required.

01 Ceremonial hall
02 Plan
03 Ceremonial hall pool

01

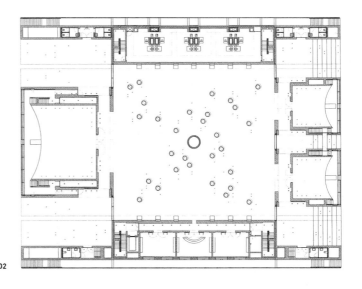

02

03

Harrison Residence and Winery

EUCHUCA, AUSTRALIA // WARD CARTER ART + ARCHITECTURE
CONCRETE INSULATED PANEL SYSTEM (CIPS), THERMAL PROPERTIES

DESIGN INTENTION

These two buildings serve as a house and a winery and tasting room, located at the bend of the Murray River, upstream from the Goulburn River, in a very dry and hot climate of Australia. Concrete, steel, and glass are the three main materials used for the construction of these structures. Insulated composite concrete panels enclose the majority of the buildings. Simple passive solar design principles were employed: being in the southern hemisphere, the house is oriented toward the north with a large roof overhang, permitting the entry of winter sunshine but excluding the high-angled summer sun. The design objectives gave priority to building economy and using the materials' thermal properties to achieve energy efficiency. Also, because the site is open to the public, the materials are intended to relate attractively to site characteristics.

MATERIALITY

All contemporary buildings employ some degree of prefabrication, from pre-assembled windows pre-set into frames to manufactured housing which can arrive at the site ready for connection to utilities and occupation, reducing overall construction time considerably. Prefabrication off site allows for economies of scale and for a construction process largely unaffected by changing weather conditions. Each piece is prepared in a controlled setting with close dimensional tolerances and other intrinsic advantages compared to site-cast concrete construction, resulting in a consistent level of quality.

Concrete insulated panels, one type of prefabricated wall system, combines the insulation value of rigid foam with the strength of concrete, which by itself does not have the requisite thermal properties for buildings needed in many climates. Prefabricated wall systems are transported to the site and are then typically installed mechanically. They are usually load-bearing or, as in this case, they are both self-supporting and are held in place by a steel frame.

Construction time was further reduced by not having to construct two different wall systems, one for an exterior skin and another for an interior finish. Instead, the CIPS panels, providing both interior and exterior finish, were selected to ensure an efficient, stable year-round internal temperature, especially critical for wine production. Composite concrete panels offer an R-value (thermal resistance) of between six and eight. They also offer high thermal inertia and low thermal conductivity—all desirable properties for this region. The value of the composite precast panels as a thermal regulation strategy is demonstrated by the absence of central cooling or heating in either the winery or the residence. The only means of heating is a single slow combustion wood stove in the living room of the residence, fueled by wood from the property.

Concrete in its natural state is a neutral gray color that blends well with the Australian bush, an arid landscape that is filled with gnarled and twisted river red gum trees. Insulated composite concrete panels are an economic and efficient system that provides finishes, structure, and thermal performance all in one installation. Electrical, plumbing, and other utilities, however, can be problematic. Here they are either carefully cast into wall panels or more often are placed within partition cavities.

Because the number of precast elements is small, economies of scale were not the highest priority. This is advantageous because the conventional approach, emphasizing mass production of identical elements, was not necessary. The erection of precast walls and steel frame was achieved quickly and efficiently. Precast panel sizes were optimal to provide the scale and variability required by the design without being so large as to make transport and placement difficult.

There is an evident rigor in the detailing of this kit-of-parts strategy, with all materials exposed without alteration and with material dimensions being evident, making explicit to occupants and visitors the means of construction. Both buildings are simple rectangular volumes, taking advantage of the planar elements used for their construction.

TECHNICAL

Exterior walls are made of composite precast concrete panels which are 10.5 in. (267 mm) thick, comprised of 2.5 in. (63 mm) outer veneer of concrete, 2 in. (51 mm) closed cell foam insulation, and 6 in. (152 mm) structural concrete layer. They are cast to become a monolithic unit with minimal thermal links between the inner and outer layers of concrete. Interior precast elements are a single layer of uninsulated concrete.

Exterior materials here will remain attractive for some time. All of the precast concrete is exposed on both sides with only a clear sealant. Steel framing members and metal roofing are all galvanized, and insulated glass and aluminum curtainwalls and sash are used where transparency is called for. In this climate, exterior maintenance needs will be minimal.

Precast panels in the residence are generally building height; intermediate floors are bolted to steel fittings embedded in the precast concrete. Planar precast walls form a sheltering south wall and are arranged in a series of parallel planes to partition interior spaces, each of which has a wide view of the vineyards to the north. Ground floors use simple thickened edge slabs; load-bearing walls of this size do not require extraordinary foundations.

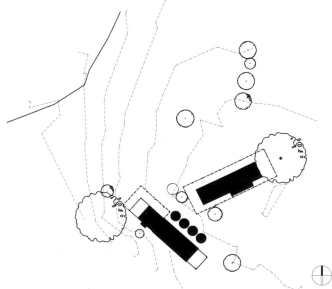

01 Site plan
02 Section
03 View from northwest

01

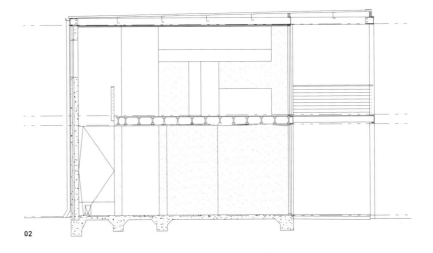

02

03

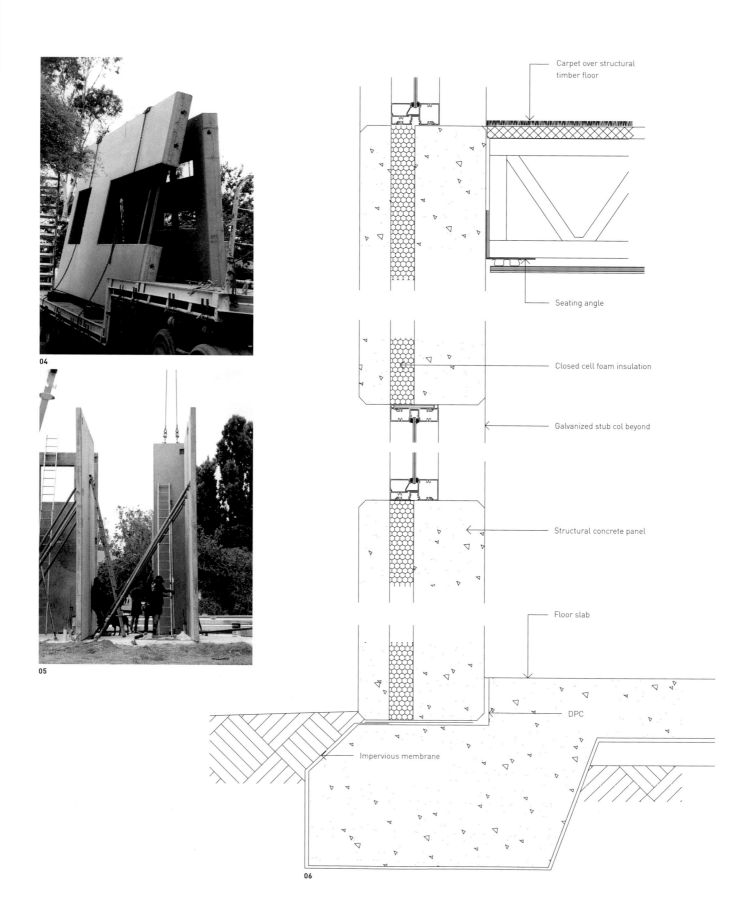

04

05

Carpet over structural
timber floor

Seating angle

Closed cell foam insulation

Galvanized stub col beyond

Structural concrete panel

Floor slab

DPC

Impervious membrane

06

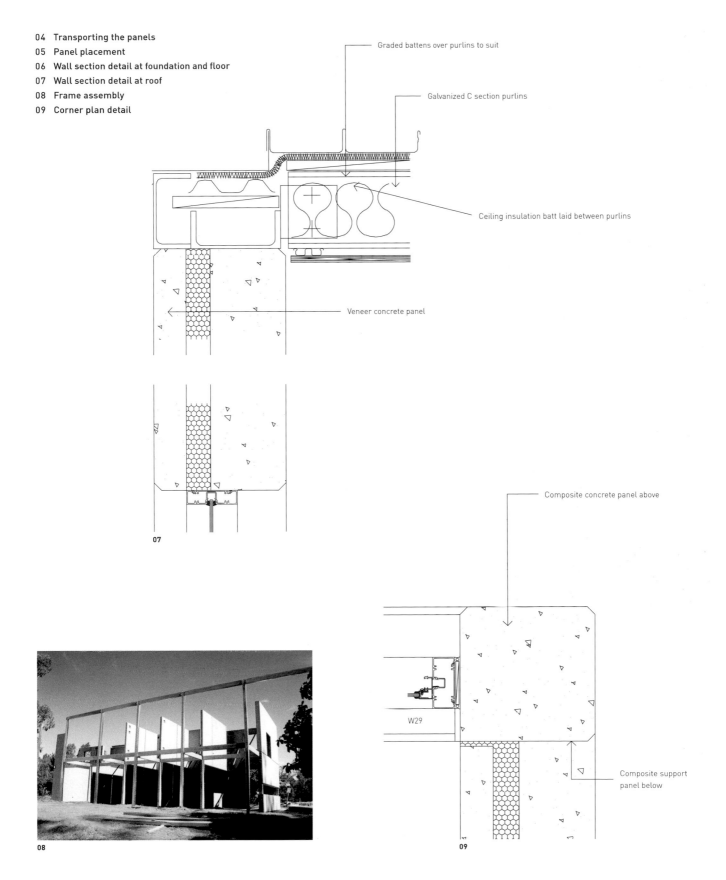

Graded battens over purlins to suit

Galvanized C section purlins

Ceiling insulation batt laid between purlins

Veneer concrete panel

07

Composite concrete panel above

W29

Composite support panel below

08

09

Retirement Home

BASEL, SWITZERLAND // STEINMANN & SCHMID ARCHITEKTEN
PRECAST CONCRETE PANELS, PRECISION

DESIGN INTENTION

This addition to a retirement home was erected between two existing structures built in the 1950s. The existing buildings are residential, while the new structure needed to contain an apartment for the home's director on the upper floor and a general reception area on the lower floor. The new building is sited to create new exterior paths, entrances, and outdoor spaces. The design goals were for the building to have a feeling of openness and to mesh with the existing structures in its locale.

MATERIALITY

Precast concrete panels are the central feature of the new building, performing all of the technical functions of the exterior wall system in one element. They provide the structure interior and exterior finishes, and create detail in anticipation of other systems in the building such as the electrical, plumbing, and HVAC. They are resistant to moisture and thermal fluctuations. Using these prefabricated panels, large openings such as floor-to-ceiling windows enhance the connection between interior and exterior spaces.

The concrete panels were cast and cured offsite and then shipped to the construction site. This method allowed for a control of quality during the casting and curing, and assured a more consistent finish on the panels, though it added some cost due to transportation. The windows are of generous size, in part because they are, like the precast panels, story height. The windows and doors occur between rather than within the concrete panels. Casting the concrete offsite also allowed for the use of high-quality formwork made of steel rather than wood, which is more typical of onsite formwork. This resulted in greater dimensional accuracy and an enhanced surface finish. Once the panels were delivered to the site, they were quickly put in place by crane.

Precast concrete construction is typically composed of large repetitive elements in order to reduce costs. In this project the relatively small dimensions of the precast elements give considerable variety to the design and express the residential scale. The building elements and their configuration are not excessively repetitive. Openings for windows and doors do not need to align between floors because the panels are only story height, and the floor plates were designed to transfer loads a short distance horizontally. The wall panels are uniform in thickness and height for a given story. They vary somewhat in width, however, giving the designer latitude in the configuration of rooms and openings. This gives the overall building a varied elevation. The small precast elements at floor and roof levels are repetitive in sectional profile except for their height. In both cases, the precast concrete elements gain considerable design flexibility by allowing one dimension to be a variable.

TECHNICAL

In this project the elements were manufactured nearby. Their relatively small sizes reduced the weight of each piece. Both of these factors made element transport and placement easier to achieve using conventional equipment.

The wall panels were precast in three layers on a smooth, horizontal metal casting bed. First the 3.94 in. (10 cm) thick outer layer was cast, then a rigid 4.72 in. (12 cm) thick insulation/vapor barrier panel was placed, and lastly the 4.72 in. (12 cm) thick interior concrete surface was cast. Stainless steel anchors link the two layers of concrete. The inner layer is load-bearing; the outer layer, which is pigmented with a 3.7 percent color admixture, is not. The seams between adjoining precast elements are .39 in. (1 cm).

All wall panels are the height of one story, approximately 8.9 ft. (2.71 m). Separate precast elements varying in height from 15 to 24 in. (37 to 60 cm) occur at the edges of floor and roof slabs to articulate the variety of conditions where upper and lower wall panels meet, to detail window or door openings, and to shape the parapet. Retractable blinds are concealed in recesses behind these panels above glazed openings on sunny exposures.

Elevated cast-in-place slabs bear on the precast panel below them. Second-floor wall panels could not be placed until the second-floor slab was cast and cured. Steel pins link the precast elements with the cast-in-place slabs. All interior partitions are made of plastered masonry.

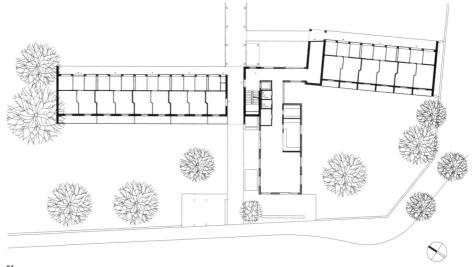

01 Site plan
02 South elevation
03 Northwest corner

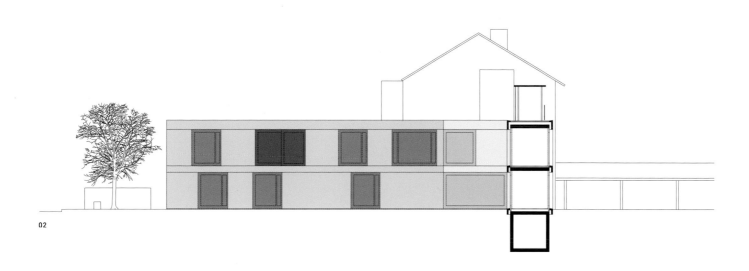

02

03

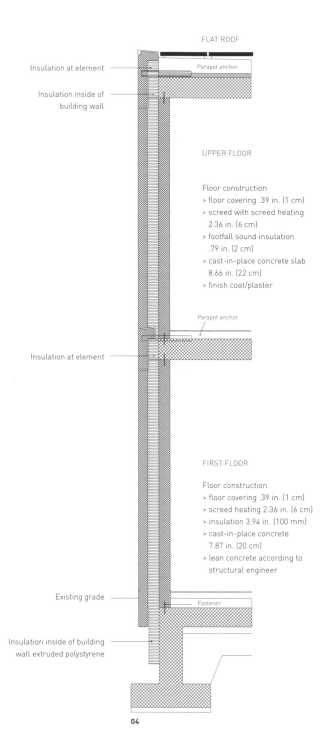

FLAT ROOF

Insulation at element

Insulation inside of building wall

Parapet anchor

UPPER FLOOR

Floor construction
> floor covering .39 in. (1 cm)
> screed with screed heating
  2.36 in. (6 cm)
> footfall sound insulation
  .79 in. (2 cm)
> cast-in-place concrete slab
  8.66 in. (22 cm)
> finish coat/plaster

Parapet anchor

Insulation at element

FIRST FLOOR

Floor construction
> floor covering .39 in. (1 cm)
> screed heating 2.36 in. (6 cm)
> insulation 3.94 in. (100 mm)
> cast-in-place concrete
  7.87 in. (20 cm)
> lean concrete according to
  structural engineer

Existing grade

Fastener

Insulation inside of building
wall extruded polystyrene

04

05

06

07

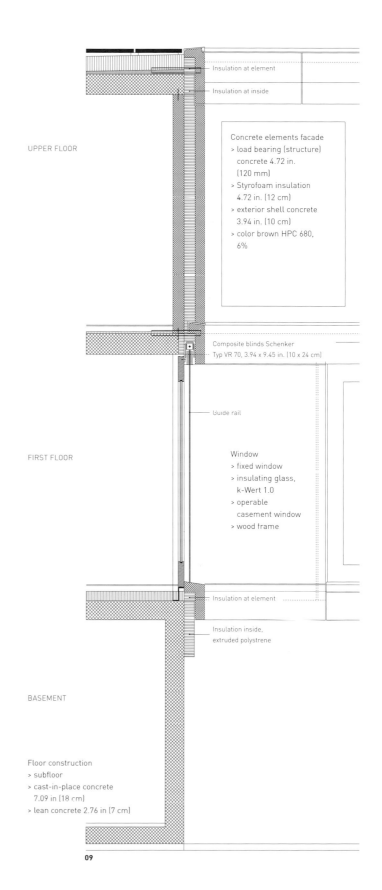

UPPER FLOOR

Insulation at element

Insulation at inside

Concrete elements facade
> load bearing (structure)
  concrete 4.72 in.
  (120 mm)
> Styrofoam insulation
  4.72 in. (12 cm)
> exterior shell concrete
  3.94 in. (10 cm)
> color brown HPC 680,
  6%

Composite blinds Schenker
Typ VR 70, 3.94 x 9.45 in. (10 x 24 cm)

Guide rail

FIRST FLOOR

Window
> fixed window
> insulating glass,
  k-Wert 1.0
> operable
  casement window
> wood frame

Insulation at element

Insulation inside,
extruded polystrene

BASEMENT

Floor construction
> subfloor
> cast-in-place concrete
  7.09 in (18 cm)
> lean concrete 2.76 in (7 cm)

08

09

Falmouth Recreation Center

FALMOUTH, MASSACHUSETTS, USA // THE GALANTE ARCHITECTURE STUDIO
COMPOSITE FIBER-REINFORCED CONCRETE CLADDING

DESIGN INTENTION

This youth recreation center and sports facility is located on a long, sloped site between an existing gymnasium and playing fields. The building looks out onto these sport fields and contains a café, fitness center, office space, computer classroom, game room, lounge, and locker facilities. This municipal building was required to use renewable energy sources, which entailed equipping the structure with passive and active solar systems and photovoltaic electrical systems. Faced with a limited budget, the challenge was to create a sports and recreation center that engaged the existing playing fields and site. Composite fiber-reinforced concrete panels were selected that express strength both as a practical maintenance issue and as a metaphor for sports. Each individual concrete panel combines into a single strong edifice, just as one player contributes to the overall strength of a team.

MATERIALITY

Composite concrete panel cladding was chosen not only for its expression of robustness but also for its literal physical durability. The panels are like shingles applied to the planar walls of the building. A prominently exposed steel frame with lateral bracing is the primary structure and is allowed to pass by windows and openings to fully express the strength and purpose of the steel, and to reveal that the composite concrete panels are not structural.

The character of the composite concrete panels as a thin cladding rather than a monolithic load-bearing wall is expressed in several prominent details: their edges are exposed at corners and at window and door openings; they lap shingle-style, revealing their lower edge and casting a thin shadow on the elevation; the fasteners are frequent and small, as is appropriate for a panel; and the primary structural frame is evident from both outside and inside the building.

The cladding strategy relies chiefly on the concrete panels to repel precipitation, but also includes an air cavity behind them, through which condensation can drain and evaporation can occur. Water is shed by a typical weathering sheet covering the sheathing.

Simple creative details turn the basic panels into an expressive shell. Explicit diagrams were prepared by the architect for the installation and fastening of all panels. This assured proper support but also acknowledged that every fastener would become ornament in the building. It was necessary to precisely place each stud in the exterior walls to receive the prescribed locations of fasteners in the running bond pattern of the concrete panels.

The module of the concrete panels determined the building's overall wall lengths and heights. Windows were selected that matched this module and were installed so that the concrete panels covered their frames, minimizing interruption of the geometric pattern of cladding panels.

TECHNICAL

Concrete has little tensile strength; reinforcement with a mesh of glass fibers imparts tensile capacity and ductility, allowing the panels to be very thin compared to their surface area. The fibers also allow the material to be easily manipulated with standard tools. The 4 x 8 ft. (1.22 x 2.44 m) panel dimension was set by building industry standards in the mid-twentieth century to accommodate the arm span and carrying capacity of the average construction worker. It is also compatible with the conventional modules of light frame construction, as was used here for the steel stud assembly.

Thin concrete panels offer excellent weathering and fire resistive qualities. While composite fiber reinforced panels lack the compressive strength of cast-in-place concrete, they are easier to handle, easy to cut and fasten, and do not require a sophisticated supporting structure.

Glass-fiber reinforced concrete panels used here have a natural cementitious finish, with no embossed texture. The wall is protected from precipitation by the concrete panels, which have washered fasteners, silicone-sealed vertical joints, and horizontal joints that are lapped shingle-style 6 in. (152 mm).

Composite concrete panels were secured using 2 in. (51 mm) stainless steel self-tapping square drive fasteners with .12 in. (3.17 mm) thick black neoprene washers behind. Fasteners are anchored at 16 in. (406 mm) on center horizontally and 21 in. (533 mm) vertically into pressure treated wood furring strips. The furring strips were clad with an EPDM (ethylene propylene diene monomer) membrane to repel moisture and isolate the concrete panel from the wood. The furring strips were anchored through exterior gypsum sheathing into metal studs.

01 Transverse section through addition
02 West elevation
03 Interior view

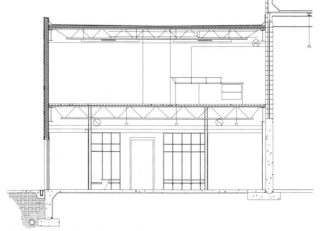

02

03

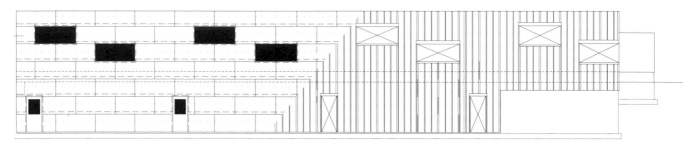

04

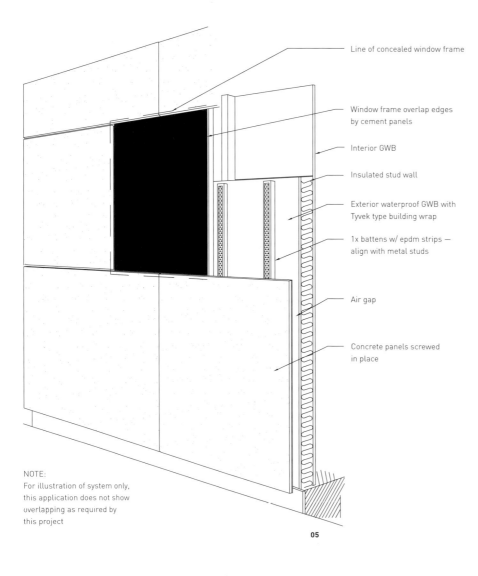

Line of concealed window frame

Window frame overlap edges by cement panels

Interior GWB

Insulated stud wall

Exterior waterproof GWB with Tyvek type building wrap

1x battens w/ epdm strips — align with metal studs

Air gap

Concrete panels screwed in place

NOTE:
For illustration of system only, this application does not show overlapping as required by this project

05

06

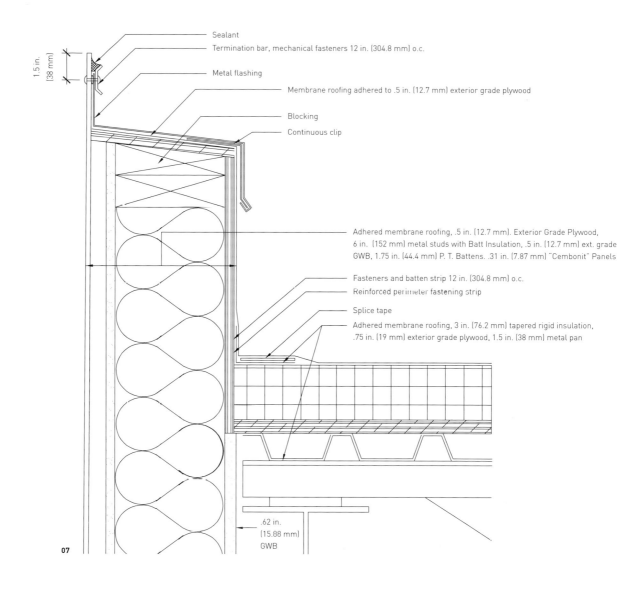

1.5 in.
(38 mm)

Sealant

Termination bar, mechanical fasteners 12 in. (304.8 mm) o.c.

Metal flashing

Membrane roofing adhered to .5 in. (12.7 mm) exterior grade plywood

Blocking

Continuous clip

Adhered membrane roofing, .5 in. (12.7 mm). Exterior Grade Plywood,
6 in. (152 mm) metal studs with Batt Insulation, .5 in. (12.7 mm) ext. grade
GWB, 1.75 in. (44.4 mm) P. T. Battens. .31 in. (7.87 mm) "Cembonit" Panels

Fasteners and batten strip 12 in. (304.8 mm) o.c.

Reinforced perimeter fastening strip

Splice tape

Adhered membrane roofing, 3 in. (76.2 mm) tapered rigid insulation,
.75 in. (19 mm) exterior grade plywood, 1.5 in. (38 mm) metal pan

.62 in.
(15.88 mm)
GWB

07

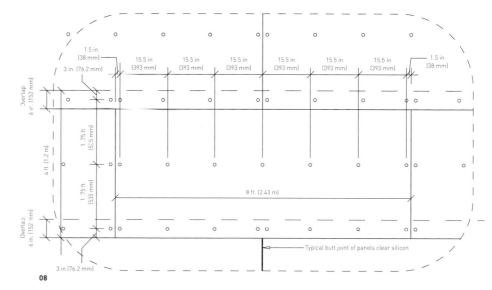

1.5 in.
(38 mm)

3 in. (76.2 mm)

15.5 in
(393 mm)

15.5 in
(393 mm)

15.5 in
(393 mm)

15.5 in
(393 mm)

15.5 in
(393 mm)

15.5 in
(393 mm)

1.5 in
(38 mm)

Overlap:
6 in. (152 mm)

1.75 ft
(5.5 mm)

4 ft (1.2 m)

1.75 ft
(535 mm)

8 ft. (2.43 m)

Overlap:
6 in. (152 mm)

3 in (76.2 mm)

Typical butt joint of panels clear silicon

08

04 West façade panel layout
05 Exterior wall assembly
06 Corner window detail
07 Roof parapet detail
08 Concrete panel typical fastener detail

Price O'Reilly House

REDFERN, NEW SOUTH WALES, AUSTRALIA // ENGELEN MOORE
COMPOSITE FIBER-REINFORCED CONCRETE CLADDING

DESIGN INTENTION

This two-story house and studio was built on a vacant block of land formerly occupied by two terrace houses. The street contains a mix of residential and commercial building types including terrace houses, warehouses, and apartments of varying ages and scales. As it was to be a residential infill building, the Local Council insisted that it read as two terrace-type houses rather than as a single element which may typologically have resembled a warehouse. The architect's aim was to ensure that this house fit its contextual role on the street while still fulfilling the needs of being a home and photography studio for the owners.

MATERIALITY

The striking play of residential versus warehouse scales is achieved through the use of two concrete products. Inexpensive concrete masonry units form the exterior surfaces of the two long walls, which are perpendicular to the street and thus are not visible in the primary elevations. This material provides the required fire separation with the neighboring properties as well as needed acoustic control. The second concrete product is .35 in. (9 mm) thick composite fiber cement sheets, a product that combines the compressive strength of concrete with the tensile strength of lightweight glass fibers. It is easily cut, nailed, screwed, and sanded with common tools and conventional construction methods. The joints between these sheets are filled with an epoxy, sanded smooth, and painted white to achieve a pristine planar appearance. Combined with a similar interior surface of gypsum board, the effect is a monolithic and pure shape that reveals little about material or scale. The intrinsic attributes of the interior and exterior wall materials are repressed in favor of the expression of the pure form.

The internal planning reflects the two-bay arrangement of the front elevation, while the rear elevation expresses a full 19.68 ft. high x 22.97 ft. wide (6 x 7 m) internal volume. There was a very limited budget for this project, so a simple strategy was developed in which a low-cost shell would be constructed, comprised of concrete block external walls on the long sides with gypsum-lined interior faces. The public end elevations are steel-framed and clad with compressed fiber cement sheets. The shell is painted white throughout and contains a series of more refined and rigorously detailed elements, differentiated by their aluminum or gray paint finish. The composite cement fiber boards are the exterior equivalent of gypsum board, used here to clad the interior spaces in a similarly smooth, abstract manner. Together, they produce a minimalist expression remarkably free of any sense of materiality.

TECHNICAL

Reinforced with alkali-resistant glass fibers, compressed fiber cement board offers many of the surface qualities of concrete, but in a simpler panelized form. Some manufacturers offer a variety of embossed textures on this product. These panels can be used as a wall surface or as sheathing below other finishes. Sheathing is a structural covering that is typically installed on the outside surface of a building's framing. It can provide lateral support, increase rigidity, and act as a base for any desired finishes.

Glass fiber reinforced concrete panels used here are .31 x 35.4 x 71 in. (9 x 900 x 1,800 mm) with no embossed texture. Composite fiber cement sheets are used as cladding only. The primary structural system in areas clad with cement board cladding is a steel frame, with galvanized studs as secondary structure.

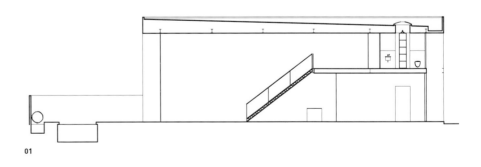

01

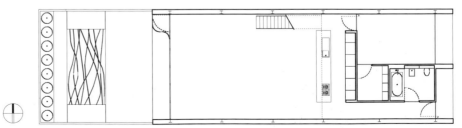

01 Longitudinal section
02 Plan
03 Open rear facade
04 View through open back doors
05 Wall section at doors

02

03

04

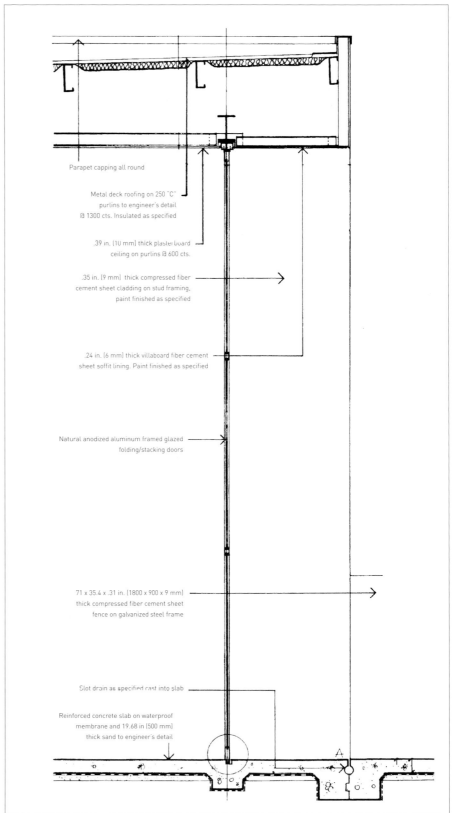

05

Parapet capping all round

Metal deck roofing on 250 "C"
purlins to engineer's detail
@ 1300 cts. Insulated as specified

.39 in. (10 mm) thick plaster board
ceiling on purlins @ 600 cts.

.35 in. (9 mm) thick compressed fiber
cement sheet cladding on stud framing,
paint finished as specified

.24 in. (6 mm) thick villaboard fiber cement
sheet soffit lining. Paint finished as specified

Natural anodized aluminum framed glazed
folding/stacking doors

71 x 35.4 x .31 in. (1800 x 900 x 9 mm)
thick compressed fiber cement sheet
fence on galvanized steel frame

Slot drain as specified cast into slab

Reinforced concrete slab on waterproof
membrane and 19.68 in (500 mm)
thick sand to engineer's detail

Yamaguchi Prefecture Pavilion

AJISU-CHO, JAPAN // KATSUFUMI KUBOTA
COMPOSITE FIBER REINFORCED CONCRETE CLADDING, JOINTS

DESIGN INTENTION

This public pavilion was constructed for a local exposition with the simple program of a theater, lobby, and art gallery. Over a period of just three months, it was used intensely by some 2.5 million visitors. The temporary nature of the exposition required that the pavilion be easily dismantled and moved to another location in the future. It was also necessary, however, that the structure be able to withstand possible earthquakes, snow, and high wind loads coming off the adjacent ocean. The design intention was to provide a serene and pure space where the land, water, and sky could be framed by the pure forms of the building. The pavilion's simple lines and large clean planes create a flowing, open space with constant framed views of the ocean and sky.

MATERIALITY

Material selection needed to be simple given the impermanence and relatively low budget of the facility. Steel was used for the primary structure, providing strength and an overall skeleton that could accommodate the extreme climatic and seismic conditions. Permanent connections such as welds were kept to a minimum. Composite fiber reinforced cement board, a lightweight and economical concrete material, gives the building its clean, simple planes and lines. It is an ideal material choice for this building given the desire to create large, flat planes that are lightweight, easily dismantled, and rebuilt. The steel primary and secondary structures can be built and dismantled with relative ease, and provide needed ductility and strength, while the cladding system renders the intended form and quality of finish without being heavy or expensive. The resulting building form does not appear to be temporary or to be made using a kit-of-parts approach. The quality of its minimalist details is a tribute to the skill of the crafts-people, and proof that relatively modest materials can be used to produce refined results.

TECHNICAL

Composite fiber reinforced concrete panels are used on exterior and interior wall and ceiling surfaces of the pavilion. This accommodates the wide moisture and thermal range anticipated in this partially open pavilion. The cladding sheets were a standard size of 2.98 x 9.94 ft. (.91 x 3.03 m) with a thickness of .47 in. (12 mm). This material can achieve this sharp edge profile (see detail drawing), which would be very difficult to achieve in cast-in-place or precast concrete.

The glass-fiber-reinforced concrete panels are applied over galvanized steel stud framing. All fasteners are countersunk, joints taped, filled with elastic compound, sanded, and painted to achieve a pure, flush form. Some walls in this pavilion are 125 feet long x 45 feet tall (38.1 x 13.7 m)—the maximum length possible without prescribed movement joints. The nearly invisible joints between cladding panels accommodate movement, obviating the need for prominent movement joints.

The high wind loads and possible seismic stress on the building required flexibility to allow for movement. Seams between the sheets of cement board are .20 in. (5 mm) spaces that are covered by fiber mesh tape and an elastic putty. This joint absorbs anticipated movement but is almost unnoticed when finished.

The planar roof assembly is 20 in. (50.8 cm) thick to conceal structure and services, but tapers to an acute angle of 15 degrees along its edge, demonstrating the workability of the cladding panels used and the skill of the craftspeople.

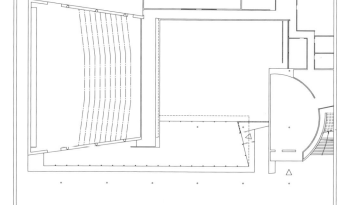

01 Ground-floor plan
02 South facade
03 Gallery interior

01

02

03

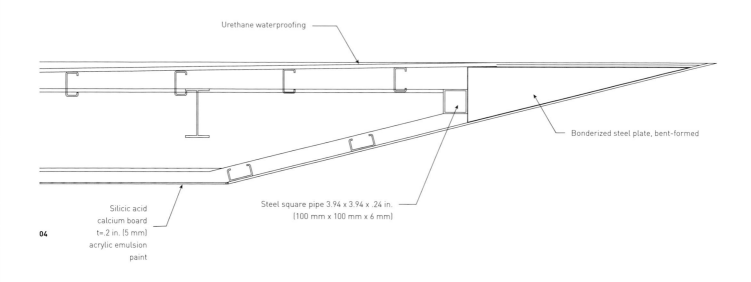

Urethane waterproofing

Bonderized steel plate, bent-formed

Silicic acid
calcium board
t=.2 in. (5 mm)
acrylic emulsion
paint

Steel square pipe 3.94 x 3.94 x .24 in.
(100 mm x 100 mm x 6 mm)

04

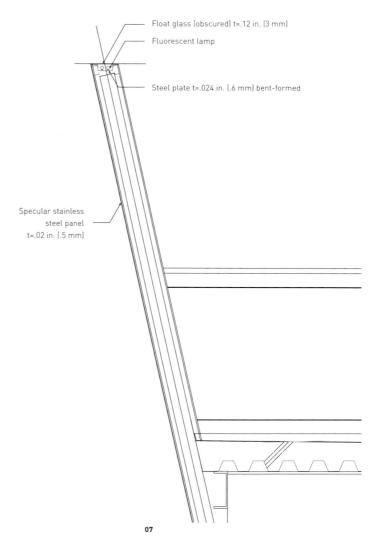

Float glass (obscured) t=.12 in. (3 mm)

Fluorescent lamp

Steel plate t=.024 in. (.6 mm) bent-formed

Specular stainless
steel panel
t=.02 in. (.5 mm)

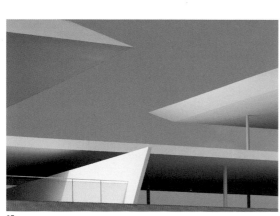

05

06

07

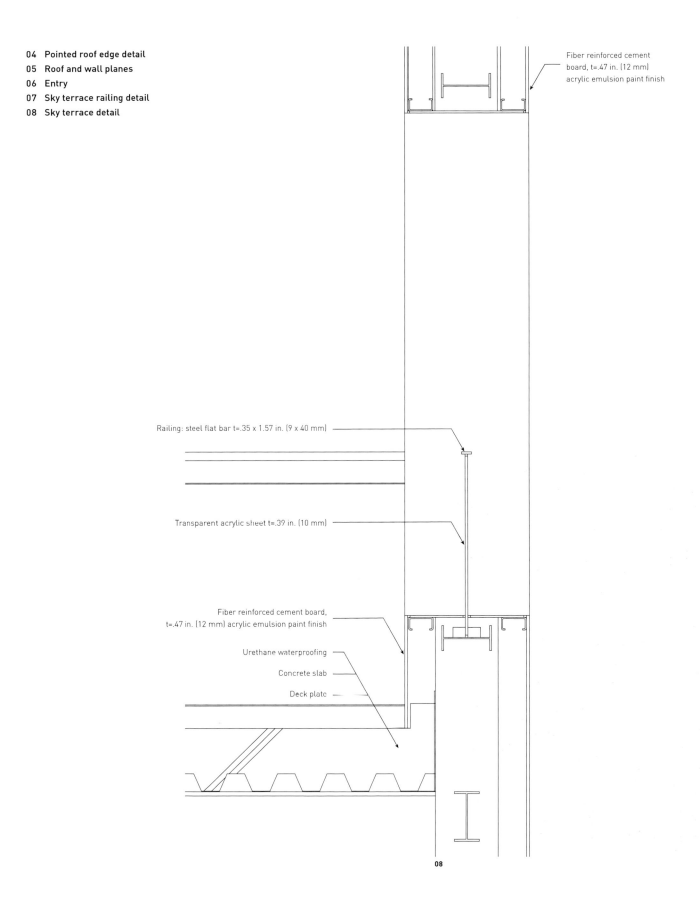

Fiber reinforced cement board, t=.47 in. (12 mm) acrylic emulsion paint finish

Railing: steel flat bar t=.35 x 1.57 in. (9 x 40 mm)

Transparent acrylic sheet t=.39 in. (10 mm)

Fiber reinforced cement board, t=.47 in. (12 mm) acrylic emulsion paint finish

Urethane waterproofing

Concrete slab

Deck plate

08

Burley Barling House

MANDURANG, VICTORIA, AUSTRALIA // WARD CARTER ART + ARCHITECTURE
RAMMED EARTH, THERMAL MASS

DESIGN INTENTION

Situated on a rocky knoll on a rural site in the Mandurang Valley, south-east of Bendigo, Australia, the Burley Barling House aspires to be environmentally sensitive, energy efficient, and have passive solar capabilities. The house is oriented along an east-west axis that intersects with a sunny north-south axis to make the most of views and solar orientation. Materials are used to respond to this dry climate and to surrounding contextual materials of the landscape, where there are moderate summer and winter temperatures with plenty of sun. Local earth is used for construction by compressing it into formwork. It is intended to be a literal link to the landscape and a means of energy efficiency. This project exhibits a mutually beneficial relationship between steel frame and load-bearing walls, demonstrated structurally as well as spatially. The walls have a strong presence and sense of stability, while the frame offers contrasting delicacy and openness.

MATERIALITY

Similar to concrete, rammed earth relies on silica/alumina/lime-based products such as Portland cement to harden, but uses local earth instead of sand and gravel aggregates and requires a smaller proportion of Portland cement and water. The principles for designing with rammed earth walls are similar to those for designing with concrete, except the compressive and tensile strengths are assumed to be reduced but are quite sufficient if loads are moderate and are uniformly distributed. Point loads may exceed bearing capacity, and thus wood or steel bearing plates may be required.

Rammed earth construction employs carefully mixed soils in the construction of the superstructure, typically in the form of relatively thick walls. Rammed earth walls provide thermal mass, an excellent tool for conserving energy in this climate. The thickness and high thermal inertia of the walls ensures that the house retains warmth in the winter and remains relatively cool in the summer. A concrete slab floor stays cool on hot days and is warmed on cold days via a radiant hot-water circulating system within the floor. The thermal inertia of massive rammed earth construction is used to shift the daily temperature curve approximately half of one cycle, thus warming interior spaces at night by the wall's thermal gain during the day. Interior concrete slabs and rammed earth walls further moderate temperatures in the summer and winter and store direct radiant energy, and a supplementary propane-fired hydronic floor heating system and slow-combustion metal-lined firebox are available if needed. Also, the embodied energy of rammed earth wall construction is significantly less than that of concrete because relatively little energy is used to produce the constituents of the rammed earth walls, and energy needed to transport the material is greatly reduced because it is of local origin.

The availability of materials and skills make this method of construction attractive in many areas. This project demonstrates that rammed earth can be used to produce finished facilities of very high quality and durability. Wall thickness, height, position relative to roof overhangs, and solar exposure are all coordinated with finesse, demonstrating that this material can be rendered with a very high level of craft. Consistency of mix, placement, and compaction minimize the evidence of the normal "strata" of the rammed earth wall which can occur due to the series of compacted material lifts required by the process.

TECHNICAL

Earth that is well suited to rammed earth construction has a mixture of clay, sand, and fine aggregate without organic materials. In this case, local soils consisting of fine gravels, laterite soils, and soil blends with less than 2 percent organic content were used. Clay and silt content material (particle size .03–.19 in. [.75–4.75 mm]) was not less than 50 percent, and gravel content (.19 in.–.30 in. [4.75–7.5 mm]) was not above 30 percent. Portland cement (8–10 percent by volume) supplemented the local minerals. Moisture content at the time of placement was between 8 and 16 percent. All mixing was prepared on site; a pneumatic ram was used to consolidate the mix into formwork and eliminate air pockets. Trial mixes were tested for strength, determining a minimum strength of 363 psi (2.5 MPa).

The rammed earth walls are 11.8 in. (300 mm) thick in all locations, with no steel reinforcing bars within the walls. However, steel support brackets, bars, and tie down rods are imbedded into the rammed earth to provide support where joined to galvanized steel columns and beams. Inverted steel T lintels are used to span over openings in the walls. The walls and frame are mutually dependent for structural stability against lateral loads.

All exposed horizontal and vertical corners of the walls are chamfered. The tops of the walls are either covered by the roof or are capped with galvanized steel copings. Rammed earth is used in both exterior and interior wall applications, and is exposed at the window sills for up to half of the wall thickness. In exterior applications, a damp-proof barrier isolates the rammed earth wall from the thickened edge slab foundation below.

Modular formwork similar to that used in concrete wall construction is used for rammed earth wall construction. It is lined with marine grade plywood; subtle patterns of the wood surface and fasteners impart textural detail and scale to the rammed earth. The wall dimensions are compatible with formwork dimensions of 11.8 x 23.6 in. (300 x 600 mm). The walls are cured for a minimum of twelve hours before stripping formwork.

01 North elevation
02 Rammed earth wall
03 Plan
04 North elevation

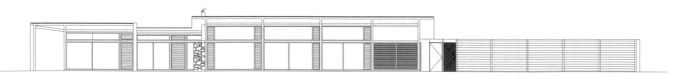

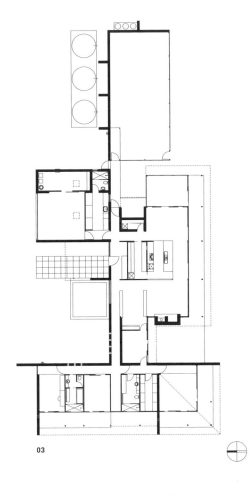

03

02

04

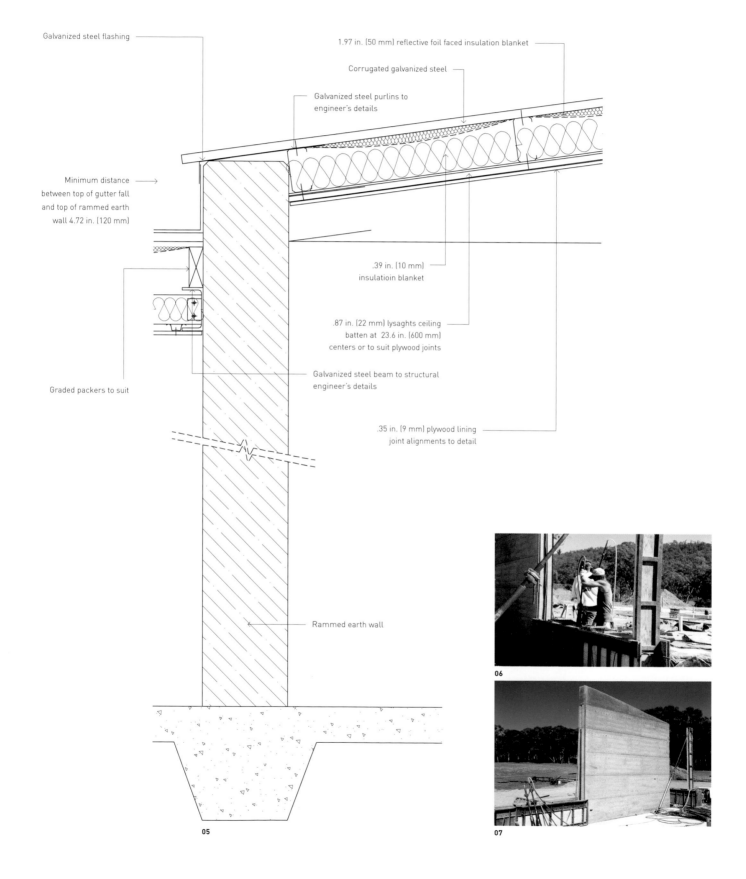

Galvanized steel flashing

1.97 in. (50 mm) reflective foil faced insulation blanket

Corrugated galvanized steel

Galvanized steel purlins to
engineer's details

Minimum distance
between top of gutter fall
and top of rammed earth
wall 4.72 in. (120 mm)

.39 in. (10 mm)
insulatioin blanket

.87 in. (22 mm) lysaghts ceiling
batten at 23.6 in. (600 mm)
centers or to suit plywood joints

Graded packers to suit

Galvanized steel beam to structural
engineer's details

.35 in. (9 mm) plywood lining
joint alignments to detail

Rammed earth wall

05

06

07

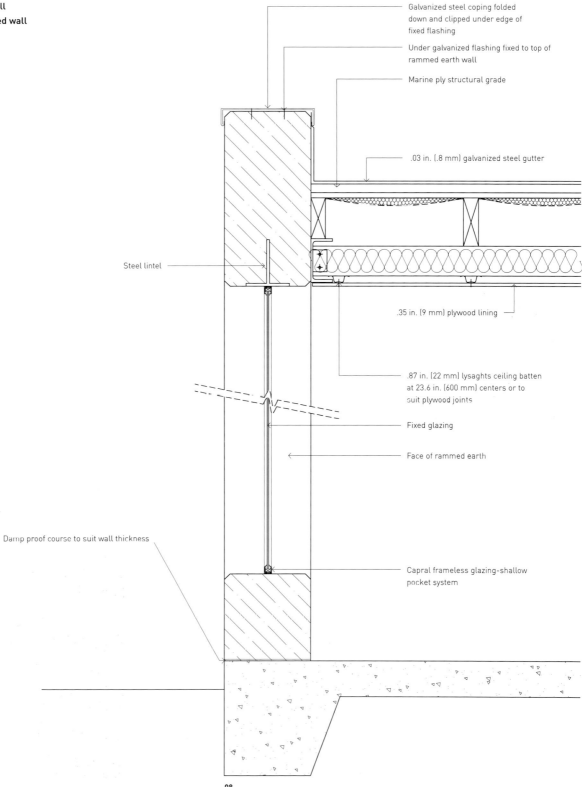

Galvanized steel coping folded
down and clipped under edge of
fixed flashing

Under galvanized flashing fixed to top of
rammed earth wall

Marine ply structural grade

.03 in. (.8 mm) galvanized steel gutter

Steel lintel

.35 in. (9 mm) plywood lining

.87 in. (22 mm) lysaghts ceiling batten
at 23.6 in. (600 mm) centers or to
suit plywood joints

Fixed glazing

Face of rammed earth

Damp proof course to suit wall thickness

Capral frameless glazing-shallow
pocket system

08

WOOD

THE BASICS

The tree remains one of the most critical plants to the human on earth. Through history, the tree has provided fruit for food and wood for shelter, protection from the elements, and a source for a wide range of tools. Wood is natural, organic, lightweight, strong, readily accessible, and simple to work with in construction. Its wide variety of colors, textures, grain patterns, and fragrances give designers a versatile and adaptable expressive tool for construction. Its warm aesthetic and easy workability has made it an appealing architectural material for centuries.

The basic anatomical structure of wood includes fibers and cells. This structure, along with its chemical composition, determines the strength and technical characteristics of a particular type of wood. Wood is *anisotropic*, which means that its inherent qualities are dependant on the direction of the grain. For example, its strength is one hundred times greater in tension and four times greater in compression in the direction with the grain than it is at a right angle to the grain, while shear strength is greater across the grain than it is in parallel, making it more vulnerable to horizontal shear than to vertical shear. Solid wood members are strongest when cut and used with the grain of the wood, while cross-grain pieces are weaker. A weaker piece of wood will typically withstand one-third more force in compression than it will in tension parallel to the grain. Perpendicular to the grain, the compressive force is only about one-fifth to one-half of the allowable compressive force parallel to the grain.

Most wood used in structural framing is softwood, while hardwood is generally used for finish woodwork, furniture, and the finer details in construction. Softwoods, such as pine, fir, spruce, or cedar, are less expensive and more plentiful, while hardwoods, such as oak, cherry, ash, walnut, poplar, or birch, generally have a finer grain, a better appearance, and are more expensive. Such a generalization is difficult to make, however, as literally thousands of types of wood are used for different purposes around the world, depending on locale, availability, and quality.

Before a piece of wood leaves the mill it is graded for either its structural strength and stiffness or for its aesthetics, depending on its intended use. *Lumber*—a sawn piece of wood—is sold by size, by species, and by *grade*, its ranking based on standards regarding structural strength or appearance. Structural lumber is graded either by a trained inspector or by a machine and is judged on its density and strength. The wood is then stamped with an industry-wide standard indication before leaving the mill. The grading allows a designer to discriminate among different qualities of woods so as to economically use them for a particular use. The way in which a piece of lumber will be used can determine what grade is most viable. For example, structural members with a long span demand a different wood product than lumber for blocking or minimal structural needs. For this reason, it would not be uncommon to use several different species or grades of wood in one project, depending on their applications. Other factors to be considered when selecting lumber for structural purposes are the environmental conditions (temperature and moisture levels) in which the wood is to be located, the size and shape of the wood members, and the estimated loading cycles on the wood member.

The way in which wood is cut to become a piece of lumber also affects its ultimate strength. *Plainsawn* lumber is cut in a series of parallel planes through the log; this is a sawing method that gives the maximum yield and greatest amount of cut wood from the log. Plainsawn lumber can have a raised grain or a variety of grain patterns in each piece, tends to cup or twist more, and can shrink or swell in width. *Quartersawn* lumber is made by cutting quadrants of a log on the diagonal, at an angle generally radiating from the center of the log. This gives a more even grain pattern but leaves more waste in the cutting, making it more costly than plainsawn. Quartersawn wood is less prone to cup, twist, or warp, has less of a raised grain than plainsawn lumber, and is usually desirable for flooring and finish details because of its tight, consistent grain and fine appearance.

Flaws in a piece of wood such as knots, splits, checks, or warps affect its strength, grading, and appearance. These defects are largely due to natural characteristics, with some influence by the preparation process. This in turn affects where and how individual pieces of wood are used. Almost every piece of wood has some sort of discontinuity or flaw resulting from its growth process or how it is manufactured. *Knots*, indicating where branches were once attached to the wood member, are the most common wood defect. *Knotholes* are holes that are a result of knots that have dropped out of the wood. Both knots and knotholes compromise the structural integrity of a wood member; their size and number affect the grade of a piece of wood. Processing wood can also cause many defects, most as a result of *seasoning*—the controlled method of reducing the moisture content in wood members—in which shrinkage stresses cause distortions such as bowing, cupping, twisting, and crooking.

Knowledgeable carpenters are able to judge a piece of wood to determine whether the level of defects in a wood member is allowable for its intended use.

The amount of moisture in a piece of wood affects many of its characteristics. Wood expands as its moisture content rises and shrinks as it lowers. This must always be taken into account when designing and detailing any wood structure, since inevitably wood will shrink or swell depending on its moisture content. Dry lumber has increased strength and resistance to decay, fungi, and insects. This can be done either through the relatively slow process of air-drying or through the use of kilns, as is typical for most wood products today.

Many of today's advances in the wood industry, such as *glue laminates*, plywood, and other engineered wood products, were invented to compensate for some of the material's natural faults and limitations. Wood is highly resistant to acids, bases, salts, and other chemicals. The connection materials that are often used in wood buildings must also be considered in their reaction to chemicals and their corrosion resistance. Chemical treatments increase wood's resistance to fire, decay, and insect infestation. There is also an ever-growing industry of plastics and synthetic wood products that attempt to mimic its aesthetic, such as products for flooring, trim, and siding, as the ethical and environmental issues surrounding the cutting and clearing of trees have been cause of important debate concerning the preservation of many wood species and natural habitats.

HISTORY

Wood as an architectural material is one of the most diverse and abundant in the history of construction. It is also the only truly organic major architectural material. For thousands of years wood has been the most conventional building material along with stone and clay. Wood has typically been plentiful and readily used by man for construction. Today it is the primary source of energy for 40 percent of the world's population, most particularly in underdeveloped areas. For decades wood has played a key role in the construction of road systems, bridges, railroads, and the construction process of most buildings. In the United States almost all of the 1.25 million houses built each year are constructed of light wood framing, according to a recent study conducted by the Society of American Foresters.

Wood construction can be traced to the beginning of civilization though archeology in the crude structures of the pit dwellings, simple earth structures covered with wood members for shelter. Other early wood structures include yurts, teepees, and lean-tos. Early structures in Greece, India, Northern Europe, and Japan were then typically constructed of masonry walls with a timber roof. Vitruvius, the Roman architect and author of *De Architectura* (27 BC), talks about the primitive hut in his writings, which perhaps is the first written historical record of the use of wood in a structure. It was not until the Middle Ages when braced wood frames began to be used for walls. The hand-hewn practice of the cruck frame and the braced frame were two early timber framing methods that evolved in Europe, which laid the foundation for the framing methods we still use today.

For over two thousand years timber framing was the method of building with wood. It originated with the realization that timbers from the forest could be hand-hewn into square log shapes and joined with mortise and tennon, dovetail, or pegged joints. In places where there were thick forests, such as Europe, Japan, China, and India, the method of building with timber became a craft, with each geographic area developing its own style and process. For example during the Middle Ages in England, in order to conserve wood, shorter wood members were used with infilled masonry, a technique now identified with the Tudor period of the sixteenth century. By the 1600s craft guilds developed, teaching the art of timber framing and wood joinery, with apprentices taking great pride in their profession.

When colonists came to North America in the seventeenth century, they brought with them their various regional methods and traditions of timber framing. The abundance of trees made it easy for the new settlers to have ample supply of construction materials, as forests covered about 46 percent of the total land area in the United States in the year 1600. (Today that number has dropped to about 33 percent, due in large part to the clearing of land initially for farming and later even more so for the development of growing suburban communities.) By the mid-1800s large timber framing began to disappear due to the invention of the wire nail and circular saw, and the existence of sawmills that could inexpensively produce smaller pieces of lumber. In the 1830s in Chicago, a new method of building called balloon framing evolved, which required less skill to construct and less time to build than timber framing. It also utilized smaller trees that are more common. With the quickly growing population and the need for faster construction, balloon framing gained in popularity. It has been argued that this method also evolved due to the easy construction methods for barns and outbuildings. Eventually balloon framing evolved into *stud framing*, more commonly known as platform framing, which we use today, and allows for even smaller trees with a modular system of dimensions. This construction method was seen as fast, efficient, and economical when compared to the traditional timber framing methods.

In recent decades, the use of wood has given rise to ecological debate. On the one hand, it is a renewable resource; on the other, awareness of clearing forests and how we harvest wood can be cause for concern. The growing sensitivity to environmental responsibility, as well as the ever-rising palette of material alternatives, has contributed to a waning dominance of wood. Plywood, particleboards, and wood-simulating plastics are now a large segment of the wood industry.

Despite such competition, wood remains the most popular building material for many reasons. It is completely natural, recyclable, endlessly replenishable, and if harvested responsibly does not disturb the ecological balance of the environment. Its use can also lend a sense of connectivity to the landscape through its warmth and naturalness. This tactile material can appeal to people's psyche and senses and also fulfills the sustainability requirements many with environmental concerns seek to achieve in construction.

DESIGN CONSIDERATIONS

There are a wide range of choices and issues that can inform designing with wood. These can include the particular construction method, structural criteria, and load requirements. Choices of the type of wood species or products and their grades and ratings also effect a design's outcome. The range of wood species available is seemingly great, with choices that determine the grain, color, size, sustainability, cost, and availability of the wood itself, which varies significantly over different geographic locations. Different species have colors that can range from black to tan to red to pale cream, and no individual member ever has the same exact appearance as the next. However there are, of course, some wood types that are typically used for specific purposes—fir, pine, and spruce are most often used for structural members, while more refined woods such as cherry or birch, which are richer in appearance, are used for furniture and finish carpentry. Still other woods, such as California redwood, cypress, and red or white cedar, are more decay-resistant and therefore are often used for exterior exposures, such as roofing, wall cladding, and so forth.

Wood construction is often categorized into four methods:

→ **Log construction** is one of the oldest building construction methods in history and was used not only for dwellings but also for other structures such as churches, towers, and bridges. Today it is rarely used unless there is a desire to obtain the distinct aesthetic of a log structure. Log walls are either stacked with solid logs or spaced and filled with other insulating materials such as mud or plaster chinking. The log itself can either be left as a round shape or can be edge sawn for a more solid stacking connection. Log construction is characterized by its corner joints that interlock with a dovetail or cross-lap connection. These joints were historically carved by hand, though in log house "kits" today they are precisely cut by machinery to achieve uniformity and economy.

→ **Timber-frame construction** is built story-by-story with sills, posts, beams, and struts erected at each level. This method historically consisted of oversized handmade mortise and tennon joints in which a large portion of the interacting wood members are subtracted to fit one inside of the other. Today most of these connections are computer processed, making them more accurate and economical. Today steel connectors are oftentimes used in place of the traditional mortise and tennon and pegged connections.

Timber-framed buildings cannot span the same distance with the same amount of material as steel, nor give a smooth continuity of material as concrete, but they can give a unique aesthetic, a natural fragrance, and a general "environmental" connotation unlike any other material by leaving a natural material exposed in a recognizable state. It is more exceptional today to see a heavy timber-framed building because heavy timber must compete economically with a wider range of structural materials. Additionally the environmental implications of destroying our older growth forests have given the timber industry limited supply of raw material. Recently there has been a rejuvenation of the timber-framing craft where centuries-old methods of joinery and the art of historical construction methods have been revived and put to practice. Building codes have a classification for heavy timber (type IV) that allow greater height and area than is the case for light wood frame (type V).

→ **Balloon framing** involves using wood members that continue through two or more stories in height. The roof and floor members attach to continuous members or studs running from sill to roof. The length of these studs makes them difficult to erect efficiently, and the spacing between them can act as multiple unintended fire and smoke flues, increasing the risk of more rapidly spreading a fire to upper floors. This method is often found in older structures and is not commonly used today.

→ **Platform framing** is a floor-by-floor process traditionally used for buildings no higher than three stories, and is the most common method of wood construction in North America today, accounting for almost 95 percent of wood construction. The wall frame is formed with story-height studs that are joined together with a sole plate at the bottom and double wall plates above, and then covered on both sides with plywood or another wood sheathing product to stiffen the frame. The walls are then most often covered on both sides with finishing materials. One of the advantages of platform framing is the use of shorter, standardized pieces of lumber, such as 8 ft. (2.43 m) "studs," which are more available, less expensive, and easier to handle. Another advantage is that each floor is constructed one at a time, allowing for the floor below to act as a framing platform for the next. Other advantages are that it uses simple nailing connections. Today the majority of homes are built with a platform framing, though there is a huge range of new products available in the wood industry, including the panelized construction industry, which includes structural insulated panels (SIPs) and other types of wood panel products.

Wood structures are susceptible to damage by fungi, insects, and fire. The threat of insects and fungi both increase due to the level of moisture content of wood and duration of time which the wood is exposed to moisture. The best protection against both of these damaging elements is to use dry wood products and ensure that the wood is kept dry during construction and thereafter. In a living tree, the sapwood contains approximately 30 percent or more moisture. Certain species of wood, such as redwood, cedar, bald cypress, black walnut, and black locust, are naturally resistant to decay and fungi because they have chemical extractions that combat biological attack. Some, such as redwood, red cedar, and bald cypress, are also naturally resistant to insects due to natural oils in the wood that act as preservatives. Most wood-attacking organisms need both oxygen and moisture to survive. To reduce the problems caused by these organisms, wood must be kept away from the ground, crawl-spaces and attics should be ventilated, and wood should be kept clear from any possible water near drainage areas and areas where there could be possible moisture from leaking pipes.

For decay and insect resistance, areas that are close to the ground, or outdoor structures such as fences, decks, docks, or porches, wood can be impregnated with preservatives through a high-pressure injection process. To protect against moisture, a pressure treatment is the most effective means. There are also preservative treatments that can be applied without pressure to the surface of a piece of wood to protect it from decay and insects. There are three types of preservatives that can be applied to wood:

→ **Water-based preservatives** leave the wood odorless and ready to be painted and also do not leach out or leak into the environment.

→ **Oil-based preservatives**, which are highly toxic, may alter the color of wood, but can be painted to offset this.

→ **Creosote preservatives** are usually used in marine and saltwater applications. They give the wood a dark-colored, oily surface, and a strong odor that remains for a long period of time. Environmental restrictions greatly limit use of this method today.

For a fire retardant treatment, lumber is placed in a pressure vessel and impregnated with chemical salts, which reduce its flammability. Fire-retardant lumber is usually not used in detached single-family home construction but is used most often in nonstructural partitions and other interior locations of other constructions needing fire resistance.

TYPES

Wood as a material is classified into two major categories: *softwoods* and *hardwoods*, which actually do not refer to the materials' relative hardness or strength. Most softwoods have spiky leaves or needles and are usually ever-greens, although there are exceptions to the rule, such as western larch, which loses its needles every year. Softwoods are usually also *coniferous*, which means that their seeds (conifers) are enclosed in cones. They generally grow much quicker, are softer, and are easier to work with than hardwoods. Some common softwoods include fir, pine, cedar, Douglas fir, redwood, hemlock, and spruce. Hardwoods generally have flat, broad leaves and have seeds that are enclosed in fruit or nuts, such as acorns. Hardwoods usually are characterized by being *deciduous*, or losing their leaves each season, although again, there are a few exceptions, such as the Pacific Madrone and Tanoak, both found in the northwestern United States. Another distinction between the hardwoods and softwoods is that the former contain a more complex system of pores or vessels while the latter have a simple structure of large cells. Both hardwoods and softwoods have examples of strong and durable species, but hardwoods are generally more durable as a reflection of their slower rates of growth and tighter annual ring patterns. Some common hardwoods include beech, oak, ash, elm, sycamore, birch, balsa and walnut.

Softwoods are typically used for general construction purposes while hardwoods are usually used for flooring, paneling, trim pieces, and other finishing elements. Hardwoods are sometimes sliced into thin veneers and joined to lesser expensive woods for cost savings.

LUMBER

Lumber in the United States is sized in inches by *nominal dimensions* rather than actual dimensions; nominal dimensions are not written with inch marks while actual dimensions are. For instance, a 2x4 is approximately 1.5 x 3.5 in. (38.1 x 88.9 mm), although slight variation is standard. Those in the construction profession simply refer to the nominal dimension, with the understanding that they are not actual. In fact, because there are so many variables affecting the condition of wood, such as moisture and manufacturing techniques, it is never wise to assume that even the actual dimensions are to be taken literally. The best detailing specifies a wood detail with a *tolerance*, or allowed deviation, so that the wood members can have slight variation in dimensions. When a designer specifies wood for a construction project they must designate the species, the grade, the seasoning (moisture content percentage), the surfacing (how a piece of wood should be finished on its surface), the nominal size, and if there are any treatments to the wood. The construction manager or contactor will then order the wood from a lumber resource by specifying the lengths and number of pieces of wood for each length. The following are some common terms for wood members:

→ **Boards** are pieces of lumber that are less than two inches in nominal thickness. They are usually graded for appearance rather than their strength and are used for trim, siding, and sub-flooring purposes.

→ **Dimensional lumber** ranges from 2 to 4 inches (50.8–101.6 mm) of nominal thickness. These are usually available in 2-foot (60.9 cm) increments in length with common lengths ranging from 8 to 16 feet (243.8–487.7 cm). This lumber is usually graded for strength rather than appearance and is used for general construction needs.

→ **Timber** is wood members that are nominally 5 by 5 inches or larger in thickness. These are graded for their strength.

→ **Structural solid wood** is a load-bearing wood that is rigorously graded with capacity requirements. Spruce, fir, pine, and larch are some of the common wood species used for structural wood members.

LAMINATED WOOD

Laminated wood is a structural type consisting of built-up layers of wood that have been glued together to form an engineered and stress-rated member. Laminated wood is often preferred to solid wood members due to its consistent appearance, availability in different sizes, and water resistance. *Glue-laminated* wood (or *glulam*) is comprised of many small chips of wood glued together in different directions to create a girder or other structural members. The different orientations of these wood pieces provide greater strength than a single piece of wood of the same size and also allow for sizes and lengths unlimited by log sizes. The wood is fully sea-soned (dried) before being laminated to ensure a high-quality member. Glulams are specified by their quality and size much like typical timber. High-quality glulams will use a specific type of wood and have a greater strength or size. The development of glulams was a significant advancement in the twentieth century wood construction industry, allowing for longer spans and for shapes that the natural material cannot provide.

PANEL PRODUCTS

Panel products are an efficient use of wood and are easy to install. They are also less vulnerable to swelling and shrinkage due to moisture and temperature changes. There are three general groups of wood panel products: plywood, composite panels, and non-veneer panels. These categories are classified as structural wood panels, which are specified either by their thickness or a span rating, both indicated on a stamp that is placed on each wood panel. The span rating is an indication of a structural panel's load-bearing capacity and gives a common industry marker for the many different types of panels made of different wood species.

→ **Plywood** is made up of multiple wood veneers glued together, alternating grain direction ninety degrees for each adjacent veneer. There are always an odd number of veneers, with the grain of the front and back always parallel to the longer dimension of the sheet. Plywood is generally made from wood veneer sheets rotary sliced from logs and then kiln-dried to an approximate moisture content of 5 percent. These sheets are then glued and pressed together under elevated temperatures and high pressures to create a solid board. The plywood sheets are then trimmed, sanded, graded, and stamped. Plywood grades are rated by the American Plywood Association with the letters N, A, B, C, or D, with N being a smooth, natural finish; A, a smooth, paint-grade finish; B, a smooth finish with knots and plugs; C, a sheathing grade, unsanded; and D, a grade limited to interior panel use. The standard plywood sheet is 4 by 8 feet (121.9 x 243.8 cm) and can range in thickness from .25 to 1.125 inches (6.35 to 28.57 mm).

One of the main advantages of plywood is its high uniform strength in relation to its weight. Its unique cross-layered structure in addition to the adhesives used give it a high strength. It is also less susceptible to shrinkage, swelling, and warping than a solid wood member. Plywood is readily available and is an economical way to frame a building. It also affords a way to create curved shapes to be framed in a project. Disadvantages include its weight and unwieldiness, and unless a high grade is selected plywood can have voids or inconsistencies in its structure. It is an environmentally friendly material in that it puts waste and wood scraps from mills to good use. It is also an attractive material because it is 100% biodegradable and has an environmentally friendly manufacturing process. Chemicals used to treat and glue in the products are of concern because they may give off unwanted gasses inside a building and may have other adverse effects on the environment.

→ **Composite panels** have two or more parallel veneer sheets that are bonded together with a core of recon-stituted wood fibers through a synthetic adhesive using heat and pressure. Composite panels are available in a vast range of different types. Panels can differ by the type of wood used to construct them, their thickness, and their structural capability. Some composite panels are available with insulation inserted into the sheet or with a different material, such as aluminum, attached to one side to construct an all-inclusive wall panel.

→ There are three basic **non-veneered wood panels** available, each having different classes or grades: **Oriented Strand Board (OSB)** is made up of long strands of wood particles that are glued and compressed together in a resin into three to five layers; **waferboard** is made up of large flakes of wood, also glued and compressed together; and **particleboard** is made up of smaller wood particles than OSB and wafer-board and has a finer appearance.

MANUFACTURED WOOD COMPONENTS

Manufactured wood components combine dimensional lumber, structural panel products, wood connectors, and other wood products to create a more efficient building component that is a complete wood member.

→ **Trusses** are structural roof and floor components that usually combine 2x4s or 2x6s with toothed plate con-nectors (see p. XX). An advantage of using a truss structural system is that it uses less wood than a conventional rafters-and-joists structural system. Additionally they are usually engineered by the manufacturer after a designer submits the span, roof pitch, and the desired overhang detail. A disad-vantage of using trusses is that their struts can make attic spaces unusable.

→ **Plywood I-beams** and **box beams** can be used in place of traditional rafters or joists for long-span framing. These manufactured components can be custom designed and use timber resources more efficiently than conventional wood components.

→ **Panel and box components** have become more and more prevalent in the construction industry as entire walls, floors, and roofs can be prefabricated off site. Some panel components can also be prefabricated to include insulation, windows, wiring, and exterior or interior finish material. The panel industry has expanded rapidly, making a wide range of options and variations of panel components available for different construction types. This customization of panels not only addresses a building's more particular needs but also allows a designer more affordable yet varied options in the prefabrication industry. Panelization places more of the work in a factory than at the construction site. Designers need to adjust their approach to-ward materials and construction details accordingly.

CONNECTORS

Nails, screws, bolts, toothed plates, and adhesives are used to connect wood. Wood fasteners are often noted as the weakest component of wood construction, rarely being as strong as a monolithic material or the wood mem-ber itself. Historically, pegged or mortise and tennon connections were used to connect wood, both of which compromised the strength of a wood member due to the removal of material from each member.

→ **Nails** are available in a wide range of sizes, materials, and shapes, geared to a particular use or purpose. Fastening with nails is the fastest and easiest way to connect wood members, requiring no pre-drilling or preparation, as they are driven into wood members with a hammer or a pneumatic gun. Nails are most often made of mild steel, but are available in a variety of other metals such as aluminum, copper, zinc, brass, or stainless steel. While the rest of the world measures a nail's diameter and length in millimeters, in the U.S. they are measured in a term called *pennies* and designated as *d*. A 2d nail is one inch (25 mm) long, a 6d nail is two inches (51 mm) long, and a 10d nail is three inches (76 mm) long. The two types most often used in con-struction are *common* and *finish* nails. Common nails have flat heads, are used in most construction framing, and are not intended to be exposed to the environment. Galvanized nails have a protective zinc coating on them to inhibit rust and corrosion. Finish nails are not meant to be seen; they have a tiny head and are used in finish woodwork such as casework and interior detailing. Other types of nails are box nails, casing nails, brad nails, roofing nails, cut nails, and concrete nails, each shaped differently in terms of its head, shaft, and point, to suit their particular use.

→ **Screws** generally yield a stronger and tighter connection than nails due to their threaded shaft, which is placed directly into wood or into pre-drilled holes and then screwed into place. Wood screws take longer to install than nails, but because they have threads they have more holding strength and are somewhat easier and less damaging to remove. The more threads they have, the stronger they are. They are typically used for light fram-ing, finish work, cabinetry, furniture, or drywall. Drywall screws, which are typically used for connecting dry-wall to wood or light steel members, are small in size but can be inserted with a power screwdriver without pre-drilling. Screws should be approximately .125 inch (3.175 mm) less in length than the combined thickness of the two elements being joined. Screws are classified by use (wood, metal, drywall, set screws, machine), type of head (flat, round, oval, slotted, Phillips, pan, or hex socket), finish (steel, aluminum, stainless steel, brass, bronze), lengths (.5 to 6 in., 13 to 153 mm), and diameter (up to 24 gauge).

→ **Bolts** are threaded connectors that have round heads on one end and receive a threaded nut on the other. *Nuts* are threaded to receive the end of the bolt. Bolts are typically used for major structural connections when screws and nails are insufficient. They vary in length from .5 to 30 in. (13–762 mm), with diameters up to 1.25 in. (31.75 mm), and can have flat, round, square, or hexagonal heads. Different types of nuts include cap, wing, square, or hexagon nuts. *Washers*, which are flat metal disks, are sometimes used with bolts to distribute the compressive forces across a larger area of the wood members being connected. Washers are also used as spacing devices or to provide a seal between two materials. While most bolts use a nut to secure the end of the connection, *lag bolts* do not have nuts and are used when one end of the bolt is not accessible.

→ **Timber connectors** increase the load-carrying capacity of bolts and are typically only used in heavy timber construction. The most common timber connector is called the *split ring connector*, which is two rings that are placed in pre-drilled holes in the two connecting members and secured with a bolt to increase its strength. The split ring not only spreads the load but also allows the wood to adjust for shrinkage and expansion.

→ **Toothed plates** are most often used in the manufacturing of trusses and other prefabricated roof and floor members. These toothed fasteners act as a plate of multiple nails that splice wood members together. They are inserted into wood by hydraulic presses, pneumatic presses, or mechanical rollers, and form a strong connection with the fibers of a larger volume of the wood than would be the case with a nail or screw, thus minimizing splitting.

→ **Adhesives** are most often used in the manufacturing of plywood, cabinetry, some wood structural ele-ments, laminated woods, and other panel wood products. Adhesives may be used on the construction site in conjunction with nails or screws to make a more permanent connection or to minimize minor movement or squeaking in flooring. Adhesives that are used on a construction site include sealants or other glues that are dispersed from a gun in mastic form. The nail or other fastener secures the connection while the glue cures.

→ **Metal plate fasteners** serve a variety of uses, the most common being the *joist hanger*, which creates a strong connection at a right angle between joists and beams. These fasteners can be made of steel but are typically made of galvanized steel sheet metal. There are a wide range of sheet metal connections that join wood members for light frame construction.

Messenger House II

NOVA SCOTIA, CANADA // BRIAN MACKAY-LYONS
LIGHT WOOD FRAME, CEDAR SHINGLE CLADDING

DESIGN INTENTION

This 2,300-square-foot (214 sq. m) house is located on a ridge in Upper Kingsburg on Nova Scotia's south shore. It appears as one monolithic form in the landscape but is actually a house and a guest house, separated by a partially enclosed court. The house is appropriate to the site not through mediation or imitation, but by a common awareness of the origins and daily reality of this place.

MATERIALITY

This project is deeply rooted in its place through its material palette and its construction methods. It uses reinforced concrete to anchor it to its undulating site, but everything above that is light wood frame construction. The exterior cladding uses the cedar shingles common to this area, and with details that relate it to its vernacular neighbors.

Despite using traditional materials and building methods the house exhibits an austere aesthetic, chiefly through its monolithic massing, and secondly through its minimalist detailing. From a distance the details are not prominent, but on closer examination, they show insight in the way that they resolve needs with an economy of means. At both scales the unnecessary is eliminated; formal purity is the result.

The plan permits this house to be an insular volume when it is cold and windy, or a pair of volumes open to the dramatic ocean views during nicer weather. By opening its 40 ft. (12.19 m) wide barn doors, the house invites the sunny exposures and utilizes passive solar gain to heat its floor slab, moderating demand on its in-slab radiant heating system. The building acknowledges the sometimes high winds by avoiding extensive overhangs or other slender appendages. Closed service spaces such as closets and washrooms wrap the northeast sides of the living spaces, buffering them against the cold and making the best southwest views available to the served spaces.

TECHNICAL

Conventional residential framing systems are used in most of this house, but to achieve longer spans and larger spaces in some locations steel framing and engineered wood products are employed. Light wood framing readily incorporates these elements, using them to add spatial variety with only modest increase in cost or difficulty.

Only a modest 4 inches (102 mm) of each eastern white cedar shingle is exposed to the weather, meaning that at any point on the wall at least two layers of shingles are present to intercept unwanted water or air. Below the cedar shingles are layers of perforated building felt and plywood sheathing, then insulated 2x6 (51 x 152 mm) stud framing. Toward the interior, there is a vapor barrier, then painted .5 in. (13 mm) gypsum board. The wall is essentially a multilayered barrier, with a redundancy of elements acknowledging that none will be perfect. Wall materials generally increase in porosity toward the exterior, allowing any moisture that enters the wall to migrate back toward the exterior where it can evaporate harmlessly.

The roof is similar in concept to the wall, but with two important differences. Its outermost surface is corrugated Galvalume roofing, which is impermeable when properly installed. Details at the perimeter of the roof protect the edges of the roof deck against weathering. Below the plywood sheathing and above the insulated roof framing layer is a continuous 2 in. (51 mm) cavity, through which outside air can enter, rise through the sloped roof plane, then exit at the upper eave. This detail brings the outside air into the roof assembly so that it can carry unwanted vapor out of the wood assembly before it can cause biological attack to occur. The sloped roof plane encourages the air to move upward and out without forced ventilation.

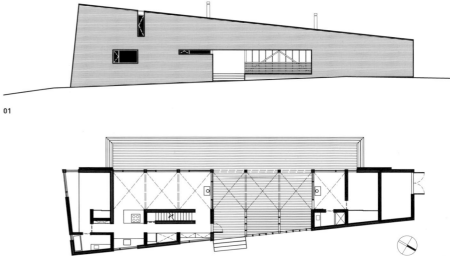

01 Northeast elevation
02 Ground-floor plan
03 View from north
04 South corner

01

02

03

04

05

06

07

1. 6 in. (15.2 cm) reinforced concrete wall
2. 2.5 in. (6.35 cm) rigid insulation
3. 1x6 spruce deckboard
4. Aluminum window system
5. 2 in. (5.08 cm) concrete topping with infloor radiant heating
6. R30 batt insulation
7. Paint grade MDF baseboard
8. Eastern White Cedar shingles (4 in. (10.16 cm) to the weather)
9. Asphalt building paper
10. .5 in. (12.7 mm) plywood sheathing
11. 2x6 exterior stud wall with R20 batt insulation
12. 3-2x10 window header
13. 6 mil vapour barrier
14. .5 in. (12.7 mm) drywall
15. 1 x 1.5 in. (2.5 x 3.8 cm) cedar blocking
16. Corrugated plastic roofing
17. Corrugated steel roofing
18. 2x3 vent strapping on 2x10 roof joists with R40 batt insulation
19. Custom metal flashing
20. Eave vent
21. Perforated venting strip
22. Galvanized metal flashing

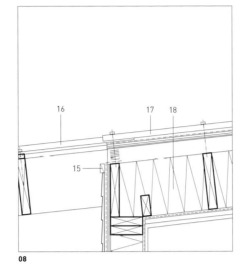
08

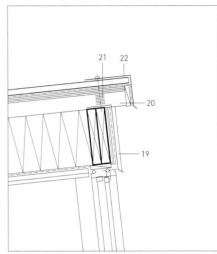
09

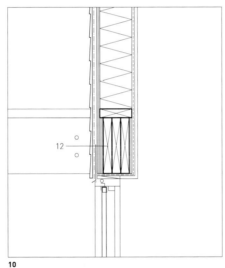
10

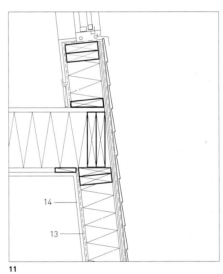
11

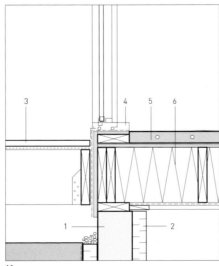
12

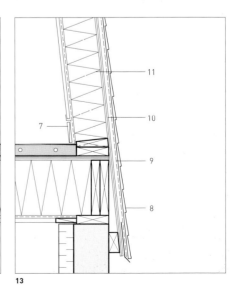
13

Bamboo Canopy

QUEENS, NEW YORK, USA // nARCHITECTS
BAMBOO, FLEXIBILITY

DESIGN INTENTION

This project was a temporary structure built at the P.S. 1 Contemporary Arts Center in Queens, New York. The canopy was built in seven weeks by the architects, volunteer students, and recent graduates from Parsons School of Design, Yale, Columbia, Harvard, and Rhode Island School of Design. The project is much more than a canopy in the traditional sense of being a structural umbrella; rather, it filled a courtyard with a range of experimental spaces through its use of bamboo.

MATERIALITY

The canopy was designed to create what the designers call a "deep landscape" that fills the entire courtyard of the Arts Center. This landscape attempts to stitch together the site, which contains the ground, concrete walls, and the sky, through the use of bamboo. Points at which the canopy comes down to the ground, or what the designers refer to as "dips" in the structure, define "rooms" that are open to the sky. These different rooms each contain a defined environment. The Pool Pad is the largest room and includes a wading pool; the Fog Pad contains nozzles that spray a mist to mimic fog; the Rock Pad is elevated and contains gravel; the Meeting Pad includes seating; the Rainforest features a sound component with intermittent water misters; and the Sand Hump maximizes exposure to both the sun and shade. The project adheres to one tectonic system while creating a series of spaces that provide varied shade, structure, and atmosphere.

The canopy is constructed of 1,100 freshly cut green Philostachys Aurea bamboo harvested in Georgia. They were cut, cleaned, and shipped in one week to maintain their freshness during construction. Once the bamboo arrived in New York, it was stored in racks, covered with an ultra-violet-resistant tarp, and watered twice a day to keep it green and flexible. This project takes a material that intrinsically wants to be a vertical line, and manipulates it to become a complex series of intersecting curves. To do so, it was important to retain its suppleness during construction. As the green bamboo dries and turns brown, loses its moisture, becomes brittle and resistant to bending. This drying process varied throughout the project due to variations in misting, exposure to the sun, and construction sequence. The objective was to set the bamboo into place before it dried, losing its flexibility.

Another of the designers' challenges was creating a set of precise geometric shapes with a material that has inherently variable properties. Much of the construction process involved adapting the design to accommodate the organic nature of this unpredictable material. Each arc in the project was first digitally modeled in a three-dimensional CAD program and then exported to two-dimensional drawings. The ideals of this digital model then met the circumstantial characteristics of the bamboo. Steel pipes at the base of the bamboo were fabricated off site then installed into the raised Pads before the bamboo was inserted. Cedar decking, expanded polystyrene with polyurethane sealer, and stainless steel wire were other materials used.

TECHNICAL

Bamboo has been utilized for centuries as a structural material in buildings. It is an abundant and economical renewable resource. It has a very favorable cross section, in which nearly all of its material is distant from the neutral axis that runs down the center of its cylindrical form, making it a nearly ideal column design with favorable axial strength. However, good columns do not necessarily make good beams. To create spans for these canopies, the linear elements were spliced together to form intersecting arches of varied configurations, forming a network of many members. By forming a network and tying the members with wire at the intersections, the designers took advantage of bamboo's intrinsic axial strength and avoided its vulnerability to bending.

The structure uses 30,800 linear feet (9,388 m) of bamboo, which is bound together with 37,000 feet (11,278 m) of stainless steel wire. Bamboo poles tapered along their average 22 ft. (6.71 m) length from a diameter of 1.25–1.5 in. (32–38 mm) at the thick end to .13–.25 in. (3–6 mm) at the thin end. The physical properties of the material change continuously along this length as its cross section changes. The designers exploited this by placing the smaller-diameter portions in locations where the radius of curvature was shortest. This is a design challenge seldom addressed by users of factory-produced steel or contemporary composites, or even milled lumber, whose properties are more consistent than the tapering pieces of bamboo.

Further, no two pieces of any natural material, including bamboo, will have the same physical properties. The designers recognized this and utilized a method in which a considerable amount of trial and error was incorporated into the construction process, while generally holding true to the digital model. In two locations, the Rock Pad and Meeting Pad, the architects added dips in the canopy in order to achieve the longest spanning arcs and to stabilize the structure.

01   Bamboo splice types
02   Pool pad
03   View from above the bamboo canopy

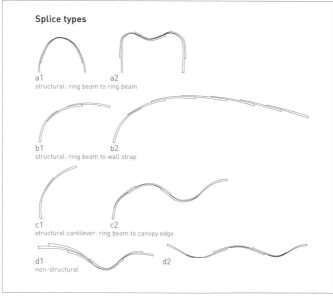

Splice types

a1   a2
structural: ring beam to ring beam

b1   b2
structural: ring beam to wall strap

c1   c2
structural cantilever: ring beam to canopy edge

d1   d2
non-structural

01

02

03

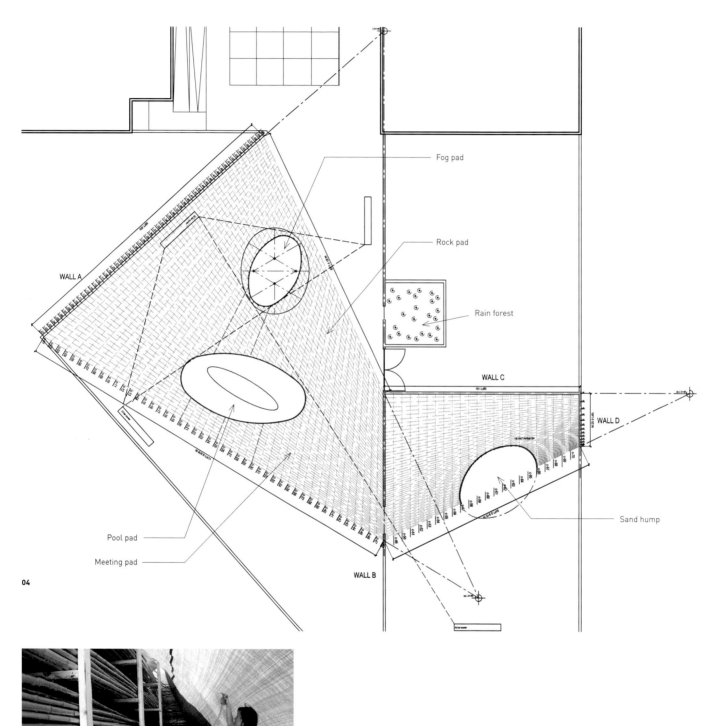

Fog pad

Rock pad

Rain forest

WALL A

WALL C

WALL D

Sand hump

Pool pad

Meeting pad

WALL B

04

05

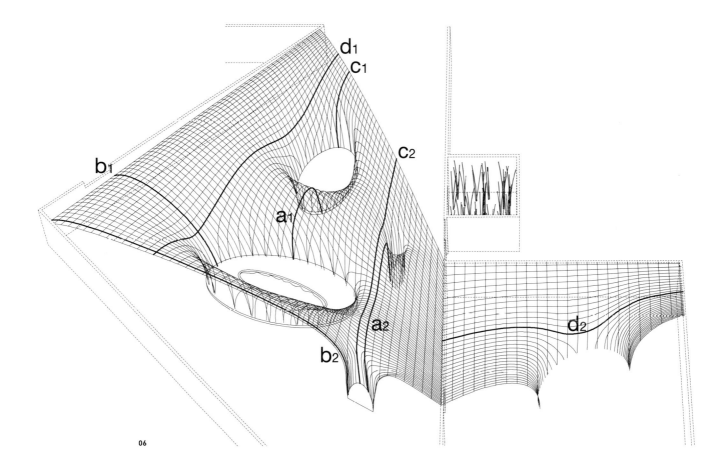

06

07

08

GucklHupf

MONDSEE, AUSTRIA // HANS PETER WÖRNDL
MARINE-GRADE PLYWOOD PANELS

DESIGN INTENTION

This small 13 x 22 x 23 ft. (4 x 6 x 7 m) experimental structure was built to explore the transformation of space in response to changing conditions. Based on the architect's metaphorical idea of a "work in progress," the attempt was to create a "living" object that is always in flux and is not intended to be permanent. It was designed for the Festival of the Regions, by the Mondsee Lake in northern Austria, as an artistic, cultural, and architectural manifestation of an unusual or unknown object. It has since been disassembled and stored. The structure could be closed down to be a solid and voidless rectangular box, but then could be opened up in a variety of different forms to create different spatial and light conditions. For six weeks in the summer, the structure was used for music performances, poetry readings, and small gatherings. During the other summer weeks, it was used as a weekend lake house. During the winter months it was transformed to hold and store a boat.

MATERIALITY

Marine-grade plywood panels clad the structure. These finished wood panels give an appearance of a wood box that was carefully and exactly fitted together. The notion of a box that slides, pivots, swings, and moves agrees with the nature of the wood panels. The plywood panels act as a wrapping that can be peeled away or pulled up to open and close the space. It is an ideal material for this, since it is relatively lightweight, has an appearance of solid wood, and is relatively uniform in its appearance and shape.

TECHNICAL

The wood framework for this project was built of 4.72 x 4.72 in. (12 x 12 cm) posts and 2.36 x 4.72 in. (6 x 12 cm) joists. Cladding was made of sandwich panels composed of plywood with Okume, an African hardwood, on the inner and outer faces with a rigid foam insulation core, all on a pine frame with some steel reinforcement. The sandwich assembly improved thermal performance and moderated the inherent tendency for the plywood to distort out of plane. A series of dowels, flaps, and stainless steel cables allow this structure to move, transform, and convert to different conditions.

The marine-grade plywood used knotfree veneers and fully waterproof structural adhesive, making it a premium panel where strength is a priority. Panels were 4.1 ft. x 8.2 ft. (125 x 250 cm), secured with Phillips drive screws. A high-quality clear marine sealer was applied to the wood.

01

02

01 Structure opened
02 Structure closed
03 Section
04 Plan

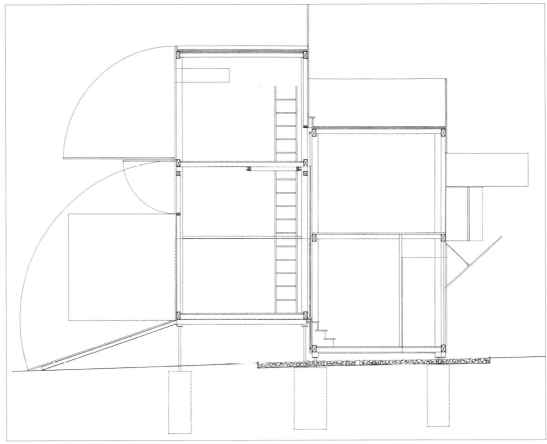

03

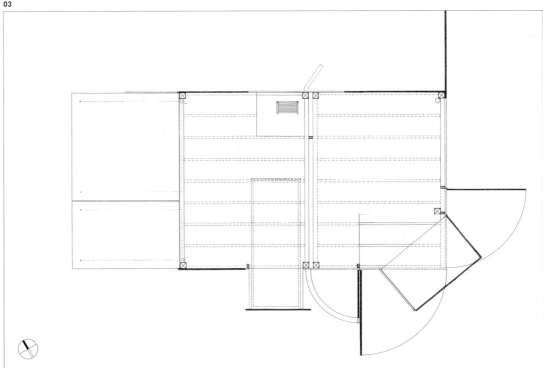

04

House in Kromeriz

KROMERIZ, CZECH REPUBLIC // ARCHTEAM
TIMBER FRAME, LAYERED INFILL WALL

DESIGN INTENTION

This house is located on a long and narrow lot in the historic village of Kromeriz, which is located in the South Moravian lowland of the southeastern part of the Czech Republic. The goal of the designers was to create a house that best fits the existing site shape with a tectonic clarity. The longitudinal north elevation is opaque while the entry and short elevations are glazed and open to gardens on the site. This allows unobstructed views all the way through the house and through this long, narrow site. As one experiences the 710-square-foot (66 sq. m) house and its simple open floor plan, there is a clear understanding of its timber construction and how wood connections are made. It is viewed by the designer as a piece of furniture within a garden.

MATERIALITY

The house has a continuous concrete foundation, but the remaining structure is built entirely of wood. A timber framework carries the loads of the house. A timber-framed canopy marks the entrance and is a clear expression of the wood construction seen throughout the house. Laminated plywood panels clad the exterior walls, and interior wall and ceiling surfaces are faced with softwood veneer panels, carefully cut to match the grid of structure. Floor surfaces are thick tongue-and-groove plywood with a veneer matching the wall and ceiling treatment. The interior and exterior faces of the end walls are painted inside and outside; other wood surfaces are finished with a clear sealer. The membrane roof is slightly sloped and is covered with raised seam titanium-zinc roofing.

TECHNICAL

The primary structural system in this building is a stout timber frame consisting of timber columns and spaced beams in a compact orthogonal grid. The frame becomes stable by diagonal braces in the wall planes, and by the triangulated floor and canopy structure in the horizontal planes.

The light wood framing within the timber frame is multilayered, with the 2.4 x 2.4 in. (60 x 60 mm) studs receiving additional horizontal wood furring of the same size on both sides before interior and exterior finishes are applied. This makes the wall assemblies thick enough to envelope the timber columns, and also makes it possible to achieve an effective thermal break in this sometimes chilly climate. Thermal insulation fills the space between the studs but also between horizontal furring members, making it so that no wood framing contacts both interior and exterior surfaces. Likewise, building services can travel vertically or horizontally within this wall without interfering with either framing or insulation systems. The exterior plywood is ventilated on its interior face using .78 x 2.4 in. (20 x 60 mm) vertical battens.

The timber columns and beam intersections use either traditional subtractive joinery or exposed steel plates with bolted connections. These wood members have also checked somewhat—split longitudinally due to tangential shrinkage—which is normal as their moisture content drops after milling. This rustic character contrasts with the refined expression of the glossy finished veneers of the non-structural finishes throughout the interior. Details throughout the house are minimal, allowing the character of the materials, the interior spaces, and the view of the landscape to be appreciated.

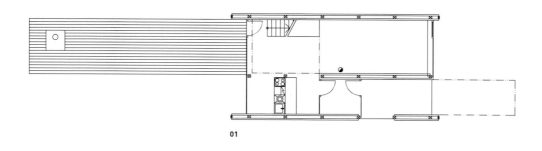

01

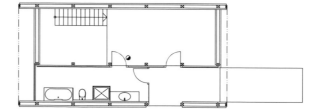

02

01   Ground-floor plan
02   Second-floor plan
03   Exterior view
04   Entry canopy

03

04

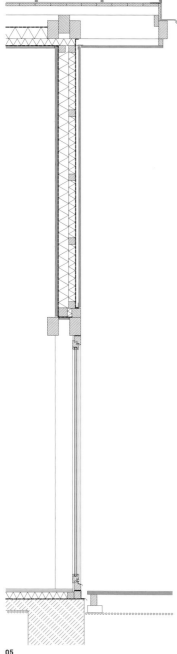

05

06

05 Wall section
06 Interior view
07 Building section

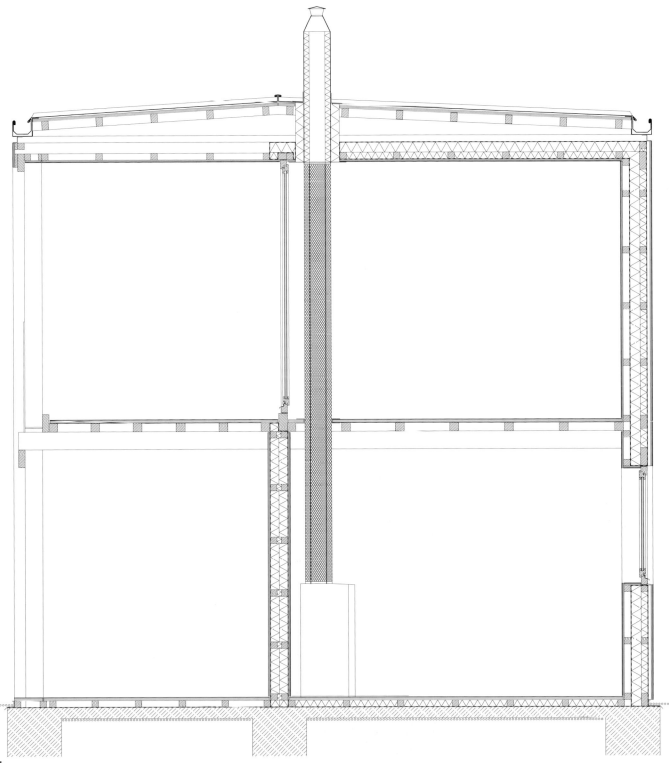

Think Tank

SKIBBEREEN, COUNTY CORK, IRELAND // GUMUCHDJIAN ARCHITECTS
POST-AND-BEAM, WOOD AND STEEL FRAME, CEDAR BOARD ROOFING

DESIGN INTENTION

This small retreat was designed for a filmmaker as a place to withdraw to for contemplation and reading. It is 592 square feet (55 sq. m) and sits atop a stone plinth on the River Ilen, against a backdrop of lush green trees and adjacent to a freshwater pool. Inspired by the structural precedence of boathouses and Japanese pavilions, the design goal was to create a simple open plan that is built of a bold wood construction that has been reinterpreted for a modern use.

MATERIALITY

This iconic post-and-beam structure builds upon a traditional diagram with modernist spatial features and materiality. It is the essence of shelter: base, frame, and roof. In general the project handsomely merges with its context, serving both as a retreat and as a birdwatching "hide." But up close it reveals innovation and sophistication in its details, incorporating contemporary amenities without doing harm to the purity of the basic form. Some construction materials are durable and never-changing, such as the stone plinth upon which the pavilion is built. Other materials are ever-changing in response to nature. The red cedar exterior materials darken when the drizzle begins, only to be bleached again as the sun returns to dry them. Over time this material will change from its warm hue to a cool dove gray, near that of the stone in the plinth. Beyond its aesthetic qualities, red cedar is also a good selection for a structure near water in a temperate wet climate, due to its inherent anti-decay properties.

The openness of the basic frame is enhanced by the absence of engaging walls or the clutter of program within. Insulated glass is the weather barrier on all walls, with screens made of red cedar on all or part of three elevations to filter light and view. Even the slender spaces between the roof rafters and ceiling are glazed, silhouetting the frame with clarity.

TECHNICAL

The columns in this pavilion are actually steel sections, wrapped in fine iroko wood. This contemporary solution provides a moment-resisting frame, eliminating need for shear walls or diagonal bracing, which would not be possible if the columns were made of a stout piece of timber. The wrapped columns also provide a small vertical chase through which minor building services can be concealed. Beams and rafters are one-piece heavy timber elements also made of iroko wood.

The roof uses the familiar red cedar material often used as shingles, but here in an unfamiliar configuration: a series of eave-to-ridge boards that interlock in a roman tilelike manner. This reduces vulnerability to wind-driven rain that can push moisture into the numerous small spaces in conventional cedar shingle roofing. The relieved back on the boards produces a c-shaped profile that will reduce the chance that the wood will distort by cupping as its moisture content changes. The cedar roofing is elevated over a cavity, permitting drying of the wood from the underside, and limiting the chance that moisture will migrate deeper into the assembly. A bituminous felt layer isolates this cavity from the plywood and thermal insulation below, making the cedar roofing layer become a variation of the rain screen wall. A hidden gutter made of copper sheet metal collects water at the bottom of both the cavity and the roof surface, preventing water from blemishing the cedar fascia or other surfaces below. The roof ridge is made of cedar boards oriented longitudinally, which interlock with the upper ends of the roof boarding to cover their end grain. In this narrow building, ventilation of the cavity can occur laterally across the ridge, from eave to eave.

The roof boards are 1.38 in. x 7.09 in.(35 x 180 mm), and are full length, so they have no splices along their length. Cedar slats in screens over the glass in some locations are 1.18 in. x 3.94 in.(30 x 100 mm), secured to a frame very near the fixed glass skin.

01 View from pier
02 Exterior view
03 Transverse section

01

02

Vertical and horizontal sections
1. Roof construction: two 1.38 x 7.09 in. (35 x 180 mm)
    interlocking cedar boarding ventilated cavity; .98 x 1.77 in.
    (25 x 45 mm) battens and counter-battens on
    .08 in. (2 mm) bituminous felt waterproof layer
    .79 in. (20 mm) plywood sheets
    3.94 in. (100 mm) glass-wool thermal insulation
    .98 in. (25 mm) cedar tongued-and-grooved boarding
2. .94 x 11.02 in. (24 x 280 mm) cedar verge fascia board
3. 3.94 x 3.94 in. (100 x 100 mm) softwood bearer
4. .08 in. (2 mm) sheet copper gutter, bent to shape, behind
    1.77 x 11.02 in. (45 x 280 mm) cedar eaves fascia board
5. 7.07 x 7.87 in. (200 x 200 mm) iroko rafters x beams
6. 11.81 x 7.87 in. (300 x 200 mm) iroko plate
7. Sliding door with double glazing: .24 in. (6 mm) safety glass;
    .47 in. (12 mm) cavity; .31 in. (8 mm) lam. safety glass
8. 1.18 x 3.94 in. (30 x 100 mm) cedar slats in front
    of fixed glazing
9. Subfloor convector
10. 7.87 x 11.81 in. (200 x 300 mm) column:
    5.03 x 7.79 in. (128 x 198 mm) galvanized
    steel I-section in iroko casing
11. Fixed glazing to end wall: .74 in.
    (19 mm) safety glass

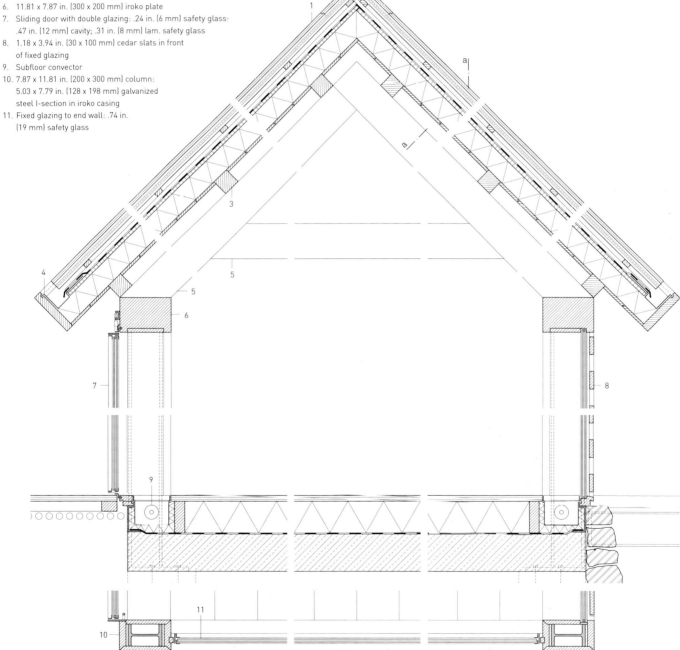

BTV Commercial and Residential Building

WOLFURT, GERMANY // BAUMSCHLAGER & EBERLE
LARCH LATTICE PANELS, MOVABLE SCREENS

DESIGN INTENTION

This multipurpose building is sited perpendicular to a fairly busy thoroughfare in the village of Wolfurt in southern Germany. The design goal was to create a multiuse residential and commercial building that fits contextually into the character of the village. Through the use of a movable larch wood slat wrapping, the building is able to achieve a lightness and softness while creating an ever-changing facade. The front portion of the building facing the public street contains a bank while the rear, which is oriented toward a garden, contains apartment units of varying size. The glass storefront of the bank is the only portion of the building that is completely open and not wrapped in the wood lattice system. A concrete service core intersects the building and is in sharp contrast to the light and ethereal nature of the wood facade.

MATERIALITY

The building reads clearly as a glass box that has been wrapped in a system of larch lattice panels that are able to move and slide horizontally, changing the interior spaces by playing with the light and shadow. This lattice acts as a sunshield but also gives a level of privacy when desired.

The lattice treatment is used in all locations other than the public exposure of the commercial space on the lower level, and at the service core. It is used on elevations that will not receive direct sunlight, and even over opaque wall substrates. The wood lattice therefore becomes the single architectural cladding solution for nearly all environmental and programmatic situations. The result is a building that at first seems abstract and siteless, but which becomes more tangible through the warmth of the delicate wood treatment and through animation by occupants manipulating the panels to meet their personal needs.

TECHNICAL

The larch lattice is composed of horizontal wood strips secured to a frame made of vertical steel channels. Movable panels are equipped with rollers that are guided in tracks at the top and bottom of each panel. At the top the roller assembly is attached to each vertical steel channel; at the bottom it is attached to the bottom-most piece of wood lattice. Lattice panels that are fixed in location are identical except that they are secured with steel angles rather than roller assemblies. The lattice panels are positioned in two planes, allowing movable panels to move easily past fixed ones. The innermost lattice is 1.64 ft.(50 cm) from the glass enclosure walls on the building, providing adequate space for maintenance personnel to perform needed service.

Screws secure the wood lattice elements to the steel channels from the interior, leaving no fasteners exposed to the exterior face. The wood is oiled but unpainted; over time the larch will become a soft gray color. The larch lattice elements are 1.57 in. wide x 1.77 in. tall (40 x 45 mm), with a 1.10 in. (28 mm) space between each piece. The lattice panels are 4.92 ft. tall x 11.81 ft. wide (1.5 x 3.6 m)—one half the building's story height and equal to the structural bay dimension. Movable lattice panels allow occupants to open the upper portion of the exterior wall to light and view.

Each piece of wood in the lattice is a rhombus in section, giving the upper surface a slope toward the exterior to shed precipitation, and giving the lower outside edge an acute-angle drip edge, to better release any moisture. This shape also gives occupants a view angled slightly downward toward street activity, and helps to block unwanted sunlight.

01 Plan
02 Southeast corner
03 West elevation

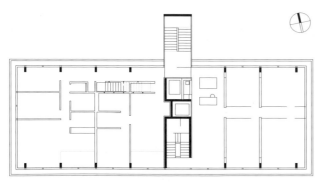

01

02

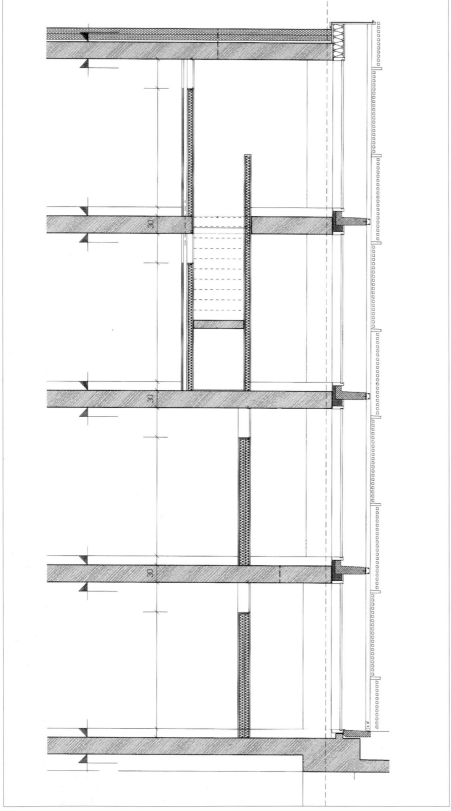

04 Wall section
05 Screen track detail
06 View between screen and
glass facade

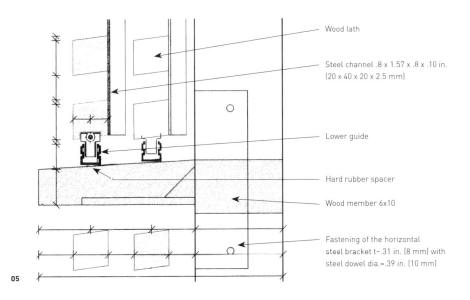

Wood lath

Steel channel .8 x 1.57 x .8 x .10 in.
(20 x 40 x 20 x 2.5 mm)

Lower guide

Hard rubber spacer

Wood member 6x10

Fastening of the horizontal
steel bracket t~.31 in. (8 mm) with
steel dowel dia.=.39 in. (10 mm)

05

ILMASI School

GARBSEN, GERMANY // DESPANG ARCHITEKTEN
PREFABRICATED FIR WOOD PANEL, GLUELAM BEAMS

INTENTION

This school for physically and mentally handicapped children accommodates approximately one hundred children, all with distinctive needs and challenges, and forty teachers. The designer's goal was to create a passive and serene environment for a large educational program. A series of low wood buildings with shed roofs and a series of distinct courtyards meander on the site with an almost natural sense of always belonging there. Through the use of wood, the landscape, and the courtyards, this building creates a link to nature and a calming character by creating a variety of subtle connections between the internal and external spaces.

MATERIALITY

An unusual prefabricated load-bearing wood panel is used for most of the enclosure. Fir lumber with a vertical profile is used to sheath most walls and ceilings, a dark stained oak is used for doors, and floors are wood parquet or stone. The senses of the occupants are meant to be productively stimulated by the tactile richness and the play of light over the vertically textured wall surfaces. These surfaces are also intended to enhance acoustic quality within the school, and are durable enough to withstand the anticipated wear. The designer also reasons that fire threat is reduced because the wood is more massive in this project than in conventional light frame construction. Sprinklers were nonetheless installed as a precaution.

The interior and exterior faces of the walls have an identical materiality and appearance, despite being made in significantly different ways. Both use vertically profiled fir wood as the material, but the structural panels on the interior are made by subtracting or rabbeting the corner of each piece of lumber, whereas the outside faces are non-structural, and are made by adding small pieces of fir to a plane of like material, making its overall thickness less than that of the structural panel.

TECHNICAL

The load-bearing panels consist of 2.36 x 5.19 in. (60 x 130 mm) fir boards nailed face-to-face to form a dense plane of wood. These panels support an upper floor and roof, serve as thermal mass in the building, and are exposed as the interior wall finish. More than 14,000 sq. ft. (1,400 sq. m) of wall area was made using these fir panels. The client wished to avoid using non-renewable construction materials and to utilize a material of local origin.

Fir is not a species of wood that is intrinsically resistant to biological attack. The architect therefore took precautions to prevent moisture intrusion and other prudent measures to lengthen the life of the assembly. Outside of the structural wood panel is a sophisticated strategy to provide thermal insulation and moisture control of the exterior walls. Thermal insulation is provided by two layers of wood framing and insulation, oriented vertically and horizontally to avoid any continuous members conducting heat from inside to outside. Inside of this insulation is the vapor barrier; outside of it is the air barrier.

Lessons from masonry cavity walls are applied to the wood exterior veneer, which acts as a rain screen in this building. The ribbed wood exterior face of the wall is supported on a series of horizontal furring strips that maintain a cavity behind the veneer, through which air and moisture can freely move. The wood veneer repels most of the weather, but the backup cavity provides a second avenue for it to exit before reaching critical elements within the assembly. The air barrier bounds the cavity toward the interior, preventing air infiltration and discouraging moisture from entering the insulation layer. Vents at the top of the cavity and weeps at the bottom permit air and moisture to move without marring the outside appearance.

Glue laminated wood beams span some of the courtyards to support a translucent ETFE plastic foil roof treatment. These structural elements are consistent in material with the wall materials, and are slender so that the quantity of light into the courtyard and adjoining spaces is abundant. Where screens are desired, such as over some windows, next to stairs, and around exterior mechanical equipment, the designer used a variation of the basic ribbed wood wall treatment. Screens are made by omitting either 50 or 66 percent of the pieces of wood, producing voids in elevation but still knitting the screen together with the adjoining solid wood walls.

01 Building section
02 Exterior view
03 Wood siding assembly
04 Transparent wood screen
05 Window detail

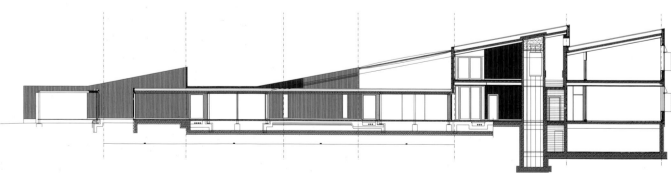

02

03

04

05

06 **Wall section**
07 **Roof assembly**
08 **Plan detail at window**

Wall assembly
> 1.18 x 1.18 in. (30 x 30 mm) pine strips
> .79 in. (20 mm) pine boarding
> 1.57 x 2.36 in. (40 x 60 mm) pine counter-battens
  (all pine members thermally treated)
> Windproof layer
> 2.36 x 2.36 in. (60 x 60 mm) wood bearers
> 2x 2.36 in. (60 mm) rock-wool insulation
> .79 in. (20 mm) oriented strand board
> 2.36 x 5.12 in. (60 x 130 mm) rabbeted stacked planks,
  oiled (with 2 per cent white pigment)

Floor Assembly
> .87 in. (22 mm) smoked-oak parquet
> 2.44 in. (62 mm) screed
> 1.38 in. (35 mm) impact-sound insulation
> 4.72 in. (120 mm) reinforced concrete slab on
  5.51 in. (140 mm) filling
> .79 in. (20 mm) chipboard
> 3.94 x 5.51 in. (100 x 140 mm) timber beams
  between steel
> I-beams 11.81 in. (300 mm) deep
> 1.18 x 1.18 in. (30 x 30 mm) softwood bearers
> .79 in. (20 mm) softwood bearing

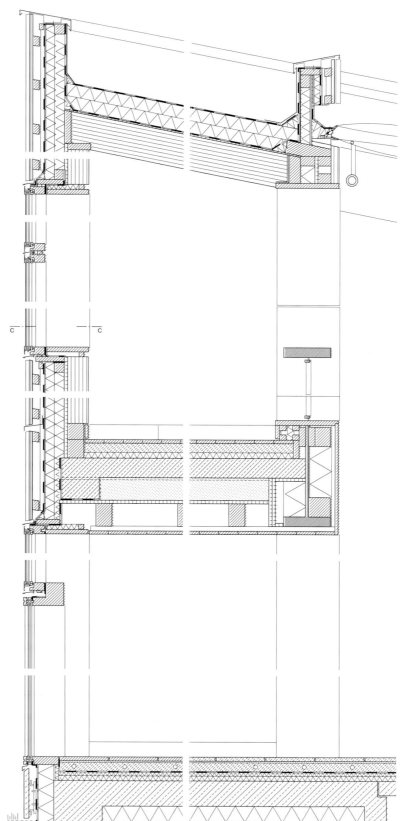

Roof assembly
> 3.15 in. (80 mm) substrate soil layer
> 2.76 in. (70 mm) water retaining
  drainage layer
> Plastic roof sealing layer
> 7.09 in. (180 mm) two-layer rock wool
  insulation
> Bituminious sealing layer
> 2.36 x 7.09 in. (60 x 180 mm) rabbeted
  stacked planks

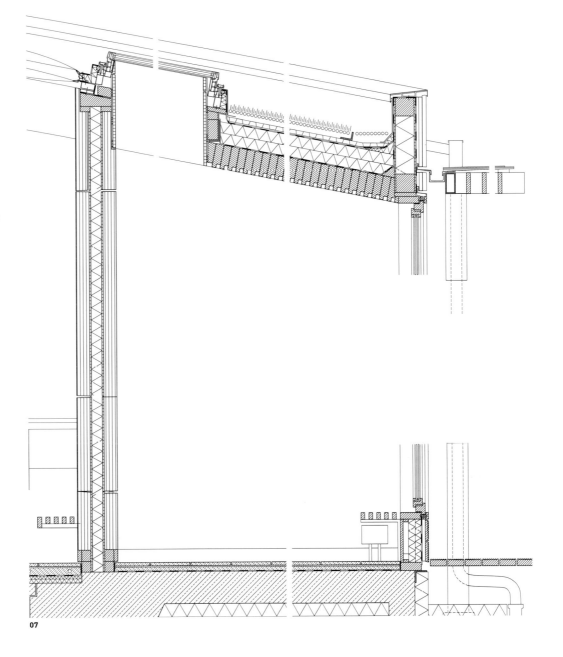

07

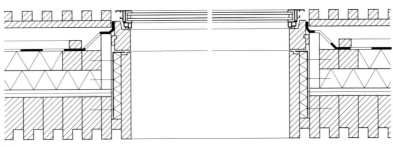

08

Sirch Woodworking Manufacturing

BÖHEN, GERMANY // BAUMSCHLAGER & EBERLE
STRESSED-SKIN CONSTRUCTION, SIBERIAN LARCH SLAT WRAP

DESIGN INTENTION

This building serves as a laboratory and wood storage for a lumber company in a rural area of the German Allgau region. The designers wanted to create a large wood frame to encompass the building and thus create a viewing box for the rural landscape. The building appears to be a wood vessel that is floating on the landscape with a transparent base. The intention was for the building to be a subtle and unassuming presence in this pastoral area.

MATERIALITY

The lower level was constructed of concrete retaining walls on three sides that embed the building into the hillside. The other lower-level facade is clad with a translucent polycarbonate, giving the appearance that the building is hovering on the landscape. The upper level appears to be a floating wood box that is wrapped with perimeter frame columns infilled with glass. The building is covered on the long elevations with a system of Siberian larch slats, while the short elevations are large glass panels that allow light into the building, also emphasizing the wrapping nature of the larch slats. Interior spaces are open for woodworking processes, storage, and for administrative functions. A remarkably unencumbered interior space is available on both floors.

TECHNICAL

Above ground level, the structural system is a timber frame whose planning module carries over to control all enclosure and fenestration features of this simple building. Window mullions are also the columns that support upper-floor and roof loads above. Slats that screen the glazed east and west elevations are shop-fabricated into panels that coincide with the 6.56 ft. (2 m) interval of the mullions.

Floor and roof spanning systems are 15.7 in. (40 cm) deep stressed-skin construction, allowing them to span the up to 50 ft. (15 m) space without columns. The depth-to-span ratio of 1:38 is exceptional for wood construction. In this application, the plywood above and below the spanning members combine with those members to form an integrated structural unit referred by the architect as a "multibox timber element."

The slats cover not only the broad east and west elevations, but also the entire roof and part of the soffit below the overhanging portions of the second floor. This contributes a consistent appearance to all sides of the building, and reduces the impact of sunlight on building surfaces and interior spaces. The slats are made of Siberian larch, an especially stiff and hard species of softwood, approximately 50 percent more dense than eastern white pine. The slats are a slender .94 in. x 5.51 in. (24 x 140 mm), with a 3.7 in. (94 mm) space between each. They are carefully mitered at their corners to avoid exposure of end grain to the weather. In rare locations where the upper end of a slat is not covered by another slat, such as at the west entry, a small sheet metal cap is installed. The slats are held off of the enclosure wall 6.3 in. (160 mm), providing a chase through which roof drainage and other minor services may reside without affecting the elevation or the interior space.

01 East-west section
02 Day view
03 Night view
04 Upper-floor plan showing large spanning open plan
05 North glass wall

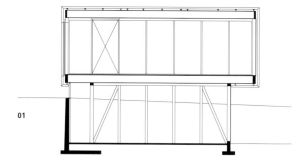

01

02

03

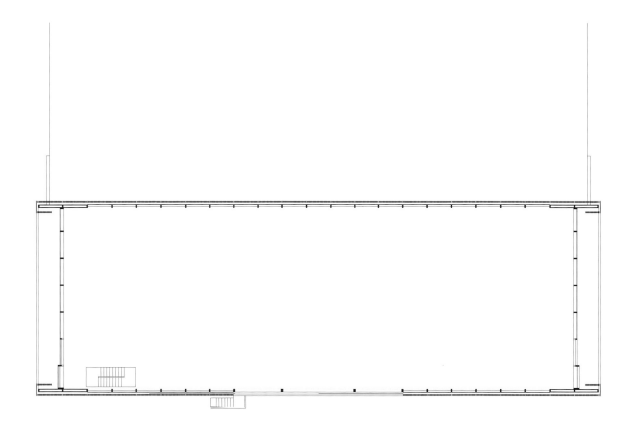

04

05

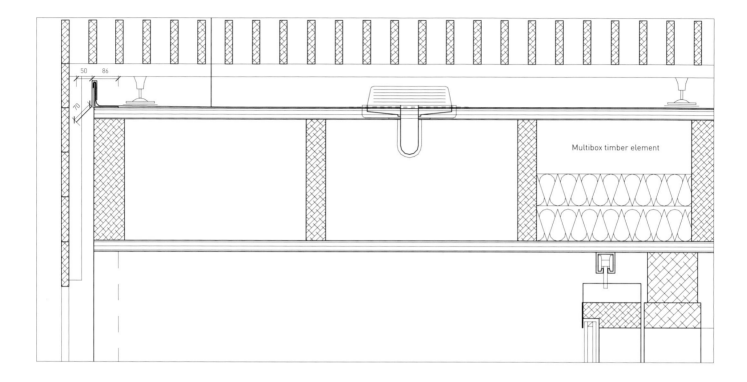

50　86

70

Multibox timber element

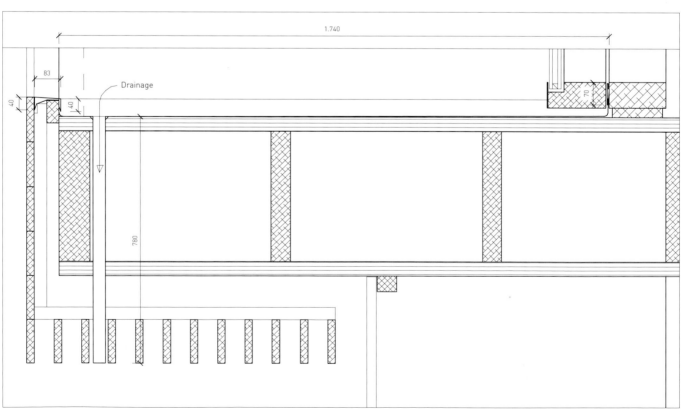

1.740

83

40　40

Drainage

70

780

06 Section at balcony
07 Slat detailing
08 Section at east wall

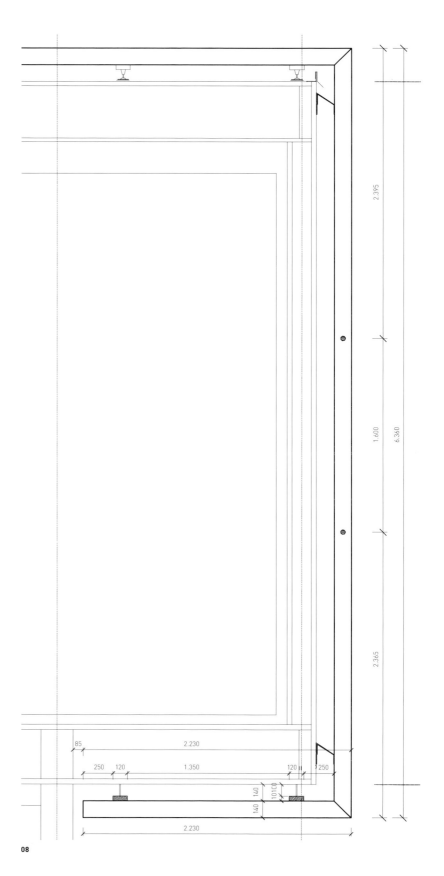

07

08

METALS

THE BASICS

Metals are elements made by the refinement of minerals, each with unique qualities derived from their constituents and the process used to produce them. Unlike wood or stone or many other materials, metals are entropic—they can be re-covered, re-formed, or mixed together to form totally new metal types. Metals that contain iron are called *ferrous* metals, such as steel, cast iron, and wrought iron. Ferrous metals are generally the strongest metals but tend to oxidize easily. *Nonferrous* metals contain no iron, such as aluminum, copper, and lead. These metals are usually easy to work with and are considered more attractive. Generally nonferrous metals are more costly, however they tend to form a protective oxide layer on their surface to prevent excessive corrosion. Most architectural metals are alloys or mixtures of various elements, controlled to yield optimum qualities for a particular application. Metals have a great range of properties. They can be lustrous, ductile, conductive of heat and electricity, corrode by oxidation, vulnerable to heat, and are considered the strongest architectural material.

Minerals that contain a mixture of a metallic elements and various impurities are called *ore*. The process of extracting metal from ore is called *smelting*. Combinations of metals, or a base metal mixed with traces of others are called *alloys*. The predominate elements used in architecture are iron, aluminum, copper, zinc, and titanium. Metals are seldom used in their pure state, but rather as alloys that offer more strength and durability. Most often these elements are alloyed with others to yield optimum qualities for a particular application.

Metals can be worked with the following methods and processes:

→ **Casting**—in which molten metal is poured into a mold to achieve a desired shape
→ **Forging**—in which hot metal is forced into a die to achieve a desired shape
→ **Rolling**—in which hot or cold metal passes through a series of rollers to give it a profile
→ **Extruding**—in which metal is pushed through a die, squeezing it to a desired cross section
→ **Drawing**—in which metal is pulled rather than pushed through the die, to produce wires, tubing, or rods

HISTORY

Metal is one of the oldest materials to be manipulated by man, and has been used for its strength and versatility. For centuries metals have been shaped into tools, weapons, and different practical objects. Copper, one of the harder historic metals, was first used for tools, followed by bronze, which is a copper alloy. Gold and silver, which are soft metals were only used for decorative purposes as they primarily are today. The Greeks used bronze and iron for tying stone blocks together without mortar, and the Romans used lead and copper for water pipes and roofing. But it was not until the eighteenth century when iron could be processed economically that metal's role in architecture became substantial, as it was manufactured for structural beams, columns, and machinery. By the nineteenth century, structural iron and steel were becoming common. When reinforced concrete was invented in the 1860s, the marriage of steel and concrete revolutionized the construction industry: longer spans and taller buildings were possible as never before.

Copper is thought to be one of the first metals ever used—archaeologists have found evidence of its use stretching back as far as 6000 BC. For most of history, copper was the prime construction metal due to its combination of strength and durability. The first evidence of copper production techniques appeared in 6000–4000 BC in the eastern Mediterranean area (present-day Turkey), where copper was extracted and forged into finished tools. In 5000 BC Egyptians became very skilled with working copper by smelting in wood-fired furnaces and creating tools, jewelry, and other ornaments. It was the Romans, however, who first used copper in a major architectural application. They mastered soldering and brazing techniques and created some different fluxes to clean and remove oxides from copper's surface. The Pantheon, built by Marcus Agrippa in 27 BC, and later rebuilt by Hadrian in 120 AD, had a copper roof and cornice, which remained intact until the beginning of the Word War II. As history progressed, copper's use increased primarily for the roofs in many Renaissance buildings and the steep roofs of the Gothic cathedrals and churches. More recently, the Statue of Liberty was constructed of copper sheets over an iron framework. Copper's primacy did not fade until the second half of the twentieth century, when iron, as a steel alloy, became the most common construction metal, followed by aluminum, with copper falling to the third most used metal in architecture.

Zinc was first used by the Romans in 200 BC as a copper alloy to make brass, but was not commercially produced as an architectural metal until the 1650s. It is a blue-white–colored metal that is relatively brittle and will oxidize to a self-protecting gray surface. The first production method for zinc was in a sheet form, but the result was extremely brittle and cracked easily. The hot-rolling process reduced zinc's brittleness and increased its strength as an architectural metal. It was first used architecturally in Europe during the Industrial Revolution, primarily in roofing and details. Brass, developed in the seventeenth century, contains up to 40 percent zinc and is most often used for finishes, fixtures, and ornamental objects. It was most commonly seen in the form of roof tile or ornamentation. The United States, where copper was much more widely used, did not develop zinc sheet production until 1838, relying until that point on imports to meet modest demand for this metal.

It can be argued that the development of steel was one of the most pivotal moments in the history of architecture, giving a freedom of design and space and opening up structural possibilities in countless new ways. With the construction of Joseph Paxton's Crystal Palace in London in 1851, cast iron and wrought iron, later refined to what we know today as steel, was shown to be a new construction material with capabilities like no other. Iron, which is not abundant in pure form in the earth's crust, was historically a metal used only for tools. The largest source of pure iron, in fact, can be found in meteorites—not a particularly reliable source. Therefore the most common way to obtain iron was the smelting of iron ore, which is very common all over the world. In the Middle Ages, most of the iron refined from ore used a method that acted somewhat like a blast furnace. Crushed iron ore and charcoal were placed in a stone vault and molten iron (also called pig iron) would drop to the bottom and release into molds. The use of charcoal added traces of carbon to the iron, which altered its workability. Interestingly, the use of wood to produce charcoal for iron smelting was one of the main causes of world deforestation. Late in the nineteenth century, charcoal was replaced by coke, a residue of coal used for fuel. The iron produced at this time was almost a pure iron—it was very malleable since it had little carbon. It was called *wrought iron* and was used mainly for tools and weapons for centuries. Large productions of wrought iron were produced in Europe after the 1300s. While wrought iron is almost pure iron, iron produced in a blast furnace with 2 to 4 percent carbon is called *cast iron*. The Chinese discovered cast iron in the sixth century BC, but the process of production did not fully evolve until the twelfth century in Europe. Cast iron is much more brittle, difficult to work, and has a lower melting point than wrought iron. A malleable, low-carbon iron alloy was sometimes produced in a blast furnace. This metal, which was approximately 1 percent carbon, was historically the closest metalworkers came to producing what we know today as steel. Iron was considered expensive until the late eighteenth century, when cheaper manufacturing processes emerged. Whether these advances spurred the Industrial Revolution or vice versa is debatable. In the early 1800s cast iron structural members became a viable alternative to load-bearing masonry walls.

In the mid-1800s steel was used for only very specific non-architectural applications, such as swords or scissors. Early production of steel was unpredictable, not very homogenous, and thought of as a very demanding process. Only in certain geographic areas such as some parts of Asia were these select batches of steel produced with any success. In 1855 Englishman Henry Bessemer designed the first converter for processing steel, which by today's classifications was really cast iron. Steel began to be produced in large quantities after Bessemer discovered how to add and control the amount of carbon. It was first produced by either adding carbon to molten wrought iron or by preventing carbon from oxidizing in the pig iron. In the United States, Andrew Carnegie of U.S. Steel and Edgar Thompson of Bethlehem Steel both helped feed the Industrial Revolution by producing large quantities of steel in the 1800s. Steel began to be used in railroad tracks, bridges, shipbuilding, and eventually skyscrapers.

Bauxite, from which aluminum is refined, is one of the most common metallic elements in the earth's crust and yet was not known to the ancient world. It was first produced in 1845 as a precious metal, but did not become widely used in construction until the past century. Prior to the twentieth century, purifying aluminum, which is not naturally unearthed in a usable state, was a very expensive and lengthy process. Today, it is second only to iron as the most used metal in construction.

Titanium was first discovered in 1791 by William Gregor, an English chemist and mineralogist. His discovery was not widely known until 1795, however, when it was "rediscovered" by Martin Klaproth, a German chemist. Klaproth named the metal *titanium* after the Titans, the family of giants that was overthrown by the gods in Greek mythology. Interestingly, he named it so because of the difficulty in removing the impurities and oxygen to reduce titanium to a pure state, not because of the high strength with which we associate it today. Initially, titanium was only used in paints as a pigment supplement. The metal has many tiny impurities that made it a brittle material and difficult to work. It first became commercially available in 1951 and was developed to be four times harder than steel. Mass production of titanium began in World War II by Dr. William Kroll, a German who fled Nazi Germany and came to the United States. In the early 1950s titanium was considered purely an aerospace material, given its light weight and high strength. It was not until the 1990s that titanium was considered a realistic architectural material, when its price dropped and its production techniques were refined.

DESIGN CONSIDERATIONS

In architecture, metals have developed and grown into a huge industry producing materials for an unprec-edent-ed range of applications. It is too general to speak about "metal" as if it were one simple material, given its enor-mously wide range of types, colors, qualities, and properties. As a category, metals are architecturally unique for being relatively lightweight and malleable as well as strong. They can also be used sculpturally, allowing for free-form designs. Metals are available in a variety of surface finishes—the range of color, texture, and luster allows architects an immense degree of flexibility. With today's variety of finishes and coatings, a designer can almost prescribe exactly how a metal should appear on a building, then find the product that will yield that appearance.

Beyond aesthetics, however, there is a long list of functional considerations when choosing a metal for a building. Despite the many product options and technological advances in applying metals in architecture, designers must be mindful of limitations associated with each material. How will it perform as a structural component? How will it react to different temperatures or to adjacent materials? How will it weather? How will its color, luster, and reflectivity endure? *Oil canning*, or the waviness that occurs in a metal surface, sometimes occurs in large stretches of metal and can be an inherent characteristic of metal products, should also be considered in the design process, or measures must be taken to prevent it.

The qualities of reflectivity, weathering, and finish can create a wildly diverse amount of design possibilities. Notably, the aging of metals is often seen as an inherent material quality of beauty. The familiar image of the vernacular barn and its rusted, colorful metal roof is a common architectural expression of the venerable and of a particular material culture. Architectural appreciation is often linked to a building material's expression of maturity and aesthetic age. In other circumstances, retaining a metal's original luster and finish and suppressing any declaration of age is a clear design intention. Weathering is therefore an important consideration.

The process of bimetallic corrosion is complex and can be affected by a number of factors, including the surrounding environment, variations in composition, any coatings and finishes, and contact with other materials, the principle being that different metals expand at different rates as they warm. *Galvanic action*, which is the corrosion process that occurs when two unlike metals and moisture are present, is an electric current flowing from the *anode*, which corrodes, to the *cathode*, which gives the ions to the atmosphere. When two metals are in contact, the one that is higher in the Galvanic Series will become the anode and will corrode. The current flows from the positive (high end of the table) to the negative (low end of the table). For instance, when iron and copper are in contact, iron will become the anode and will quickly corrode (see Table 1, p.156).

Metals, like other materials, expand and contract due to changes in temperatures. These changes are quantified and are represented numerically as *coefficients of thermal expansion*. These are ratios that give the amount of change per length of material per degree of change in temperature. The coefficient of thermal expansion for structural steel is .0000065 in./in./degree F (.000017 mm/mm/degree C), and for stainless steel is .0000099 in./in./degree F (.0000173 mm/mm/degree C). The greater the difference in thermal coefficient of materials being joined, the greater the need for details that accommodate thermal movement (see Table 2, p.156). If not relieved, these stresses may cause a loss of integrity of the enclosure or structural system.

TYPES

The metal industry is a mammoth enterprise that continues to grow and evolve. Research yields new alloys and new uses for metals constantly, and prices and manufacturing processes are always changing—all critical factors when architects make selections of materials. Whether as banal as an aluminum window frame or as expressive as the patina of a copper wall panel, metals are a potent design tools.

IRON AND STEEL

Steel, one of the strongest and most affordable materials, is a ferrous metal, meaning it contains iron. It is used in all types of buildings and in all aspects of construction. Compared to other building materials, steel has a favorable strength-to-weight ratio, and it offers the greatest strength per volume. It combines optimum strength with elasticity and is most often used for light and heavy structural framing, in addition to other building elements such as windows, doors, and hardware. It is easily drilled, tapped, welded, fastened, and shaped. Its most important architectural characteristics are its strength, stiffness, and fire and corrosion resistance, all properties that can be further influenced by alloying and coatings.

Most steels today are produced and categorized as a *standard* steel, which are then subcategorized as *carbon* or *alloy* steels. The more carbon a steel has, the greater its strength and hardness, though the more difficult it is to cold-work or weld. Alloy steel contains more than 1 percent of carbon or other elements than the standards set for carbon steel. Construction steel is a combination of carbon and iron (98 to 99 percent iron and 0.16 to 1.7 percent carbon). More common and more affordable, carbon steels are used for structural and mechanical applications, while alloy steels are most often used for fixtures and finishing parts such as door handles, pulls, or counter tops. The most common alloy steel is *stainless steel*, which is harder, stronger, and more corrosion-resistant than others. *High-strength, low-alloy* steel (HSLA) is also a common alloy steel, more commonly known as *Cor-ten*, and is not only extremely strong but has a high resistance to progressive corrosion due to a layer of dense red/orange-colored oxide that develops on its surface.

Wrought Iron has a low carbon content (0.02 percent) and is almost a pure iron. It is a ductile material and is easily worked and forged when red hot. It is highly resistant to corrosion, yet cannot be welded or cast. Wrought iron is made when iron ore is heated on a charcoal fire until it turns into a soft spongy state, not entirely melted. This spongelike condition can then be worked or wrought into a form in what is called a *white heat* state.

Wrought iron is most commonly used for ornamental work such as grilles, hardware, gates, and railings. A small amount of wrought iron is still made today in the traditional fashion, but most metal called "wrought iron" today is really mild steel with a low carbon content that can be formed into shapes by machine, putting many blacksmiths and their trade to rest.

Most steel is called *mild steel* and has a carbon content of .15–.25 percent. A common strength grade steel as determined by the American Society for Testing and Materials is ASTM A36, with a yield point (the point at which a material begins to permanently deform) of 36,000 psi (248.2 Mpa). A typical higher-strength steel, ASTM A572, which is a low-alloy, has a yield point of 50,000 psi (344.7 Mpa).

Cast Iron has a higher carbon content (approximately 1.8 to 4.5 percent), making the metal more brittle and difficult to work or forge when hot. Cast iron is an alloy of iron and iron carbide and is considered corrosion resistant and strong in compression. Due to its high amounts of carbon, cast iron is very easily cast, allowing for intricate molds. However, once it has solidified it cannot be worked. It is very hard and has good compressive strength but inferior elasticity; it also provides a tough surface that is less prone to rust than steel, despite it being very brittle and having a low tensile strength. Originally cast iron was made for both structural and decorative purposes, but its low melting point and brittleness make it undesirable as a structural material. It is still made and used often today, more often for architectural decorative details, piping, plumbing fixtures, grates, street furniture, and rainwater fixtures.

Stainless steel is an alloy steel that contains between 12 and 20 percent chromium and other elements such as nickel, copper, molybdenum, and aluminum. It may be cast into slabs; hot-rolled into plates, bars, or sheets; cold-rolled into thin sections; welded; and otherwise readily formed. Because of its strength and low maintenance requirements, stainless steel is often used for curtain walls, sanitary fixtures, sinks, hardware, flashing, and trim. Its high corrosion resistance makes it suitable for masonry accessories as well. Since the cost of stainless steel usually precludes its use structurally, it is more often used in smaller or visible applications such as fasteners, hardware, and building products such as kitchen appliances and limited areas of cladding.

Cor-ten steel is an alloy metal in which a small amount of copper (.25–.55 percent) and other elements are added to steel. The yield strength of Cor-ten steel is greater than that of mild steel. It is considered a weathering steel because the exposed surface quickly oxidizes in the atmosphere, forming a dense, shallow, passive barrier against further corrosion. It does not require painting or other treatment, though it does tend to stain materials adjacent to it with reddish-brown ferrous residue as the rusty surface is eroded slightly by precipitation.

Manufacturing Steel

The raw materials for producing steel are iron ore, coke (a residue of coal burning), and limestone. There are two standard processes for manufacturing steel: the *basic oxygen process*, used to make the bulk of standard-grade steel, uses an oxygen point to blow pressurized oxygen into a furnace containing pig iron and scrap metal; and the *electric arc furnace process*, which produces high-quality special steels like stainless steel, uses carbon electrodes to create a powerful electric arc that melts the metal. Both processes allow for the removal of unwanted elements and the addition of desired elements, carbon being the most common additive. Steel usually contains trace elements of other byproducts from refinement, such as sulfur and silicon.

Steel can be heat-treated to form alloys with other metals to change its quality. Metals that are alloyed with steel and the qualities created include:

→ **Aluminum**—improves surface hardening
→ **Chromium**—increases corrosion resistance and hardness
→ **Copper**—increases corrosion resistance and strength
→ **Manganese**—increases corrosion resistance and hardness
→ **Molybdenum**—increases corrosion resistance and strength
→ **Nickel**—increases tensile strength and corrosion resistance
→ **Tungsten**—increases strength at higher temperatures

After being manufactured, steel can be shaped in many different ways. Architecturally, this is classified under two main categories: *hot rolled* or *cold rolled*. Hot rolled steel is rolled out of the casting area to a specific thickness. Cold rolled steel, the most common architectural metal, is a product of the hot rolled process. After being hot rolled, the steel is run through cold rollers, stretching the grains, smoothing the surface, and making the metal more dimensionally accurate.

There are a number of ways of working steel to increase its hardness and strength. One is by a process called *cold-hardening*, which is the method of hammering or compressing steel to make it harder. Another frequently employed method, *quenching*, heats the steel and then quickly cools it in water, oil, or air, creating a very thin layer of metal crystals on the steel's surface that is harder and more brittle than the rest of the metal, thereby increasing its strength. *Tempering* is another way to increase the hardness, ductility, or strength of steel by a heating and controlled-cooling process. *Annealing* is the process of heating steel and cooling it very slowly to make a hard steel soft, usually to improve cold-working, cutting, and forming methods. Steel can also be *cast*, *forged*, *extruded*, *drawn*, and *rolled*.

Galvanization is the application of a zinc coating onto steel or iron to prevent rusting. There are two methods of galvanization. *Hot-dipped galvanizing* involves a coating that is applied by immersing the metal in a bath of molten zinc, forming a protective layer of zinc on the outside and zinc/iron alloys bonding to the steel. Repeated dipping produces a thicker coating, increasing durability. Zinc is a brittle metal, dictating that complex shapes such as corrugations should be formed before being galvanized. The surface of the zinc coating freezes into a crystalline or spangled pattern that oxidizes to a self-protecting matte gray color. If this coating is scratched or marred to the steel beneath, zinc compounds form in the scratch and heal the discontinuity, preventing oxidation. *Cold-dipping*, or *electro-galvanizing*, is a less durable process in which a thin coating of zinc is electrically created on the steel member, resulting in a shiny surface finish that is less durably bonded to the iron or steel core.

Appearance

In its most common and inexpensive form, steel has a plain gray appearance when new that will quickly react with oxygen and then scale and rust. To improve its appearance and to prevent corrosion, steel can be finished in many different ways. It can be painted, galvanized, or chemically treated to prevent oxidation and corrosion. Although it is not combustible, it will lose strength and become ductile under high heat conditions. Building codes therefore require most primary structural steel to be fireproofed. Some of these methods include enclosing steel in layers of gypsum board, encasing steel in concrete, or covering the steel with spray-on fireproofing, all of which conceal it from view.

High-quality stainless steel has an aesthetically appealing appearance but is also more expensive than carbon steel or other alloy steels. Stainless steel can be finished in a variety of ways. It can be polished, brushed, textured, patterned, or made reflective with optical effects using an electrochemical finish.

Weathering

Mild steel and low-alloy steels are highly susceptible to reacting with oxygen, causing rust, with accelerated corrosion occurring in coastal and marine locations. Corrosion resistance of steel can be improved by applying paint, powder coating, galvanizing, copper alloy, or various coatings. These can also improve the appearance by adding color or a shiny, uni-form surface. Stainless steel, on the other hand, is highly resistant to atmospheric corrosion and will retain its original luster. Its corrosion resistance is due to a thin oxide film that continually forms on its surface. This film may be permanently colored to bronze, blue, gold, red, purple, or green by a chemical and cathodic treatment.

Joining

Steel can be joined by most of the common metal joining heat processes—welding, soldering, or mechanically joined with bolts, rivets, pins, and most other mechanical fasteners. Steel is very easily welded and produces a strong bond. It can be welded using an oxygen/acetylene gas mixture or using an electric arc, which is more suitable for large steel sections such as structural steel. Smaller sections of steel can be welded with an electric arc and a metal inert gas (MIG) using a semiautomatic tool and argon gas. A similar tool using a tungsten electrode (TIG) is also available. *High-strength bolts* are bolts that are heat-treated during manufacturing to give them extra strength. Their strength is a result of their shear resistance, as opposed to how tight they are turned to prevent slippage of the two materials. Bolting is quicker, easier, and cheaper, can be done on site, and is reversible, but is sometimes not as strong.

ALUMINUM

Behind steel, aluminum is the most commonly used metal in construction. It is one of the lightest and easiest metals to manipulate, bend, shape, cast, fasten, and weld, and is also very ductile, often extruded into shapes for architectural purposes. It can easily be drilled, tapped, sawed, planed, and filed with hand tools, making it a yielding material for tradesmen to use.

Aluminum is used in many different functions and locations in architecture, the most common being roofing, cladding, flashing, curtain-wall and glazing systems, insulation, ductwork, hardware, and lighting. It is typically used for secondary building elements, but high-strength aluminum alloys are also used for structural purposes. This list continues to grow as the construction industry becomes more comfortable and creative with the material's capabilities and as it becomes more appealing to users.

Aluminum's resistance to corrosion is high, much better than steel's. It is also lighter than steel, copper, and most other metals. Aluminum's strength in relation to its weight is also better than steel. There are disadvantages to aluminum, however, including its higher cost, greater thermal expansion, and lower fire resistance as compared to steel.

Manufacturing Aluminum

Aluminum can be manipulated using all the same methods for working steel, including casting, hot rolling, and cold rolling, although it can be worked at a much lower temperature than steel because its melting point is more than a thousand degrees lower, making it a cheaper and safer material to produce. Refining aluminum takes a significant amount of electricity, which has consequently made the business of recycling the material an extensive secondary trade for the aluminum industry.

For construction purposes, aluminum is almost always turned into an aluminum alloy. It is most often alloyed with copper, manganese, zinc, silicon, magnesium, or magnesium and silicon together. Each of which are designed for specific purposes, such as for casting, added strength, or aviation purposes. The wide range of aluminum alloys are classified into three types:

→ **Non-heat-treatable alloys** are manganese and magnesium alloys. They are stronger than other aluminum alloys and are generally used for corrugated and troughed sheet roofing and cladding.

→ **Heat-treatable alloys** are aluminum-magnesium-silicon and aluminum-copper-magnesium-silicon alloys. They not as strong as non-heat-treatable alloys and have a lower corrosion resistance, but they are more resistant to fire. They are typically applied to structural and fastening uses.

→ **Casting alloys** are silicon, silicon-copper, and silicon-magnesium alloys. They are used for casting.

Aluminum's strength varies depending on the alloy used. Pure aluminum is too soft for structural use, and is therefore used only in fully supported roofing and flashing. Depending on the alloy it is married with, aluminum can be extruded through a die, allowing for a wider and more complex range of shapes and forms.

Aluminum is further classified for its tempering designation. *Temper* is the strength and hardness produced by thermal treatment and mechanical working. It is directly related to an alloy's overall strength. The temper designation is based on heat treatment, aging, and the annealing of the alloy. Aluminum is available in a large range of alloys, each created for specific purposes. These alloys are designated from 1000 to 7000 in seven categories. The number is followed by a letter that indicates the tempering designation—the most common stable series being "T" and usually designated from T1 through T10. The most common aluminum we see is 6061-T6, which contains trace elements of silicon and magnesium and is suitable for casting and fabrication.

Appearance
Aluminum is naturally a clean silver/white color, but there are also an abundant variety of finishes, such as anodizing, surface texture, plastic coating, or painted, that can result in a transparent or colored appearance. These various finishes can be mechanically or chemically applied and are not only meant for aesthetic purposes but also for protection from the environment.

The Aluminum Association created a broad designation system for aluminum finishing processes. The labeling system recognizes that almost all finishes used on aluminum can be subdivided into three major categories: mechanical finishes, chemical finishes, and coatings. Coatings are further divided into five subcategories:

→ **Mechanical finishes** can be produced at the mill during the initial rolling or extruding processes, or by subsequent finishing techniques that include polishing, grinding, or brushing. It is typically a hand-operated process in which parts and components are finished dependent on their shape and form. The mechanical finishes applied to aluminum are standardized by the Aluminum Association into four classifications: *fabricated*, meaning the aluminum is used directly from the manufacturer with no additional finishing; *buffed*, where the surface is polished; *directional textured*, referring to a texture applied to the surface in one direction; and *non-directional textured*, where any range of textures are applied to the surface.

→ **Chemical finishes** alter a metal's surface through one or more chemical solutions. There are three purposes for using a chemical finish on aluminum: to create a clean surface for a future finish; to provide a uniform electrochemical reactive surface for an anodonic coating; or to etch the surface to achieve a specific reflectivity. Because chemical finishes are applied in a batch, it is one of the least expensive processes. The Aluminum Association has labeled a chemical treatments designation into two classifications, *non-etched* and *cleaned-and-etched* chemical treatment.

→ **Coatings** are subdivided into five categories: *anodic* coatings, *resinous* and other organic coatings, *vitreous* coatings, *electroplated* and other metal coatings, and *laminated* coatings. The most common in architectural applications are described here. When aluminum is exposed to air and has no chemical finish, a thin, protective oxide film forms on its surface, which over time becomes chalky and thick. *Anodizing* aluminum is a controlled process that makes this oxide film thicker and harder, thus increasing its corrosion and abrasion resistance. Most exterior applications using aluminum alloys are anodized surfaces. Anodizing is an oxidizing process in which the metal is immersed in sulfuric acid and electrolytically made anodic by converting the surface to an oxide film. It is then sealed by boiling the metal in water. This process increases the metal's durability, traps dyes, and adheres to other finishes. The finish appearance can range from clear to a wide variety of colors, but most importantly is the aluminum's increased hardness and durability after anodization.

→ **Clear-coat anodizing** is the most common and economical process of anodizing. Today's technology has allowed for computerized monitoring equipment to help the anodizing process.

→ **Plastic coatings**, which are usually polyesters and fall under the "laminated coating" category, are applied electrostatically as a powder and then heat-cured to a self-cleaning finish. This is done for glazing systems, cladding panels, and rainwater components in buildings. Plastic coatings can give aluminum a range of colors, as can other finishes such as enamel or lacquer finishes. These finishes give a durable protection layer and a color to the metal, and often disguise the metal with the appearance of a more uniform, flat color and texture. When aluminum is painted, it should have an appropriate primer, and no lead-based paint should be used to avoid a galvanic reaction.

Weathering
Aluminum is generally resistant to corrosion due to a thin, invisible film of oxide on its surface, which forms immediately and continuously. In normal atmospheric conditions, the metal ages well, becoming a darker gray over time. It may be further improved by anodizing its surface or applying another protective coating.

While aluminum can resist harsh weather conditions, corrosion can occur through contact with other materials such as plasters, mortars, uncured cements and, most significantly, copper. Aluminum can corrode any adjacent zinc- or iron- based materials. Aluminum therefore needs to be separated from other metals to prevent a galvanic reaction. Timber that contains preservatives like water-soluble copper or mercury can also aggressively react to aluminum. Water can stain its surface, causing it to oxidize and create dark stains that do not damage the material structurally but are extremely difficult to remove. When designing with aluminum, it is wise to think about how rainwater flows over a building and whether it flows over an affecting material (especially copper), before running over aluminum.

Joining
Aluminum is difficult to solder because of oxide formation and heat dissipation. Aluminum alloys can be welded using *metal inert gas* (MIG) or *tungsten inert gas* (TIG) techniques, which are welding processes in which electricity is used to generate heat necessary to melt and attach separate metal parts. MIG welding, also called *gas metal arc welding* (GMAW), is done by sparking an electric arc between the welded parts and a consumable electrode. It uses an aluminum alloy wire as a combined electrode and filler material. TIG welding, also called *gas tungsten arc welding* (GTAW), uses a tungsten electrode and separate filler rods, making the process more flexible. Unlike MIG, the electrode is not the filler material and is a stationary rod. It is also possible to weld without a filler material with TIG. Aluminum is often mechanically fastened with, for instance, aluminum alloy (A-1) bolts and rivets, or with non-magnetic stainless steel. It can also be bonded with a strong adhesive on a prepared surface.

COPPER

Copper is usually used as an alloy combined with zinc when used in building construction. Its important advantage over ferric metals (those with iron) is its resistance to corrosion, making it a wise choice for areas in which the metal is in consistent contact with water or severe atmospheric conditions. Today, copper is primarily seen in sheet form in roof systems, cladding, and also finishing details. It is also used for finish details, gutters, and downspouts. Both brass and bronze are copper alloys, but there is an imprecise distinction between the two based on the concentrations of each element. The copper-zinc alloys that yield a more yellow surface are usually brass, while the more red and brown alloys are bronze. Brass and bronze are harder than copper and not as easy to form, yet are far softer than steel. These alloys are most commonly used externally on door frames, balustrades, window surrounds, fasteners, and other fittings. In addition to their high corrosion resistance, copper alloys are also able to take on oxidized patinas, which can create a wide variety of surface colors.

Copper is a soft and easily machined metal, yet is also strong. It is relatively dense, with high electrical conductivity. However, copper's strength-to-weight ratio is low, making it a poor structural metal. Its malleability makes it easy to fold and seam edges on thin sheets, allowing for a clean and fitted cladding skin. It is ideal for outdoor use given its corrosion resistance, but attention should be given to water that runs over the material. Runoff from copper roofs or siding can prevent the growth of plants (though it does not affect animals); additionally, copper nails or fasteners drilled into tree trunks or branches can kill the trees. A concern from copper runoff is a staining from green copper sulfate of adjacent, porous materials such as limestone, stucco, concrete, and other light-colored materials. This problem can be prevented by careful consideration of how details are designed.

Despite an overall decrease in the use of copper through the years, it is used more than ever today in electric power transmission, lighting, and wire circuitry; next to silver, copper is the most conductive metal. Since copper is a heavy material and is relatively expensive, it is usually used in thin sheets. Copper cannot carry its own weight and is usually supported by other materials such as a wood or masonry backing.

Manufacturing Copper

In North America, most copper is obtained from sulfide ores in Arizona, Utah, Montana, Michigan, and Canada. It is also mined in Chile, Germany, South Africa, New Guinea, and Russia. Copper production today is similar to its ancient manufacturing methods, though it is predictably much more efficient and purifying techniques have now been mastered. Copper is produced by first concentrating mineral ore that has been crushed and ground through a flotation or separation technique. The ore is then roasted (but not melted) in a furnace to remove contamination and other volatile materials, then it is fully melted, which removes the major contaminate, iron. The result is what is called a *matte*, which is approximately 30 percent copper in block form. The next step is a conversion process where the matte is oxidized with air to form what is a called a *blister copper*, which is approximately 99 percent pure copper. However, the copper is purified further through a process called *electrolysis refining* or *reduction*, where the blister copper is put in an electrolyte containing copper sulphate and sulphuric acid, making the blister copper an anode or electronically positive, and yielding the final, 99.9 percent pure copper. In the 1960s, another technique called *flash smelting* replaced the roasting step, in which the ore is smelted with fluxes such as silica and limestone. This process produces a high-grade copper matte more efficiently and is environmentally safer.

Copper has the highest recycling rate of any engineered material—approximately 75 percent of copper used in architecture is recycled. In fact, the rate at which copper is recycled is actually equal to the rate at which it is mined. Disadvantages to copper production include the huge amount of energy and fuel needed to power the equipment used to mine copper.

Appearance

No other metal has such unique color variations and textures as copper. Its distinct red/orange/brown hue and naturally aging surface make it an attractive design element for architects. Its longevity, lasting for decades and sometimes centuries, also makes it an appealing material choice. The progression from its natural patina to an ultimate blue-green color has made it a pleasing material to watch transform over time. Additionally, copper is often used for ornamental metalwork due to the range of color options that can be achieved through its different alloys, as well as chemical treatments. Both brass and bronze are available in an endless number of varieties, yellow brass containing 70 percent copper and 30 percent zinc, while a more brown or red bronze is usually the result of copper alloyed with aluminum, tin, silver, or nickel. Different alloys have a diverse range of physical properties, and these can be exploited to meet a variety of needs.

Weathering

Copper is most commonly seen as a roof material that patinas to an aqua-green color over time. New copper has a characteristic metallic, dark brown color. Depending on the atmosphere and location, it begins to pati-nate to a distinctive green over five to ten years. The patina is produced from sulfur compounds in the atmosphere and occurs more quickly in industrial and marine environments or in areas with higher temperatures or high moisture. In polluted areas with acid rain, dark streaks sometime appear on the surface of the metal. This staining will then mature to the green patina, bypassing the rust stages. The metal fully stops mineralizing after approximately seventy years. If desired, there are finishes to prevent this patina process and retain the original dark brown color, as well as a pre-patinated finish to achieve the green color immediately.

Copper is compatible with most building timbers, but it will corrode quickly when it is in contact with moisture and red cedar. Copper corrodes most other metals upon sustained contact. In the presence of moisture, it will corrode metals that are higher on the galvanic series table, including steel, lead, alu-minum, zinc, and cast iron.

Joining
Copper is a very malleable metal and can be easily brazed, soldered, or welded at low levels of heat. When fastening mechanically, as with all materials, an allowance for expansion must be made, otherwise stress will build up in the metal and buckling and cracking will occur.

TITANIUM
Titanium is the fourth most abundant mineral on earth, after aluminum, iron, and magnesium. It is primarily mined in the Americas, with Brazil producing 65 percent of the world's supply of *rutile*, its primary ore. Titanium used in the United States typically originates off the coast of Australia, where it is mined from the ocean floor. Interestingly, old Soviet submarines from the Cold War are also a source of titanium.

Titanium is just beginning to mature as an architectural material. Given its high production costs, it is prohibitively expensive for most building projects. It is telling to note, however, that this was also the case for aluminum just over a century ago. As production increases, the cost will likely decrease, allowing for more architectural applications.

Manufacturing
Titanium is produced by mixing the primary ore, rutile, with coke and then charging it with hot chlorine gas. The ore then goes through further purification to create a metallic "sponge" of titanium. It is then converted into an electrode, melted, and formed into a slab. (Alloying the metal would occur at this stage, once it is melted.) The slab is then reduced in thickness to desired sheets or coils varying in thickness from 0.015 to 0.25 inches (.381–6.35 mm). It can be cast and extruded, but for architectural purposes it usually is not.

Appearance
Titanium is typically a light gray color and retains its tone for years without changing. When exposed to oxygen, a very thin film forms on its surface, preserving the surface color. One unique quality of titanium is that it can be developed into shades of silver, gold, blue, or purple through an electric charge. By changing the voltage, a different shade or tone of color is created on its surface. Different tones can also be achieved through an electrolyte bath.

Weathering
Titanium has the highest corrosion resistance of any architectural metal. It is a durable material with a low coefficient of thermal expansion, causing it to be very weatherproof and resilient. Even in marine and coastal uses, titanium is unaffected by all of the more typical weathering conditions affecting other metals.

Joining
As in typical sheet-metal techniques, titanium can be formed and joined. It can also be welded, much like any other architectural metal. Because titanium will corrode steel, aluminum, galvanized steel, and other metals, stainless steel fasteners must be used when making connections.

ZINC
Zinc is a very dense and corrosion-resistant architectural material. It is non-ferrous, thus not subject to rusting. In the U.S. market today, zinc is most commonly used as a coating on steel and as an alloy with copper and titanium. It is used much more widely in the European architecture market, frequently as cast hardware, grills, details, and surface panels.

Manufacturing

Refining zinc is much like refining copper. Zinc ore is crushed into particles and then concentrated by flotation, which separates the waste from the minerals. Zinc is cast on a continuously rotating cylinder and then rolled through pressure rolls to a specified thickness. When in a pure state, zinc has a very low tensile strength, but after being pushed through rolls, which develops a directionality to the material, its strength increases considerably. It is usually alloyed with copper and titanium in furnaces for added strength.

Appearance

Pure zinc tarnishes quickly to a light blue-gray color due to the formation of a patina of basic zinc carbonate upon exposure to the atmosphere. Natural zinc has a semi-matte, light gray color which can be pre-weathered to a darker gray, while zinc alloys will tarnish to a darker gray. Zinc can also be lacquered with a polyester lacquer in the furnace to create different colors.

Weathering

When zinc is exposed to the atmosphere, the surface film of basic zinc carbonate develops, which protects the underlying metal and checks further corrosion. Zinc's corrosion resistance is due to this protective layer that develops and limits the amount of oxygen contact to the surface. Depending on the atmospheric conditions, a darker-gray patina may develop within six months to two years.

In unpolluted areas, this protective film ensures that zinc building components will have a long, maintenance-free life. In industrial environments and areas with high levels of pollution, however, the corrosion rate increases dramatically. Sulfurous and sulfuric acids react with the zinc carbonate film to form zinc sulfate, which is soluble and washes off in rain. When employed in industrial areas, zinc is therefore most often used as vertical cladding or on pitched roofs.

Zinc should not be used in contact with copper or with acid woods such as cedar and oak. It has good compatibility with other building materials, although mortars and any moist cements can increase its level of corrosion.

Joining

Because zinc has a low melting point, it makes for easy resistance welding and soldering. When fastening zinc mechanically, galvanized or stainless steel nails, screws, rivets, and clips are recommended. One should never use copper or brass fasteners or bimetallic corrosion will occur.

LEAD

Lead is a dense, soft, toxic metal of low strength. It is one of the most weather-resistant materials, even exceeding stainless steel and zinc in corrosion resistance. It is a dull-gray colored metal that is soft yet dense. Once the main material used in plumbing, and often used as a roofing surface, the use of lead in construc-tion has declined notably since the early 1900s. Use of lead is strictly controlled in water supplies and is no longer used in building interiors, including as pigment in interior paints. Lead for cladding applications is referred to as *desilverized lead*, which is a minimum of 99.85 percent lead and a maximum of .002 percent silver. Today lead is relatively expensive and is usually only used for waste pipes, coatings, and flashing. Lead's toxicity makes many of its other possible uses unsuitable. Lead sheet, used for flashing, for example, is now often made from an alloy containing 6 percent antimony, which increases its stiffness and strength. When lead is used in applications such as a roof, it must always be fully supported by another material beneath. It is not a self-supporting metal due to its weight and low stiffness. Lead can also be used in ceiling or wall panels for sound insulation and the for the absorption of vibrations. It can be produced in rolled sheets, shot, or bar forms. Its softness makes many metal fabrication processes impossible. Lead is frequently used in non-architectural applications, such as a shield from X-rays and radiation and for automobile batteries.

Lead can be easily worked, is corrosion-resistant, and is relatively impenetrable to radiation. Although it is a heavy metal, its malleability and durability may make it an appealing cladding material. It is traditionally used in construction for roofing, flashing, sound isolation, acid and radiation resistance, and in some hardware items. Lead dust and vapor are toxic to humans and must be considered when used.

TABLE 1	GALVANIC RELATIONSHIP BETWEEN METALS

ANODIC	Aluminum	Zinc and galvanized steel	Steel and iron	Cast iron	Stainless steel	Nickel	Tin	Lead	Brass	Copper	Bronze	Monel	Titanium	Gold	CATHODIC
LEAST NOBLE	←													→	MOST NOBLE

TABLE 2		COMPARISON OF METAL PROPERTIES				
METAL	SPECIFIC GRAVITY —	MELTING POINT —	TENSILE STRENGTH —	YIELD STRENGTH —	Coefficient of THERMAL EXPANSION (in. x 10^{-6}/in./°F)	Coefficient of THERMAL EXPANSION (mm x 10^{-6}/in./°C)
Aluminum	2.70	1,220 °F (660 °C)	13.0 ksi (90 MPa)	5.0 ksi (35 MPa)	13.0	24.0
Copper	8.96	1,980 °F (1,080 °C)	29.0 ksi (200 MPa)	10.0 ksi (69 MPa)	9.3	16.8
Iron and Steel	7.90	2,780 °F (1,530 °C)	39.8–272.0 ksi (276–1,882 MPa)	26.9–109 ksi (186–758 MPa)	6.6	11.7
Lead	11.34	621 °F (327 °C)	1.7 ksi (12 MPa)	0.72 ksi (5 MPa)	16.1	29.0
Stainless steel	7.90	2,640 °F (1,450 °C)	74.4–119 ksi (515–827 MPa)	3.0–79.7 ksi (207–552 MPa)	9.8	17.8
Titanium	4.51	3,049 °F (1,675 °C)	65.0 ksi (450 MPa)	75.0 ksi (520 MPa)	4.9	9.0
Zinc	7.14	788 °F (420 °C)	4.0–12.0 ksi (110–200 MPa)	14.0 ksi (97 MPa)	13.8	24.9

TABLE 3	EFFECTS OF WEATHERING/CORROSION ON METALS		
METAL	COLOR WHEN NEW	REFLECTIVITY WHEN NEW (1=Low / 5=High)	TEN-YEAR AGING RESULT
Aluminum	Medium gray	3	Little change
Aluminum (mill finish)	Gray-white	4	Dull gray
Aluminized steel	Gray-white	4	Light gray, less reflective
Carbon Steel	Dark gray-blue	2	Red rust
Commercial bronze	Red-gold	4	Gray-green
Copper	Red-brown	4	Gray-green
Galvalume	Light gray	3	Gray
Galvanized steel	Light gray	3	Gray-white or white rust
Lead	Dark gray	1	Gray-black
Monel	Medium Gray	5	Brown
Nickel silver	Gray-yellow	4	Gray-green
Stainless steel #2B	Gray or white	4	No change
Stainless steel #2D	Medium gray	3	No change
Stainless steel #3	Chrome	4	No change
Stainless steel #8	Chrome	5	No change
Terne	Gray	3	Dark gray
Tin	Gray	4	Dark gray
Titanium	Medium gray	3	No change
Zinc (natural)	Gray-blue	4	Dark blue or gray
Zinc (pre-weathered)	Dark gray-blue	2	No change

TABLE 4	RELATIVE COSTS (1=LOWEST COST / 6=HIGHEST COST)		
METAL	RELATIVE COST BY WEIGHT	COST OF FABRICATION	COST OF INSTALLATION
Aluminum	2	1	2
Lead	2	1	3
Copper	3	1	1
Zinc	3	1	3
Tin	4	1	2
Steel	1	1	1
Iron	1	2	1
Stainless steel	2	2	1
Titanium	5	2	2
Bronze	3	5	3
Gold leaf	6	N/A	4

Tram Stations

HANOVER, GERMANY // DESPANG ARCHITEKTEN
MODULAR STEEL FRAME, APPLIED SKINS

DESIGN INTENTION

For the World Expo 2000, the City of Hanover built a series of tram stations that were to be easily mass-produced, with a standardized steel structure. They were also to respond to individual locations using a variety of materials dressing the steel frames. Thirteen stations service this street-level urban rail system throughout the city. An overall urban analysis of the infrastructure along this rail line was completed by the designers to understand the size, density, and character of the areas around these stops. The stations form a "sequence of notes" along the rail line, evoking specific characteristics and associations at each location. In some stations local residents and businesses collaborated in the design, enhancing the link with the host communities. The material variety is also intended to aid residents, tourists, and passengers in identifying the different stops.

MATERIALITY

A basic steel framework was designed to form each tram station without appearing as the dominant material in any of the structures. Each location is distinguished by its unique veneer—exposed materials attached to but not contributing structurally to its backing. In some stations the cladding is a closed skin such as stone, brick, or concrete panels, while in other stations it is a translucent or filtered skin such as glass, wood slats, or metal mesh. The consistent frame for the waiting blocks and platform establish the theme for the rail line as a whole.

The primary structural system for the waiting blocks at all thirteen stations is a modular steel frame, made of conventional steel sections. It is a consistent armature upon which various service components and cladding systems can be applied. It consists of a steel plate attached to the rail platform with three square, hollow steel sections, to which steel angles are then affixed. Prefabricated elements are then attached to this basic framework. Each station has a glass awning in front and some combination of ticket machines, posting boards, and seating areas, depending on the needs of each location. The stations are adjusted dimensionally based on the size and shape of their materials and the anticipated number of users. The variety of materials is clearly a communication and graphic tool for this series of prefabricated structures to distinguish each by its use, location, and contextual character.

These stations demonstrate the universal capability of the steel frame, valued for its certainty of physical properties, its durability, and the ease with which it can be shop-fabricated. It is well matched to the "kit-of-parts" approach taken in this design. Shop fabrication of the consistent platform and enclosure frames is coupled with onsite execution of the variable cladding, optimizing both machine and hand processes.

Normal mild steel is vulnerable to oxidation in the atmosphere, especially in urban or industrial environments. It must therefore be protected either by paint or other protective coatings, or clad with other materials to minimize its exposure to hostile environmental forces. This project clearly expresses the capabilities of steel while also recognizing its vulnerabilities. The cladding that protects the steel frame becomes the dominant expression.

Variations in cladding at each station convey the character of that particular community, respond to local materials, or adjust to the levels of vandalism anticipated in different urban situations. Among the toughest cladding treatments used was woven stainless steel mesh, further protected by an anti-graffiti coating. It is quite durable, but when illuminated from within the volume, it changes from a rugged, closed-skin expression to a more delicate translucent membrane. Another station uses pre-patinated copper, whose green hues resemble the landscape of its suburban district, and whose careful joinery recalls the sheet copper craftsmanship found on some traditional residences in the area.

TECHNICAL

This frame-and-skin system allows for a great variety of exterior expressions to be used interchangeably. The skin materials are not chosen for their structural properties but for their scale and visual qualities on a building, and for their weathering resistance. The veneer materials are typically secured using concealed metal clips, anchors, or wires. Secondary frames or infill walls are used within the steel frame to support the veneers.

Each cladding system in this project called for a special strategy to secure the cladding to the steel frame due to differences in cladding thickness, weight, and compatibility with steel. For instance, to avoid bimetallic corrosion, copper cladding was isolated from the steel frame using a wood-sheathed substructure. All fittings were designed so that the cladding can be repaired or replaced. Many of the fittings were custom castings or fabrications using metal.

The physical, technical, and haptic qualities of a wide range of materials were tested under laboratory conditions before being selected by the designers. Sustainability was also a contributing factor to the design. Materials were chosen that were recyclable or renewable resources, or which have a long service life. The stations have since performed well, with less demand for repairs than expected.

01 Stations diagram   05 Glass block station
02 Metal mesh station   06 Glass station
03 Copper station   07 Glass station
04 Brick station

Typ A sitting

Typ B technics & sitting

Typ C main info & technics

Typ C info & technics

Typ F info

Back/Advertising

02

03

04

05

06

07

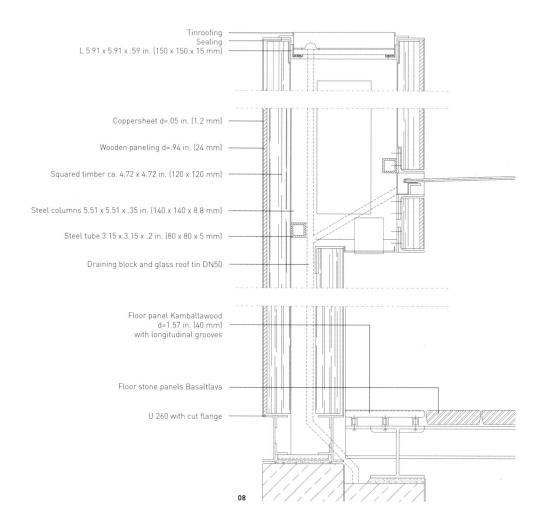

Tinroofing
Sealing
L 5.91 x 5.91 x .59 in. (150 x 150 x 15 mm)

Coppersheet d=.05 in. (1.2 mm)

Wooden paneling d=.94 in. (24 mm)

Squared timber ca. 4.72 x 4.72 in. (120 x 120 mm)

Steel columns 5.51 x 5.51 x .35 in. (140 x 140 x 8.8 mm)

Steel tube 3.15 x 3.15 x .2 in. (80 x 80 x 5 mm)

Draining block and glass roof tin DN50

Floor panel Kamballawood
d=1.57 in. (40 mm)
with longitudinal grooves

Floor stone panels Basaltlava

U 260 with cut flange

08

08 Copper cladding detail
09 Glass connection detail
10 Concrete station detail
11 Metal mesh station detail
12 Station series

09

10

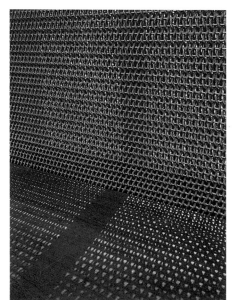

11

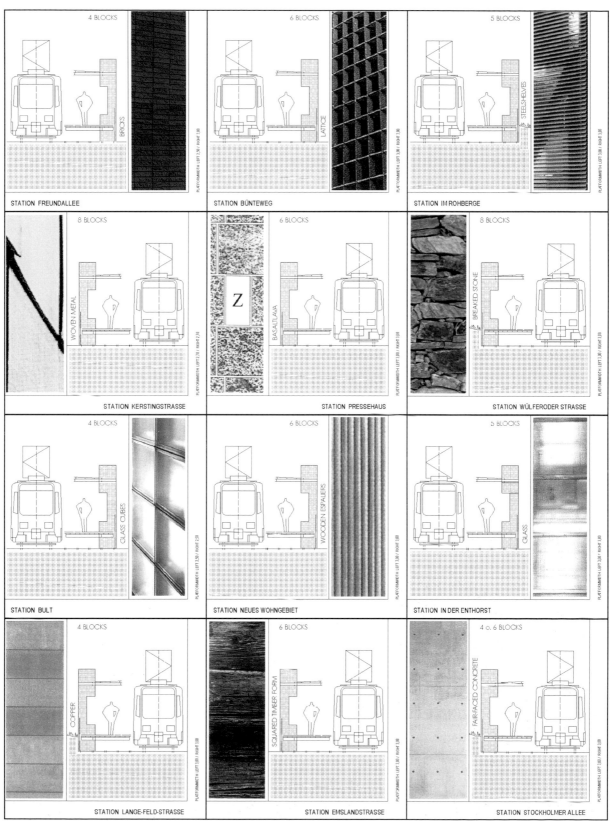

4 BLOCKS	6 BLOCKS	5 BLOCKS
BRICKS	LATTICE	STEEL SHELVES
PLATFORM WIDTH LEFT 2,50 / RIGHT 3,00	PLATFORM WIDTH LEFT 3,00 / RIGHT 3,00	PLATFORM WIDTH LEFT 3,00 / RIGHT 3,00
STATION FREUNDALLEE	STATION BÜNTEWEG	STATION IM ROHBERGE

8 BLOCKS	6 BLOCKS	8 BLOCKS
WOVEN METAL	Z BASALT LAVA	BREAKED STONE
PLATFORM WIDTH LEFT 2,70 / RIGHT 2,70		PLATFORM WIDTH LEFT 3,00 / RIGHT 3,00
STATION KERSTINGSTRASSE	STATION PRESSEHAUS	STATION WÜLFERODER STRASSE

4 BLOCKS	6 BLOCKS	5 BLOCKS
GLASS CUBES	WOODEN ESPALIERS	GLASS
PLATFORM WIDTH LEFT 2,50 / RIGHT 2,50	PLATFORM WIDTH LEFT 3,00 / RIGHT 3,00	PLATFORM WIDTH LEFT 3,00 / RIGHT 3,00
STATION BULT	STATION NEUES WOHNGEBIET	STATION IN DER ENTHORST

4 BLOCKS	6 BLOCKS	4 o. 6 BLOCKS
COPPER	SQUARED TIMBER FORM	FAIR-FACED CONCRETE
PLATFORM WIDTH LEFT 3,00 / RIGHT 3,00	PLATFORM WIDTH LEFT 3,00 / RIGHT 3,00	PLATFORM WIDTH LEFT 3,00 / RIGHT 3,00
STATION LANGE-FELD-STRASSE	STATION EMSLANDSTRASSE	STATION STOCKHOLMER ALLEE

Future Shack

VARIOUS LOCATIONS // SEAN GODSELL
STEEL CONTAINER, RE-USABILITY, TRANSPORTABILITY, MASS-PRODUCIBILITY, BOX BEAM

DESIGN INTENTION

This mass-producible prototype house modifies a steel shipping container to serve as emergency relief housing that could be expeditiously transported anywhere using standard shipping means. The recycled shipping container forms the main volume of this house, with an attached parasol roof for shading and thermal buffering. The structure is a module that can be densely packed and stockpiled, easily transported by truck or boat, and can be fully erected within twenty-four hours for a variety of needs, such as flood, fire, or earthquake relief and temporary or third-world housing. It is self-contained and packed with water tanks, a solar power cell, gas cylinders, a satellite receiver, and operable vents to allow for fresh airflow. The galvanized steel parasol roof not only provides the module with a universal symbol of "home," but can also accept thatch, mud and stick, palm, or any other local materials. The parasol roof serves as sun shading, as a mount for solar collectors, and protects rooftop equipment from weathering. Telescoping legs enable the building to be sited on uneven terrain without excavation. The module can also be fitted with a bathroom and small kitchen depending on its location and use.

MATERIALITY

This project is based on the premise that when the measurable criteria are fully addressed, the immeasurable criteria are thereby addressed as well. Details in this project are not precious: utilitarian expression is dominant. The project re-uses a product made from recyclable material, illustrating a notable quality of steel: once the raw material is refined, it has a life cycle well beyond its initial embodiment. The use of the steel shipping container is appropriate for this housing module not only for its recyclability and abundance but also for the inherent qualities of the steel itself. These modular units are durable and robust, allowing the housing module to be transported, stacked, and stored without concern for significant damage. The container also becomes a sturdy structural box beam when in use. The houses are mass-producible and can be easily adapted to the particularities of almost any given landscape or climate.

The designers have taken this recycled module and designed an accommodating home using the volumetric clarity and simplicity of the steel container. The scheme is a "decorated shed"—a simple form that is easily read. The volume is spatially open and its marine plywood interior surfaces are easily imprintable by occupants. Interior wall linings conceal pull-down beds and table, as well as utility lines and minor storage needs.

Though the steel industry historically favors mass production, most steel elements used in buildings are specially fabricated as needed. Structural steel beams and columns are seldom mass produced despite being made using stock profiles. This project utilizes mass-produced steel volumes as its basic module to achieve economies of scale that are not possible using conventional custom fabricated processes.

TECHNICAL

Box beams are an efficient use of material to achieve structural capacity. Similar to a typical I-beam, the top and bottom surfaces act as the flange while the sides act as the web of the beam. Their very deep cross section places structural material far from the neutral axis, resulting in a favorably high moment of inertia. This structural strategy is especially applicable to long spans or to cantilevers, or where stiffness is a high priority.

The shell is made of a steel frame consisting of welded steel tube sections; the frame is integrally welded to diaphragms of corrugated steel plate. The shell is rugged and strong, designed to withstand stacking, mishandling, and extreme live loading. It is protected from corrosion by rust-inhibitive paint.

The container box is 19.83 ft. long x 8 ft. wide x 8.5 ft. tall (6.05 x 2.44 x 2.59 m). Water and bottled gas are added at the time of deployment, and they are replenished as necessary. Though equipped for habitation, this deployable house may not meet applicable building codes and is not intended as permanent housing.

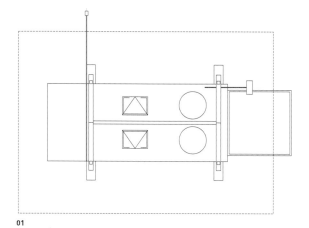

01

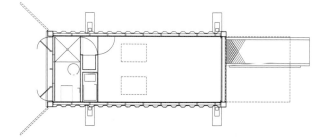

02

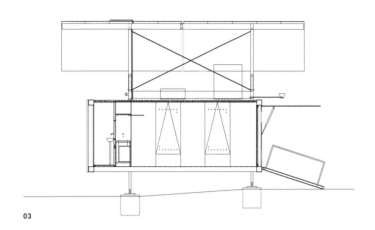

03

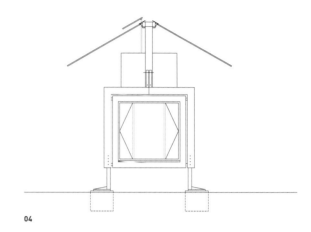

04

05

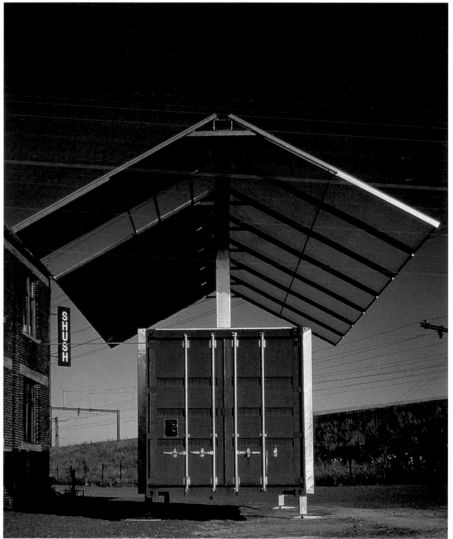

07

06

Christ Pavilion, Expo 2000

HANOVER, GERMANY; VOLKENRODA, THURINGIA, GERMANY // VON GERKAN, MARG & PARTNERS
STEEL JOINERY, TOLERANCES

DESIGN INTENTION

This Christian church was built for the World Expo 2000 in Hanover with the objective to create a largely transparent structure with spiritual content. The temporary nature of the exposition required that the building be dismantled and reassembled with ease and speed. The quality and craftsmanship evident in the building positively reflects on the skills and resources of the exhibitors from the region. When the exposition was over, the church was rebuilt on the site of a monastery in Volkenroda, Thuringia, a city some 97 miles (156 kilometers) south of its original location. This project demonstrates that well made architecture has a long life—certainly longer than the period of an Exposition. The designers and the client felt that throwaway architecture would have contradicted all sense of responsibility toward the environment, as well as the ecological spirit of Expo 2000. Good design and good construction are neither ephemeral nor temporary.

MATERIALITY

The requirement that the building be efficiently disassembled and reassembled made steel the obvious choice, given its ability to be prefabricated in parts, made to exacting precision, and its applicability to demountable connections. Additionally, steel has high resistance to compression, tension, and bending forces, permitting loads to be carried by relatively slender elements.

The node points in this project were designed to resist axial and rotational forces using a *sigma node*, a wedge-shaped slotted connector developed by the contemporary German engineer Ewald Rüter. This project was the first large-scale use of this precision joinery system, which allows rigid joining of structural elements without additional welding, bolting, or riveting, thus the members can be easily dismantled and reconnected without tools. When completed, the connection resists torsion and deformation. To resist uplift, a single pin is inserted transversely into the sigma node. The church was assembled using modular construction units based on an orthogonal three-dimensional grid.

The supporting structure for the facade consisted of a simple post-and-rail system with a double-skin glazing. The .75 in. (19 mm) thick

intermediate spaces between the glazing are used as broad exhibits filled with man-made and natural materials from the region. This mosaic of materials sandwiched between the glass walls produces varied light qualities and is also an engaging architectural application of non-architectural materials. The double-skin walls also have an insulating function and provide thermal storage mass. Portions of the diaphanous walls of this building were con- structed with an outer curtain wall and an inner skin of thinly cut trans-lucent marble slabs from Greece. Light entering through the roof, walls, and through the materials captured within the walls, results in a wide range of visual qualities.

TECHNICAL

Tolerance is an allowable deviation from the ideal because exact dimensions are not practical or are impossible to achieve. Some projects derive necessary integrity from precision engineering and must meet close tolerances throughout the making and assembly of building parts. Acceptable tolerances vary with each construction system. Conventional steel structural frames in buildings of this scale typically have tolerances of ±.38 in. (9.52 mm). Tolerances for this innovative steel frame were said to be only ±.04 in. (1 mm).

This pavilion's primary and secondary structural system forms a three-dimensional orthogonal grid 11.15 ft. (3.4 m) on center, echoing the cloisterlike geometry of the plan. The three-dimensional frame achieves rigidity through the use of moment connections at the sigma nodes and at custom-fabricated assemblies of conventional rolled shapes elsewhere. Thus the elevations and interior spaces are free of shear walls or diagonal bracing members. Electrical services are concealed in a cavity at the vertical joints between adjoining wall elements.

The same kit of parts has been assembled and used twice thus far. Large wall sections measuring 11.15 ft. wide by 22.31 ft. high (3.4 m x 6.8 m) were shipped intact from the Expo site in Hanover to the monastery site in Thuringia. The glass was protected from breakage using temporary wood cladding, but the exhibit contents remained in the glazed wall cavities.

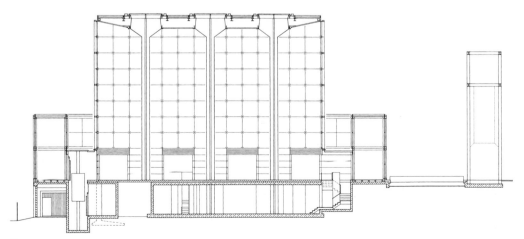

01 Pavilion section
02 Entry
03 Pavilion interior

01

02

03

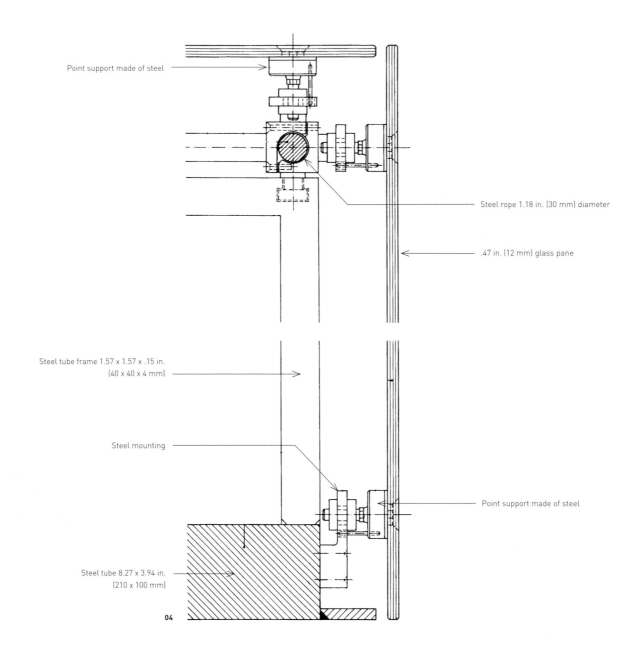

Point support made of steel

Steel rope 1.18 in. (30 mm) diameter

.47 in. (12 mm) glass pane

Steel tube frame 1.57 x 1.57 x .15 in.
(40 x 40 x 4 mm)

Steel mounting

Point support made of steel

Steel tube 8.27 x 3.94 in.
(210 x 100 mm)

04

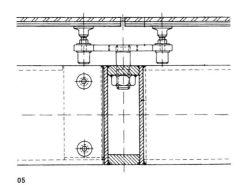

05

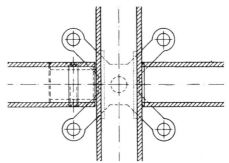

06

07

08

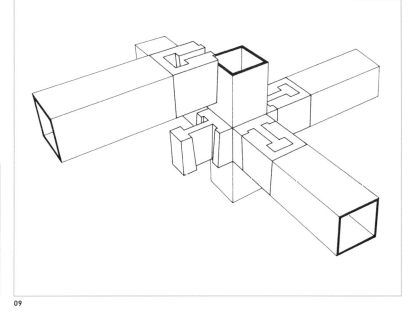
09

10

11

Kew House

KEW, MELBOURNE, AUSTRALIA // SEAN GODSELL
HIGH-STRENGTH STEEL, STRUCTURAL CAPACITY, WEATHERING

DESIGN INTENTION

This house design is a direct response to the Melbourne landscape and environment. A steel frame is designed to cantilever 18 ft. (5.5 m) over a steep site sloping toward the city, giving the building's occupants a dramatic view of the skyline. To naturally cool the interior, the design incorporates several creative strategies that work with the environment. Air is cooled by a fine-mist sprinkler system on the embankment below the house: as water evaporates, it cools the air, which rises into the building through small holes in the hardwood flooring. Sliding glass walls create breezeways, and movable industrial steel gratings are attached to the west and north (sunny) elevations, limiting direct sunlight in the summer but allowing the sun's warmth to enter in the winter, nearly eliminating the need for artificial heating during the day.

MATERIALITY

This building demonstrates steel's best attribute—its structural capacity. A material is best utilized when its inherent qualities are exploited and its inherent vulnerabilities are avoided. Here steel is employed for its optimum characteristics and then is allowed to adapt naturally to its site. A cantilever relies on both the physical properties and the cross-sectional profile of a material, which here is achieved through the steel's high strength and stiffness in a channel profile. For longer spans and greater loads, steel is usually the most economical structural material available, with a favorable strength-to-volume ratio.

The unpainted steel frame of the house is left exposed, clearly expressing the structure of the building and allowing the material to age, rust, and weather with the changing climate and conditions. However, in order to deter excessive rusting, which would reduce the cross-sectional area, the designers finished the steel after initial oxidation with a clear sealer to retain the natural weathered appearance. This captured a natural condition associated with this material, rusting, without compromising its strength.

The universal architectural ideals represented by these materials and this modern design are found in other places in the world, but the achievements of this design are uniquely possible in this specific climate, and are further enhanced by this particular site. In this sense the general ideals of the architectural language have meshed with the specific realities of this setting.

Sustainable design principles affected many aspects of this building's design and material selection, such as natural convection through operable sash and operable floor vents, shading sunny exposures during warm months. The house uses recycled ash-finish flooring and recycled wood for the deck. No air conditioning is needed, and artificial heating is used rarely. Misters can be used to cool the air as it approaches the house. Rainwater is collected off of the roof to be stored in a cistern, a standard strategy in this arid climate. Minimal maintenance is required for the building or the landscape.

TECHNICAL

The two most common causes of a loss of structural integrity in steel are corrosion and extreme heat conditions such as building fire. Common structural steel is an alloy called mild steel (ASTM A36), and has a yield strength of 36,000 psi (248.21 MPa). It is made of iron and .15–.25 percent carbon as well as small quantities of other elements such as manganese and silicon. High-strength steel (ASTM A572 Grade 50), as was used here, has a yield strength of 50,000 psi (344.74 MPa), resulting in more slender dimensions than if mild steel were used. Its constituents are similar to mild steel, except that various alloying elements are increased. It is typically hot rolled into long sections, which are then fabricated for a specific application.

If left exposed, as was the case here, steel will react with airborne moisture to create iron-oxide, or rust—a reaction that will compromise the integrity of the material if left unprotected. Rust-inhibitive primers are normally applied to mild steel elements after initial fabrication to avoid this problem. Here these primers were not applied, allowing the oxidation process to begin but then halting it before it advanced to a harmful level. This project demonstrates that the natural state for steel in the environment is actually with a layer of ferrous hydroxide (rust) on its surface.

Although steel is considered a non-combustible material, it becomes malleable and loses its strength when exposed to heat over approximately 1,000 degrees F (538 degrees C). Building codes indicate the level of fire protection required for steel elements depending upon how they are used in the building. Regulatory bodies appropriately recognize that, when used in small single-story buildings of non-hazardous uses, structural steel may be left exposed without fire protection.

The elemental assembly of post and beam elements is explicit. Steel mullions and columns are the only materials that support the roof. The infill between the steel structure is a finely detailed glass panel system that slides within the steel frame. No interior partitions contact the perimeter walls, confirming that they are nonstructural. High-strength steel is assembled and left exposed to oxidize, then a clear sealer is applied. 30 percent of the building's 59 ft. (18m) length is cantilevered, using 15 x 3.94 in. (380 x 100 mm) steel channels at roof and floor decks, assisted by a diagonal steel tension member in the plane of the beams.

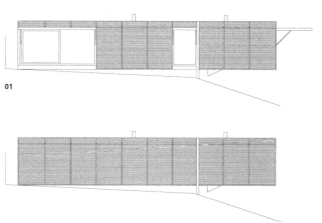

01

01 North elevation, open
02 North elevation, closed
03 Wall section
04 North entry
05 West façade
06 North façade

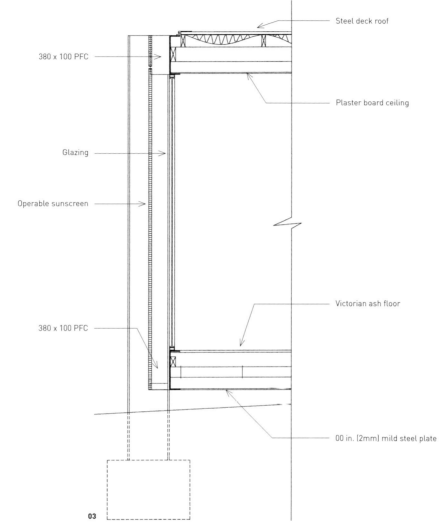

Steel deck roof

380 x 100 PFC

Plaster board ceiling

Glazing

Operable sunscreen

Victorian ash floor

380 x 100 PFC

00 in. (2mm) mild steel plate

03

04

05

06

Springtecture H

HYOGO, JAPAN // SHUHEI ENDO
GALVANIZED CORRUGATED STEEL, ANTI-CLASTIC CURVE

DESIGN INTENTION

This public facility is located in a small recreational park in the mountains in the vicinity of Osaka, Japan. The facility's building program includes men's and women's lavatories and a park-keeper's apartment. With economy of means, this small structure forms a sculptural landmark despite its modest program. The structure has no defined roof, wall, or column, appearing instead as a single flowing entity. The poetry of form and material is successful through its use of galvanized corrugated steel sheets. The structure is described by the architect as "half-tecture" (half architecture) since it is characterized by equal parts openness and enclosure. Form and space seem infinite: space escapes because the enclosure is incomplete, and the form implies a potential to be continued.

MATERIALITY

A single, versatile material does almost everything in this simple building: spirals of steel sheets make up the structure, define space, and provide enclosure using a simple language of one continuous ribbonlike material. The form is made possible with the curving and flowing of steel sheets to form the wall, column, and roof. The use of galvanized corrugated steel sheets to form this structure efficiently exploits all of the material's properties, counteracting compressive, tensile, and sheer forces as well as giving protection from weather.

Shapes that are flexible at a small scale may not be at a larger one. In this project properties associated with a particular form are juxtaposed with properties of a different material and scale. The ribbonlike structure seems to be a flexible plane but is actually quite rigid due to material properties, corrugation, and post-manufacture twisting of the metal during installation. The sheet metal begins as a relatively flexible flat plane but becomes stiffer in one axis when it is corrugated by the manufacturer, and in all axes when twisted by the fabricator and secured to the foundation on the site. Stability and structural efficiency are achieved here because of the configuration, in which elements are stabilized by opposing curvatures.

TECHNICAL

An *anti-clastic* shape is curved in two opposing directions, as a saddle, for example. Every point on the surface is fixed in space because the opposing curves restrain it from movement. This was done on site by construction workers, as opposed to during the steel's manufacturing process. Corrugation gives strength to a relatively thin sheet of material; curling it adds even more strength and stability.

The galvanized corrugated steel sheet profile is 2 in. (50 mm), with a frequency of approximately 5.9 in. (150 mm). The sheets are 8.13 ft. long x 4.26 ft. wide x .13 in. thick (2.48 m x 1.3 m x 3.2 mm). They are lapped and bolted at edges. Bolts at the long edges are at 10.31 in. (262 mm) on center; at the ends, the bolts are at intervals of 5.9 in. (150 mm) in each of two rows. The steel struts are braced and anchored where needed using steel tubes and terminate below floor/grade-level with welded steel base plates that are bolted to concrete footings.

01 Corrugated steel spirals
02 Circulation passage
03 Mathematical diagram
04 Plan
05 View from the south

01

02

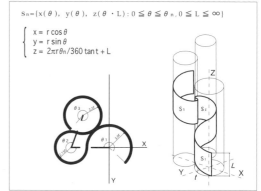

$$S_n = \{x(\theta),\ y(\theta),\ z(\theta \cdot L) : 0 \leqq \theta \leqq \theta_n, 0 \leqq L \leqq \infty\}$$

$$
\begin{cases}
x = r\cos\theta \\
y = r\sin\theta \\
z = 2\pi r\theta_n/360 \tan t + L
\end{cases}
$$

03

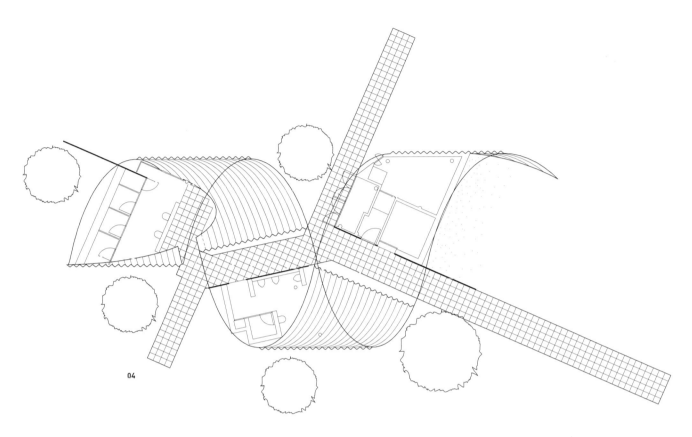

04

05

Module VII Chiller Plant, University of Pennsylvania

**PHILADELPHIA, PENNSYLVANIA // LEERS WEINZAPFEL ASSOCIATES
STAINLESS STEEL, PERFORATION**

DESIGN INTENTION

The University of Pennsylvania needed to construct a new 20,000-ton (expandable to 50,000-ton) water-chiller plant, which would be sited at a highly visible location along the Schuylkill River. The site previously contained athletic fields and now needed to also serve as a gateway landmark, giving a significant presence to the University. A continuous stainless steel screen wall wraps an elliptical plan containing the rectangular 80,000 square-foot (7,432 sq. m) chiller plant, which will be built in two phases as needed by the university. The elliptical shape echoes the curves of the passing river and highways while the materials resonate with the adjacent industrial structures. The metal screen allows for an ever-changing and sometimes ephemeral quality to the structure due to varied natural and artificial lighting conditions. During the day the screen wall glistens and is reflective of sunlight, while at night the structure becomes transparent and glows from internal illumination and an upper crown of exterior lights. The screen also helps to camouflage and break down the scale and mass of the chiller, as well as concealing incidental service equipment. It fully contains within a consolidated footprint all of the vehicular and service areas needed for the operation of the chiller, allowing for a new varsity baseball field to be built on the site as well.

MATERIALITY

The project celebrates the intrinsic complexity and industrial quality of the power plant through its configuration, materials, and detailing. The designers carefully manipulated the material, light, and color of all building elements to produce an enclosing skin that is attractive and durable but which is also varied in its character and transparency. The screen introduces a compatible material that softens the massive presence of the chiller plant.

Large panels of perforated corrugated stainless steel sheets are supported by a galvanized structural steel framework. Despite this skin appearing transparent to the eye, it substantially blocks the wind due to the small size of the holes. The enclosed building provides bracing for nearly all of the screen wall perimeter against lateral wind forces during storms. This is acheived either through direct contact or through struts attaching to the chiller building.

A conventional corrugated metal profile is used to ease installation for subcontractors. The only customization is the combination of the perfora- tion of the metal with subsequent corrugation of the perforated sheets by the manufacturer. This resulted in a custom perforated metal product that was economical because of the volume needed for the project.

Stainless steel is a highly alloyed steel that contains more than 10 percent chromium, and is characterized by its resistance to heat, oxida- tion, and corrosion. Rather than being externally coated with paint, as is common with normal steel, stainless steel uses intrinsic chemical resistance to prevent corrosion. When exposed to the atmosphere, a stable, hard, invisible film is formed on the surface, acting as a barrier against progressive corrosion. The material's relatively high initial cost is offset by its very low maintenance costs.

Stainless steel has low heat conductivity compared to other metals, but a high thermal expansion coefficient. Designers therefore need to accommodate thermal movement by placing expansion joints at appropri- ate intervals during the assembly. Here, the size of the screen walls required expansion joints and structural slip joints along the quarter-mile perimeter at four strategic points.

TECHNICAL

A collaboration between designers and a metal fabricator involved digital simulations and full-scale mockups of various screen and lighting configurations, resulting in a custom perforated metal product. The elliptical screen wall surrounds the building like a loose-fitting veil. It is 60 ft. (18.29 m) tall, framed using W14 columns at 30 ft. (9.14 m) inter- vals, with W10 beams at 16 ft. (4.88 m) intervals vertically. A secondary structure is a grid of W6 steel members supporting the stainless steel screen panels, which are bolted into aluminum strips attached to the W6 frame. Two of every three bays of screen walls were prefabricated on the ground and raised into position. The third bay, placed in between these prefabricated portions, was built in place to accommodate any variations in the dimensions. Collaborative analysis of the ellipse by the architect, the structural engineer, and the fabricator reduced the required number of custom-curved members, relying instead on less expensive straight beams.

The screen wall frame is in direct contact with the building for approximately one quarter of its length, and is elsewhere braced to the building using 6 in. (15.24 cm) diameter steel struts located 30 ft. (9.14 m) on center at rooftop level. At the ends of the ellipse, where its radius is relatively short, a horizontal steel truss braces the columns at the same elevation as the struts. The remaining portion of the screen wall is initially supported by rakers, which will be removed when the university initiates phase two of the building's construction.

The screen wall controls access to the chiller plant, conceals incidental service equipment, and serves as a welcoming symbol of the university at the threshold of the campus. The screen material is 18 gauge (.06 in. [1.52 mm]) roll-formed corrugated stainless steel sheets. The corrugated profile is .75 in. (19 mm) at a frequency of 2.75 in. (70 mm). Custom perforations are staggered circular openings, resulting in a 40 percent void. The perforations are kept small to discourage people from putting fingers in the holes or climbing up the screen wall. Screen materials are held in place with compatible aluminum attachment clips and retaining angles, secured with tamperproof screws to deter vandalism.

01   Night photo revealing inside
02   Metal mesh wall

01

02

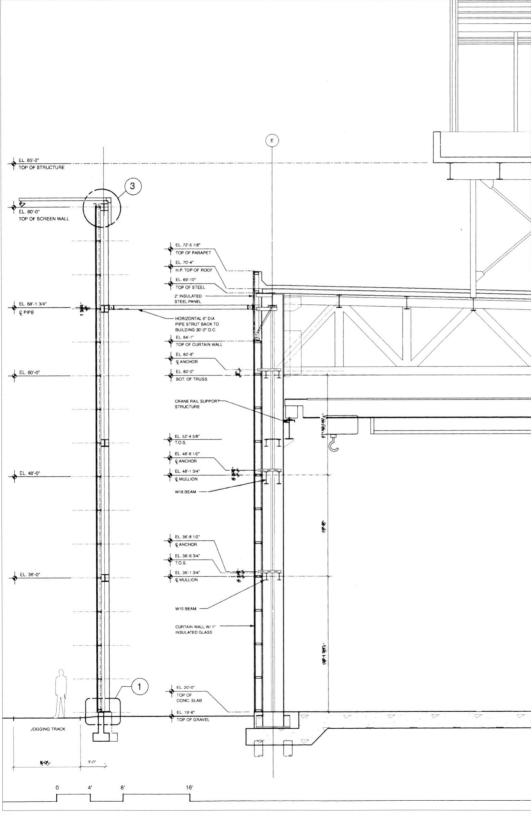

EL. 85'-2"
TOP OF STRUCTURE

EL. 80'-0"
TOP OF SCREEN WALL

EL. 72'-5 1/8"
TOP OF PARAPET

EL. 70'-4"
H.P. TOP OF ROOF

EL. 69'-10"
TOP OF STEEL

2" INSULATED
STEEL PANEL

EL. 68'-1 3/4"
℄ PIPE

HORIZONTAL 6" DIA
PIPE STRUT BACK TO
BUILDING 30'-0" O.C.

EL. 64'-1"
TOP OF CURTAIN WALL

EL. 60'-8"
℄ ANCHOR

EL. 60'-0"
BOT. OF TRUSS

EL. 60'-0"

CRANE RAIL SUPPORT
STRUCTURE

EL. 52'-4 5/8"
T.O.S.

EL. 48'-8 1/2"
℄ ANCHOR

EL. 48'-1 3/4"
℄ MULLION

EL. 48'-0"

W18 BEAM

EL. 36'-8 1/2"
℄ ANCHOR

EL. 36'-6 3/4"
T.O.S.

EL. 36'-1 3/4"
℄ MULLION

EL. 36'-0"

W10 BEAM

CURTAIN WALL W/ 1"
INSULATED GLASS

EL. 20'-0"
TOP OF
CONC. SLAB

EL. 19'-6"
TOP OF GRAVEL

JOGGING TRACK

0   4'   8'   16'

03 Wall section at screen wall and glass
curtain wall
04 Space between glass and screen
05 Floor plans showing phased growth
06 Expansion joint at screen wall

04

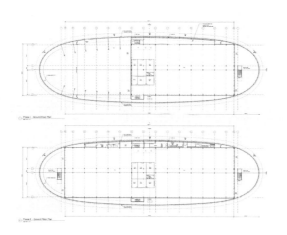

05

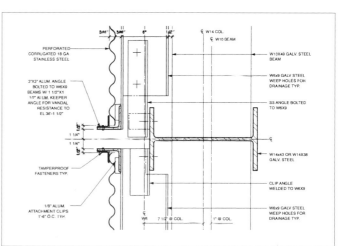

06

Sudwestmetall Reutlingen

REUTLINGEN, GERMANY // ALLMANN SATTLER WAPPNER ARCHITEKTEN
STAINLESS STEEL FLUSH-DETAILED CLADDING, MOVEMENT JOINTS, SAND BLASTING, LASER CUTTING

DESIGN INTENTION

This stainless steel-clad building houses the regional headquarters for Sudwestmetall, an association for the metalworking trades in this historically rich urban area of Germany. Other than glass, the only exterior material on this project is some variant of stainless steel product, serving various uses and configurations, right down to the automated motorized window shutters for daylight control and solar protection. The shutters have been perforated in different degrees according to the view and solar orientation; when closed, they are flush with the outer skin, achieving a pure, intact volume. The architects used the traditional forms of the surrounding historic structures as a design reference for the new building's profile. Conceptually it is a silhouette of the existing buildings to be compatible with the context, but with a homogeneous material palette and flush detailing.

MATERIALITY

This stainless steel cladding is remarkably pure, unblemished by conventional necessities such as fasteners and overt joints. The overall composition of simple iconic volumes is served by cladding these volumes in a sheer skin that minimizes articulating features. Through minimalist detailing, the observer's attention is not initially drawn to details. Instead, the dominant features are the basic composition of iconic volumes on the site and the graphic treatment of the metal and glass surfaces at ground level.

The facade is designed with a double skin of thermal glass and stainless steel sheets. The inner glass skin is made of operable glass panels; the outer stainless steel sheets are fixed on stainless steel frames, which are then hung on the structure of the building. The sheets form walls without interruption, achieving a continuous surface volume with minimal visible connections and joints. The surface reflects the colors and light of the surrounding streetscape, producing a constantly changing building surface. Thermal expansion of exterior materials usually calls for many small movement joints at frequent intervals. This building's striking appearance results from addressing the need to accommodate temperature changes of the metal using the inverse strategy: larger movement joints at less frequent intervals. Thermal movement is accommodated at joints near the building corners, and the frames that hold the sheets are hung on gliding connections, which transfer all thermal movement of the sheets into a single visible expansion joint near the edge of the facades. The building thereby de-emphasizes each individual sheet of metal to form one comprehensive mass.

In terms of massing, these building volumes are consistent with the typology of other buildings in the vicinity. In terms of materiality, however, the buildings distinguish themselves from the traditional material palette of their neighbors. The observer's tactile and visual sensibilities are stimulated by the juxtaposition of a familiar form with a material not associated with that form.

The high sheen of this metal and its resistance to dulling over time, even in an urban environment, are clearly demonstrated here. Images of buildings in the context are imparted onto the building form because of the reflectance of the metal. This adds complexity to the architectural experience and further juxtaposes form and material. Few materials can successfully be applied both on pitched roof and on vertical wall surfaces. The capability of stainless steel to be formed into continuous surfaces with excellent weathering resistance is celebrated.

TECHNICAL

This project uses a double-skin envelope on the walls and roof. Behind the nearly continuous outer layer, the inner layer is structural as well as being the moisture and thermal barrier. The metal roof and wall cladding sheets are supported off of the structural substrate approximately 14 in. (356 mm). This provides a cavity through which air can ventilate naturally to moderate temperature and humidity, and through which water collected off of the roof can be carried away through concealed gutters and leaders. Above the windows, this cavity conceals movable screens of perforated stainless steel. The building's waterproof membrane is applied to the outer surface of the underlying structural substrate, thus the metal cladding is a weatherscreen, repelling most of the precipitation, but it is not expected to prevent all moisture intrusion.

The stainless steel cladding is .16 in. (4 mm) thick and up to 22.3 ft. tall x 4.92 ft. wide (6.8 x 1.5 m). Unperforated wall and roof cladding sheets are identical. Each is bolted to the supporting structure in compression joints, milled to miter at eaves and ridge. The movable screen sections are .16 in. (4 mm) thick, 4.92 ft. (1.5 m) wide ceramic bead-blasted stainless steel sheets with laser-cut vertical butt joints. There is one large thermal expansion joint per wall surface. Expansion joints in walls are 1.97 in. (50 mm) wide; actual thermal movement anticipated at these joints is calculated to be .75 in. (19 mm). The designers were unusually thorough with their analysis. Consultants to the architect included a facade engineer and a building physics firm.

Graphic metal panels near ground level are .20 in. (5 mm) thick stainless steel sheets that are blasted with special grade corundum. To avoid causing bending in the stainless steel sheets, both sides of the stainless steel panels were shot blasted simultaneously. The 28.74 in. (730 mm) square sheets were then laser cut in highly varied floral patterns. 3,164 unique panels were economically produced using mass-customization processes. These metal panels are fixed to a steel frame as screens over vertical glazing, and to precast concrete sections as paving in the courtyard.

01 Upper-level plan
02 Court and building

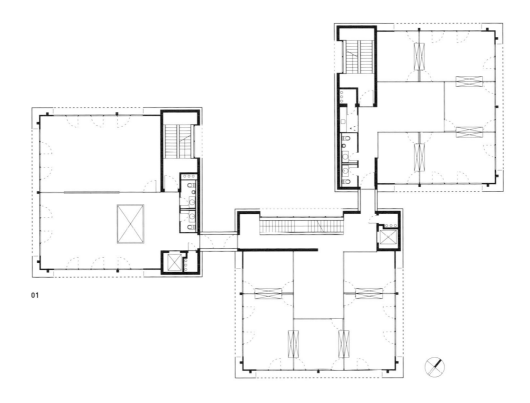

01

02

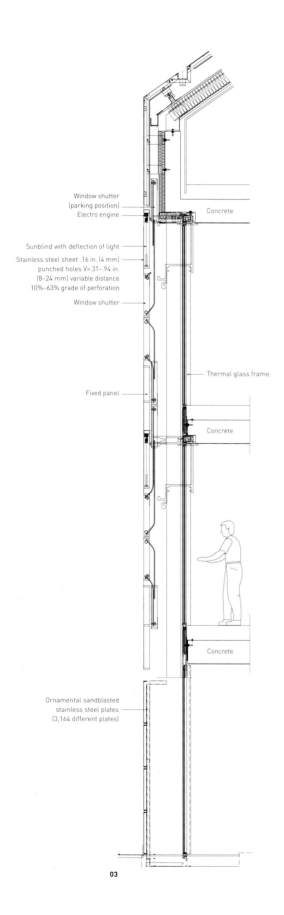

Window shutter
(parking position)

Electro engine

Sunblind with deflection of light

Stainless steel sheet .16 in. (4 mm)
punched holes V=.31–.94 in.
(8–24 mm) variable distance
10%–63% grade of perforation

Window shutter

Thermal glass frame

Fixed panel

Concrete

Concrete

Concrete

Ornamental sandblasted
stainless steel plates
(3,164 different plates)

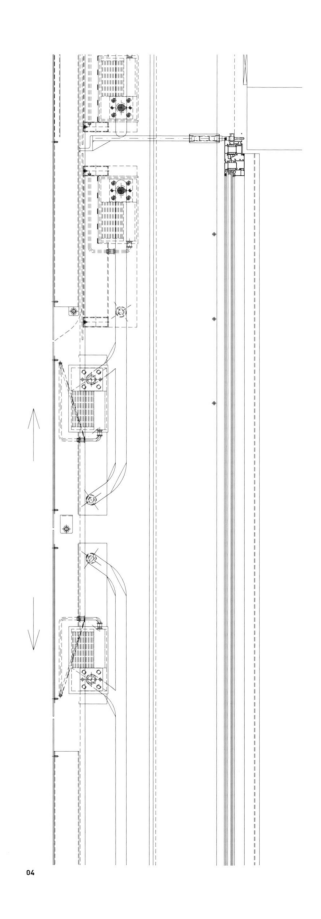

03

04

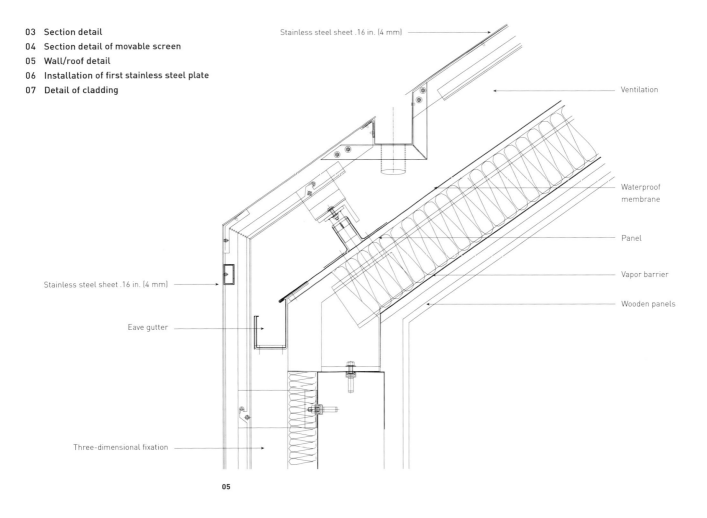

Stainless steel sheet .16 in. (4 mm)

Ventilation

Waterproof
membrane

Panel

Vapor barrier

Wooden panels

Stainless steel sheet .16 in. (4 mm)

Eave gutter

Three-dimensional fixation

05

06

07

Liner Museum

APPENZELL, SWITZERLAND // GIGON & GUYER
STAINLESS STEEL SHINGLES, SANDBLASTED SURFACES

DESIGN INTENTION

This museum is designed to house a wide range of contemporary artwork with simple, neutral spaces. The total exhibition space is divided into ten linked rooms and one larger room that serves as both lobby and lecture hall. Throughout the simple interior are white plaster-faced walls and concrete slab floors. The architect's objective was to present a structure that was compatible with the town's context while providing a suitable lighting quality for the galleries within. The sawtooth shape of the roofs references the vernacular houses in Appenzell as well as the similarly shaped roofs of the local industrial and agricultural architecture. Soft north light enters the exhibition rooms through clerestory windows set high in the gabled roof above each space, annulling the need for artificial illumination in the galleries during daylight hours.

MATERIALITY

The building is clad in sheets of stainless steel with large overlapping shingles that reference the traditional shingle facades of Appenzell architecture. This chromium-rich steel was sandblasted to reduce reflected glare in the exhibition spaces and is intended to weather to a shimmering gray as it ages. Using the same gray metal for the walls and the roofing produces an overall shape meant to correspond to the large gray mountains beyond. The reflectance of the sandblasted metal surfaces enhances the amount of daylight entering the north-facing clerestory windows, while the south-facing pitched roof surface reflect diffused light into the north-facing clerestory windows.

TECHNICAL

Sandblasting is a useful technique to soften the highly reflective surface of many metals. Small grit such as hard plastic or ceramic pearls are blown by air or steam at high pressure at the surface to produce a matte or flat finish. Modulating pressure and sandblasting techniques can result in different textures and effects as well. Areas can also be protected or masked to create contrast in textures and depth of effect. Sandblasting uses silica or other fine particles to abrade the surface of a metal. It can be used as a decorative or finishing process on metal or it can be used as a surface preparation for paint. Because sandblasting is an extremely dusty process, it is performed in controlled surroundings where the blasting particles are compressed with air and forced through a small nozzle at a high velocity. Sandblasting usually creates surfaces that are matte or have a chalky finish. However, other blasting particles such as glass beads create smooth, polished finishes, while metal shot blasting can create a random dimpled pattern.

Here, pre-formed stainless steel shingles are installed in stepped courses over all exterior surfaces, including the walls and pitched roof. They are secured using concealed clips fastened to the substrate. Where the rake end of the pitched roof meets the wall, the shingles are folded to negotiate the change in surface seamlessly. Exterior forms become patterned by the stepped courses of shingles, whose edges lap and interlock with those below, providing subtle shadows and highlights.

The interior walls and ceiling are homogeneously treated with white painted plaster, rendering the interior spaces featureless and minimizing distraction from the artwork on exhibit.

The coefficient of thermal movement for stainless steel is relatively high. By installing the sheet metal in small segments with lapped slip joints at each edge, this building easily accommodates thermal movement. The cladding is a discontinuous membrane, with watertight movement joints at relatively close intervals.

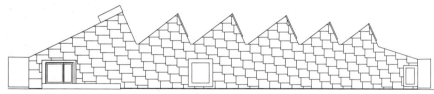

01

02

03

01 East elevation
02 Southeast corner
03 Sand blasted stainless steel cladding
04 Roof section
05 Detail of east facade

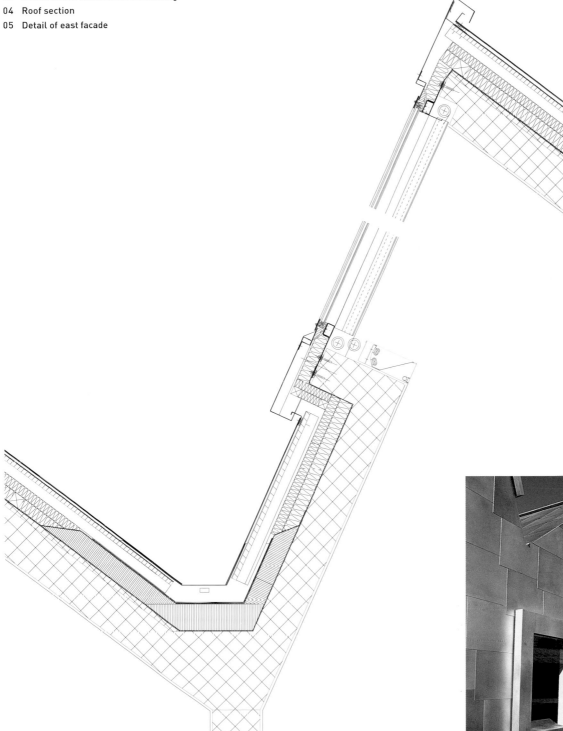

04

05

Power Station North

**SALZBURG, AUSTRIA // BÉTRIX AND CONSOLASCIO ARCHITECTS
STAINLESS STEEL, BUTT-WELDING**

DESIGN INTENTION

In 1976 a modest concrete powerhouse was built on this site located adjacent to an industrial rail line. To upgrade and enlarge the powerhouse, including the addition of living spaces, a new structure was designed with state-of-the-art thermal power technology. The original building was altered and integrated into the design of the new structure by enveloping the existing boiler room within the new outer walls. The stainless steel cladding of the new facility was intended to complement the concrete used elsewhere in the building, as both are similar in hue and value and share a smoothness to their gray exteriors. The broad surfaces of both the stainless steel and the concrete are subdivided into smaller rectangles with seams indicating the pragmatics of how they were made. However, they have contrasting inherent qualities, which the designers also intended to express.

MATERIALITY

The tectonic language consists of flat, massive structural elements made of concrete contrasting with the curving enclosure elements made of stainless steel. The duality of materials expresses the technical purpose of each element as structure or enclosure while also serving as complementary materials in the composition.

The curved metal roof and south wall are clad with .16 and .20 in. (4 and 5 mm) thick stainless steel panels that in some locations were butt-welded together and in others were folded. These welded joints were subsequently chemically treated and burnished. Appropriately, this industrial facility uses materials that are strong, durable, and very low-maintenance. The materiality of the building reflects a state-of-the-art technology characteristic of a power station.

The bold south elevation demonstrates that even subtle features of a building can enhance its appearance. In these broad surfaces of homogeneous material, with no fenestration present, it is the seams between the panels that indicate scale and which are organized to form an attractive arc across the surface, as if each "course" of metal panels were suspended from a string tied at each end of the wall.

Though literally (and often metaphorically) cold and hard, materials such as these can be softened in appearance and made more engaging by careful designers who address all aspects of a material's role in a building, beyond merely the technical domain.

TECHNICAL

Stainless steel is considered an alloy of steel that usually contains 12–27 percent chromium and nickel. It is a hard, strong, and extremely corrosion-resistant metal. It is generally harder to form and machine and is more expensive than standard mild steel. But the finish can have a range of qualities and textures from a mirror polish to a matte gray, not typical of mild steel.

Welding creates a metallurgical bond between two metals by heating them above their melting point and then placing them in direct contact. When cooled, the metals fuse to form a single member. Welding stainless steel requires considerable skill, especially when the resulting work is prominently visible in the finished project, as was the case here.

The stainless steel cladding is mounted to a series of concealed stainless steel nodes organized into an orthogonal grid at intervals of 4 ft. (1.22 m) horizontally and 4.83 ft. (1.47 m) vertically across the curving surface. These nodes are held in place by a mild steel substrate that is in turn bolted to the primary structural system. Non-conductive polymer (delrin) pads isolate the dissimilar metals to avoid bimetallic corrosion. No metal sheets on the roof or the convex south wall are flat. Most are simple curves, with some being compound curved.

01 East facade
02 Plan detail of skin assembly
03 Roof detail
04 Plan
05 West elevation

01

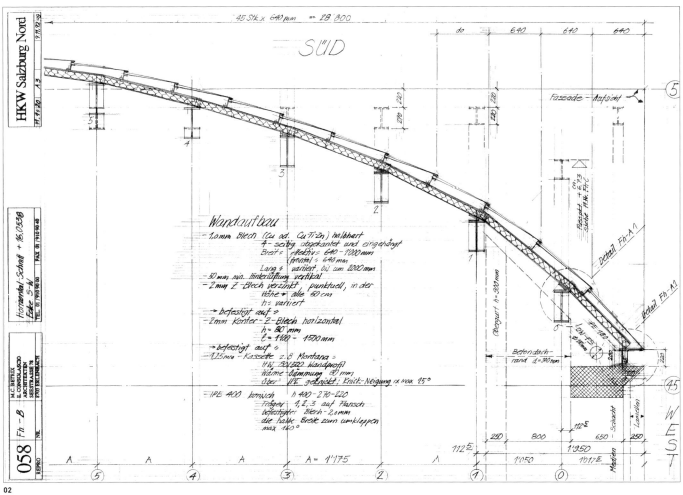

SÜD

Wandaufbau

- 1,0mm Blech (Cu od. CuTiZn) halbhart
  4-seitig abgekantet und eingehängt
  Breit = effektiv = 640 - 1000mm
  (frontal = 640 mm
  Lang + variiert bis um 2000mm
- 50 mm min. Hinterlüftung vertikal
- 2mm Z-Blech verzinkt, punktuell, in der
  Höhe → alle 60 cm
  h = variiert
  → befestigt auf =
- 2mm Konter-Z-Blech horizontal
  h = 80 mm
  ℓ = 1400 - 1500mm
  → befestigt auf =
- 1,25mm - Kassette z.B Montana =
  HW BOLERO Wandprofil
  Wärme-Dämmung 80 mm
  über IPE geknickt; Knick-Neigung α max 15°
- IPE 400 konisch h 400-270-220
  Träger 1, 2, 3 auf Flansch
  befestigter Blech-2,0mm
  die halbe Breite zum umklappen
  max 160°

02

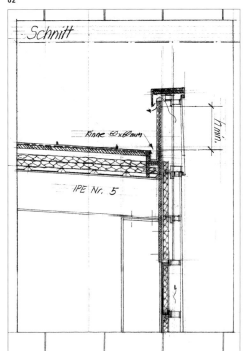

Schnitt

Rinne 60×60mm

IPE Nr. 5

03

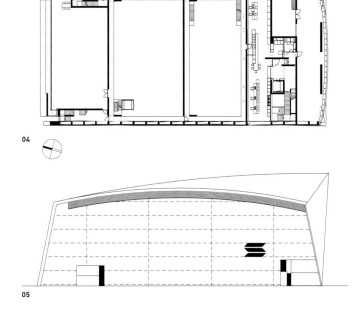

04

05

Kavel 37

BORNEO, AMSTERDAM, THE NETHERLANDS // HEREN 5 ARCHITECTEN
COR-TEN STEEL ALLOY, PERFORATED SHEET

DESIGN INTENTION

Sixty *kavels,* or lots, on the peninsula of Borneo in Amsterdam, have been divided to be sold, designed, and built as residences. One site, Kavel 37, faces a small street, while the rear looks out on a picturesque canal. Two residences occupy this site in a single volume. The design objectives were to create a residence whose public and private nature could be manipulated through kinetic architecture, and to use a cladding material to blend with the existing brick context.

MATERIALITY

Cor-ten steel is a patent-protected material in which an oxidized steel without finish is exposed to the weather. An alloy of iron, carbon, copper, and phosphorous, this material reacts with water and oxygen in the atmosphere to form a protective layer of rust on its surface. Despite its rough texture and rusted appearance, it has a high tensile strength and is more resistant to progressive corrosion than standard forms of mild steel. It is used here as a screen on both the street- and canal-side facades, with a varied degree of perforation providing desired views and privacy.

The oxidized Cor-ten steel is in harmony with the surrounding colors and textures of the existing brick homes of the harbor buildings. The perforated screens of the facade provide privacy on the street side as well as an awning on the canal side. The thick sheet metal is punched in a variety of patterns depending upon the amount of privacy required.

The facade can be opened automatically by a mechanized folding and sliding system. During the day an unhindered view of the outside is possible, while at night the inhabitants are visible as silhouettes behind the facades. The visual features of this material vary according to the orientation, the desired level of privacy, and even the time of day. Few materials are available that match this range of visual qualities, machine operation, and low maintenance.

This project demonstrates that comprehension of visual information is not lost when the view is partially obscured. Perforated and woven metal screens are an effective means of optimizing views while limiting radiant energy gain. Designers can use these products in concert with other features such as glazing and illumination to exert control over the visual experience. A given screen can be nearly opaque or nearly transparent, depending upon the illumination strategy employed.

TECHNICAL

Reinforced concrete is the primary structural material, used to make the east and west party walls, floor, and roof structural decks. The north and south elevations are substantially open, using glazing and external screens to enclose space. Both visible elevations are clad with a series of modular perforated Cor-ten "cassettes," or panels, arranged flush with the ends of the party walls. These "cassettes" subdivide the elevations into panels that are 1.64 ft. (500 mm) high, 3.22 ft. (980 mm) wide, and 1.38 in. (35 mm) deep. They are made of .08 in. (2 mm) thick Cor-ten steel that is perforated in the broad face to permit light and air to pass through.

The pattern of perforation varies depending upon the desired level of privacy. On the facade facing the water and the upper area of the street facade, the type of Cor-ten mesh used is .24 in. (6 mm) holes at .30 in. (7.5 mm) on-center (58 percent perforation) while the Cor-ten mesh used in the lower area of the street facade is .24 in. (6 mm) holes at .35 in. (9 mm) on-center (40 percent perforation). To give residents options, 40 percent of the screens are operable, controlled by the occupants using electric motors that are concealed inside the walls. Screen panels that are not operable are hung on a grid of supports that suspend it off of the underlying wall, in alignment with the operable panels.

Residue from weathered Cor-ten steel is carried by precipitation to adjoining materials, often leaving a reddish brown stain in its path. In this project, similarly colored bricks are used as pavers at the base of the wall, camouflaging this process.

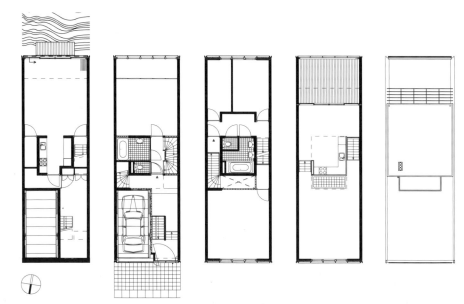

01 Floor plan
02 North-south section with elevations
03 North facade
04 South facade

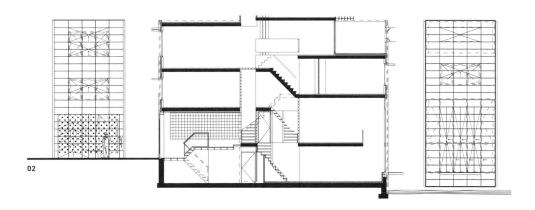

02

03

04

1. Perforated Cor-ten-steel .06 in. (1.5 mm)
2. Beam hea 200
3. Plaster board .49 in. (12.5 mm)
4. Thermal insulation rc=8.2 ft. (2.5 m) 2k/w
5. Menuiserite .2 in. (5 mm) ventilating
6. T 2.76 x 2.76 x .31 in. (70 x 70 x 8 mm)
7. Steel strip .79 x .16 in. (20 x 4 mm)
8. Freestone window sill
9. Bankirai parts .87 x 4.13 in. (22 x 105 mm)

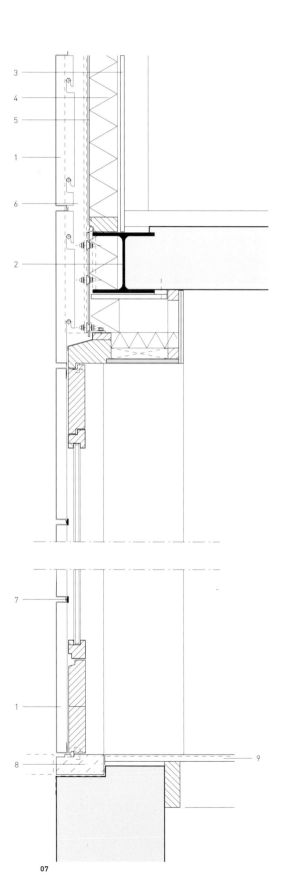

07

05

06

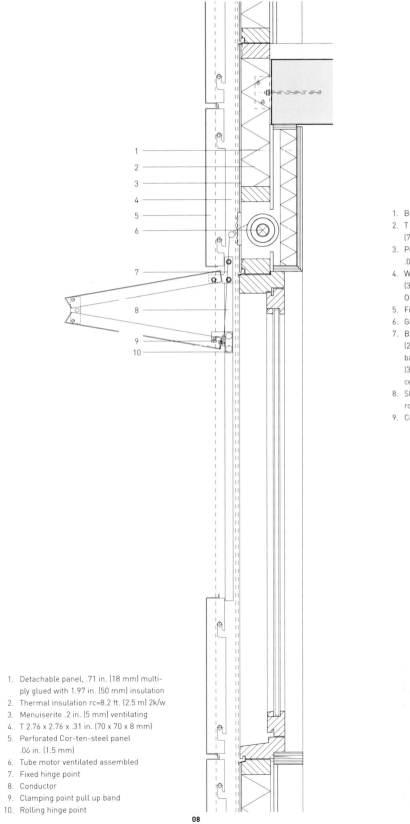

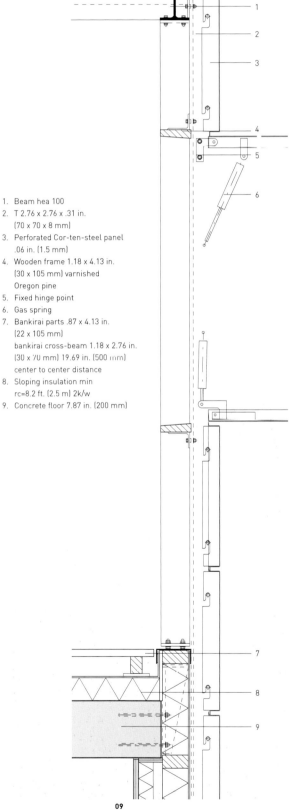

1. Beam hea 100
2. T 2.76 x 2.76 x .31 in.
   (70 x 70 x 8 mm)
3. Perforated Cor-ten-steel panel
   .06 in. (1.5 mm)
4. Wooden frame 1.18 x 4.13 in.
   (30 x 105 mm) varnished
   Oregon pine
5. Fixed hinge point
6. Gas spring
7. Bankirai parts .87 x 4.13 in.
   (22 x 105 mm)
   bankirai cross-beam 1.18 x 2.76 in.
   (30 x 70 mm) 19.69 in. (500 mm)
   center to center distance
8. Sloping insulation min
   rc=8.2 ft. (2.5 m) 2k/w
9. Concrete floor 7.87 in. (200 mm)

1. Detachable panel, .71 in. (18 mm) multi-
   ply glued with 1.97 in. (50 mm) insulation
2. Thermal insulation rc=8.2 ft. (2.5 m) 2k/w
3. Menuiserite .2 in. (5 mm) ventilating
4. T 2.76 x 2.76 x .31 in. (70 x 70 x 8 mm)
5. Perforated Cor-ten-steel panel
   .06 in. (1.5 mm)
6. Tube motor ventilated assembled
7. Fixed hinge point
8. Conductor
9. Clamping point pull up band
10. Rolling hinge point

Schemata XI

LAWRENCE, KANSAS // UNIVERSITY OF KANSAS, SCHOOL OF ARCHITECTURE AND URBAN DESIGN: STUDIO 804
COR-TEN STEEL CLADDING

DESIGN INTENTION

This house was completed by students at the University of Kansas through a design/build program during the last two semesters of their professional degree program in architecture. The project began with an intense design period in which students combined their ideas to meet the criteria given to them by their client partner, Tenants to Homeowners, Inc. This organization, dedicated to selling affordable homes, required a 1,500 square foot (139 sq. m), three-bedroom, two-bathroom home that is fully accessible in compliance with the American Disability Association (ADA) standards. Three additional objectives the students incorporated into the project were sustainable design, passive solar design, and community design issues. The design theme, a "lantern on life," drove the proposal for the house in the use of both materials and metaphor.

MATERIALITY

Sustainability and reuse of materials determined many specific design choices for this house, resulting in an interesting and rich collection of materials. The building is wrapped in Cor-ten steel, which is a proprietary metal that is designed to seal its surfaces through oxidation. The Cor-ten cladding minimizes maintenance requirements for this low-income house, which has a planned thirty-year life.

A redwood louver system salvaged from a local cooling tower was adapted and used for exterior sunscreens attached to the house. The 2x4s and plywood that were used to make the concrete formwork were reused for the framing of the house. Two bathrooms are stacked on top of each other for efficient utility layout and are constructed of steel and polycarbonate to create a glowing "lantern" at the core of the house.

Detailing any building project involves first speculating with models, carefully prepared working drawings, and specifications, but then refining the detail throughout the construction process, often not ending until the completion of construction. The final design decision is not made until the maximum amount of relevant information is available, often at the moment of construction. This is especially appropriate in a design/build endeavor such as this. Drawings prepared before construction show Cor-ten cladding being installed like shingles, with fasteners near the upper edges that are covered by the next course of shingles. In this approach, only the topmost course of shingles would have had exposed fasteners. Images of the installed elements indicate that a second line of fasteners was installed near the lower edge of each panel, also securing the top edge of the shingle below it. This adjustment reduces the need for stiffness in the panels, and holds them more snugly against the building wall.

The shingled cladding panels are held off of the wall below using treated wood furring strips oriented vertically. This allows air to circulate behind the cladding and allows moisture to drain without staining the surface of the concrete foundation wall. The metal cladding is not the waterproof barrier in this assembly; rather, it is the primary weatherscreen, repelling most but not all of the precipitation. A polymer waterproof membrane is adhered to the sheathing continuously, below the wood furring strips, where it is shielded by the metal cladding from harmful sunlight and the harshest weather.

TECHNICAL

This project's details recognize that cladding is prone to thermal movement at a greater rate than the substrate to which it is secured. The designers set the dimensions of each panel and the interval between fasteners accordingly, acknowledging that the greater the panel dimensions, the greater the amount of movement at a given joint. Sunny exposures will undergo greater thermal movement than shady exposures due to direct radiant gain. Metal cladding installed during cool weather, as was the case with many in this project, will likely become slightly larger in size during hot weather. Fastener diameters are smaller than the holes drilled in the metal to provide tolerance for minor movement; the boundaries of the metal panels are not rigidly constrained.

Cor-ten cladding panels in this building vary in size, but are generally 24 in. tall x 8 ft. wide x .1 in. thick (609 mm x 2.44 m x 2.54 mm). Plates are arranged with a lap of 3.62 in. (92 mm) at horizontal edges, and a .5 in. (13 mm) reveal at vertical edges. They are secured using Trugrip screws with neoprene washers, installed at intervals of 16 in. (406 mm) horizontally. Some cladding panels cantilever 8 in. (203 mm) from center of furring strip to edge of cladding panel.

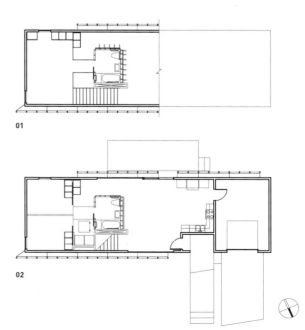

01

02

01 Ground-floor plan
02 Upper-floor plan
03 East facade
04 North facade

03

04

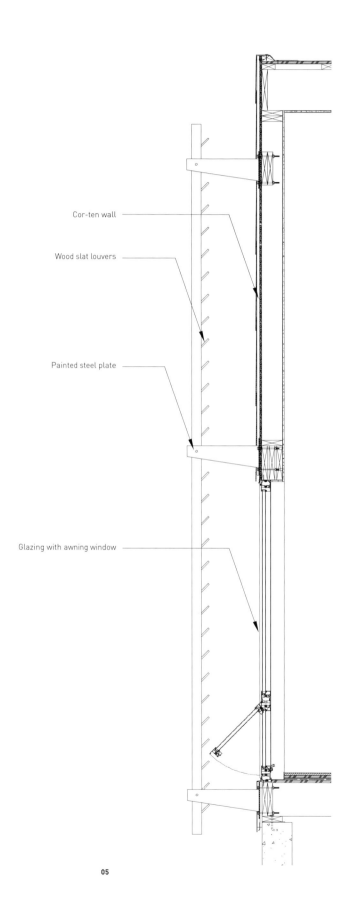

Cor-ten wall

Wood slat louvers

Painted steel plate

Glazing with awning window

05

06

07

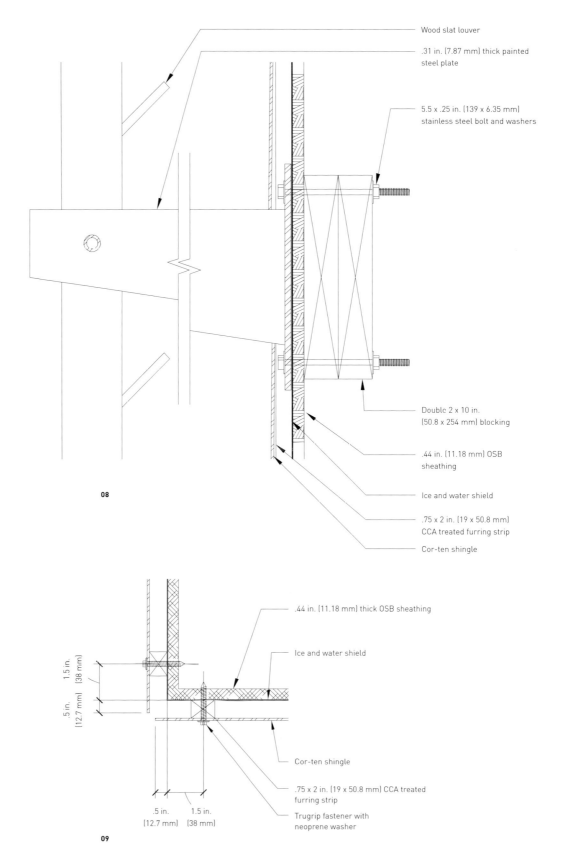

Wood slat louver

.31 in. (7.87 mm) thick painted steel plate

5.5 x .25 in. (139 x 6.35 mm) stainless steel bolt and washers

Double 2 x 10 in. (50.8 x 254 mm) blocking

.44 in. (11.18 mm) OSB sheathing

Ice and water shield

.75 x 2 in. (19 x 50.8 mm) CCA treated furring strip

Cor-ten shingle

08

.44 in. (11.18 mm) thick OSB sheathing

Ice and water shield

1.5 in. (38 mm)

.5 in. (12.7 mm)

Cor-ten shingle

.75 x 2 in. (19 x 50.8 mm) CCA treated furring strip

Trugrip fastener with neoprene washer

.5 in. (12.7 mm)

1.5 in. (38 mm)

09

05   Wall section at south wall
06   Entry
07   Cor-ten installation
08   Louver bracket detail
09   Corner detail

Aluminum Forest

HOUTEN, THE NETHERLANDS // ARCHITECTENBUREAU MICHA DE HAAS
ALUMINUM EXTRUSION, STRUCTURAL CAPABILITIES, PREFABRICATION

DESIGN INTENTION

This is the first public building whose primary bearing structure is made completely of aluminum. It consists of 368 unusually slender aluminum columns, which bear the weight of an upper structure nearly 20 feet (6 m) above the ground, containing offices, conference rooms, and demonstration areas for the Aluminum Centre. The source of inspiration for the Aluminum Forest was the Dutch landscape, specifically characteristic slender poplar trees that merge into a single mass of foliage above the trunks. The building rests partly on a sloping bank and partly over water. Sunlight reflects off of the water and onto the hundreds of columns, illuminating the space below and adding to the hovering effect of the building.

This project demonstrates the extraordinary benefits of close collaboration between architect, engineer, material manufacturer, and crafts-people. Several innovative features originated with this project, such as the patented column and cladding system used in the office walls. In other cases innovations were transferred to this architectural application from other industries, such as aerospace. For example, the strategy of using many small structural elements rather than few large ones is borrowed from aircraft design. The resulting project is a working showcase for aluminum.

MATERIALITY

The upper volume of this building has to be light while the columns that support it must be strong, making aluminum the perfect material choice for both. Several of the columns serve as drainpipes and service conduits, while others have much thicker walls and are purely structural. Although the columns appear random, they are spaced and angled with regularity. As in a forest of trees, the columns vary in diameter and the angle at which they stand. The angled columns (at 5 or 10 degrees) buttress the building against lateral movement to avoid buckling that would otherwise occur due to the slenderness of the columns. Larger columns are chosen where loads are greater, and column wall thicknesses increase with the diameter of the column. One counterintuitive characteristic of tube columns is that the thinner their wall thickness, the less likely they are to fail due to buckling. Spans in the floor above vary from 1.97 ft. (.6 m) to 11.81 ft. (3.6 m). The advantage of having many columns is that the spans in the floor deck can be very short, reducing beam sizes considerably.

Only the concrete ground slab was made on site. This slab acts as a grade beam, spreading the dispersed point loads evenly over the soft soils of the site. Since there is no precedent with such slender structural aluminum columns, extensive calculations and research was done with 3-D software to ensure the building's structural integrity. The concrete floor is cast on profiled decks made of steel, because aluminum is not compatible with the alkali compounds in fresh concrete. The roof deck is made of profiled aluminum because the lightweight concrete topping slab is not cast in direct contact with the metal deck.

Completely hidden from the eye is a highly sophisticated structural grid of specially made aluminum beams that create a platform for the open plan and carry the enclosing walls of the occupied floor. Within the building envelope, aluminum structural columns have been incorporated unobtrusively into the perimeter walls. These columns were custom-designed and extruded to integrate all of the structural and wall systems into their form. Aluminum extrusion techniques make it possible to design custom-made profiles with precise details. The columns at the perimeter of the office floor are actually an assembly of pieces that are extruded separately, but whose profiles match with sufficient precision that they snap together without fasteners. This makes initial assembly and subsequent servicing easier, and demonstrates a unique feature of aluminum extrusions.

Each component of the building was prefabricated off site, then transported and assembled mechanically on site. This allowed for any piece to be individually replaced, dismantled, or reused. Because aluminum is fully recyclable with no loss of quality, parts made with this material score well on any building lifecycle analysis.

The embodied energy associated with the initial production of aluminum is approximately six times greater than that of steel, chiefly because of the great amount of energy required to refine it. However, the service life of aluminum is attractively long; it requires minimal maintenance and can be recycled with little energy and no degradation of properties. It is often used as an exterior enclosure material, due to its intrinsic resistance to corrosion. It also attracts and holds a variety of permanent finishes, and it can be extruded into complex shapes. Traditionally, aluminum has seldom been used as a primary structural material because it has a relatively low modulus of elasticity (i.e., it is brittle and stiff), has a low melting point, and compared to steel is high in cost per unit of strength. Advantages aluminum offers for structural applications compared to steel are its low dead load; possibly reduced safety factors since designers do not need to provide allowances for corrosion; more complex and precise extruded shapes rather than simpler rolled shapes; and the varied aluminum alloys available to match physical properties with the needs of a given application.

TECHNICAL

Extrusion is a fabrication process in which a material is forced by pressure through a die to achieve a continuous profile. The low melting point and malleability of aluminum easily allows for extrusion, resulting in common shapes such as angles, channels, and tubes, as well as more complex profiles used in enclosure assemblies. Building elements most commonly made from extruded aluminum are windows, doors, roofing, and hardware. In this case extruded aluminum is used for all of the primary structural elements in the building, including tube columns, floor beams, and roof columns. Also, the trusses that frame part of the roof were made from extruded aluminum tubes joined in cast aluminum nodes. Aluminum multipanel products were used as the ceiling treatment and for the underside of the main floor.

Columns supporting the roof are at the perimeter of the enclosed space. They integrate several functions in one custom extrusion, bearing the roof load, receiving the interior and exterior finish treatments, and providing an accessible vertical conduit for electrical and data services. They were placed at an interval that matches the horizontal spanning capacity of the aluminum composite exterior panels and aluminum interior panels, so metal studs are not required. This strategy reduces heat transmission through wall framing. Thermal breaks separate the aluminum columns from the frame that supports the exterior cladding panels.

Columns supporting the floor are anodized. Concealed aluminum members are natural mill finish. Aluminum columns supporting the floor were not fire protected because the architect demonstrated that even if a few singular columns collapse, the other columns and floor beams (with some deflection) would still carry the load. The column wall thicknesses vary with the diameter of the column: 3.54 x .16 in. (90 x 4 mm), 4.72 x .20 in. (120 x 5 mm), 7.09 x .31 in. (180 x 8 mm), and 8.27 x .39 in. (210 x 10 mm).

01

02

01 View across water
02 Entry elevation

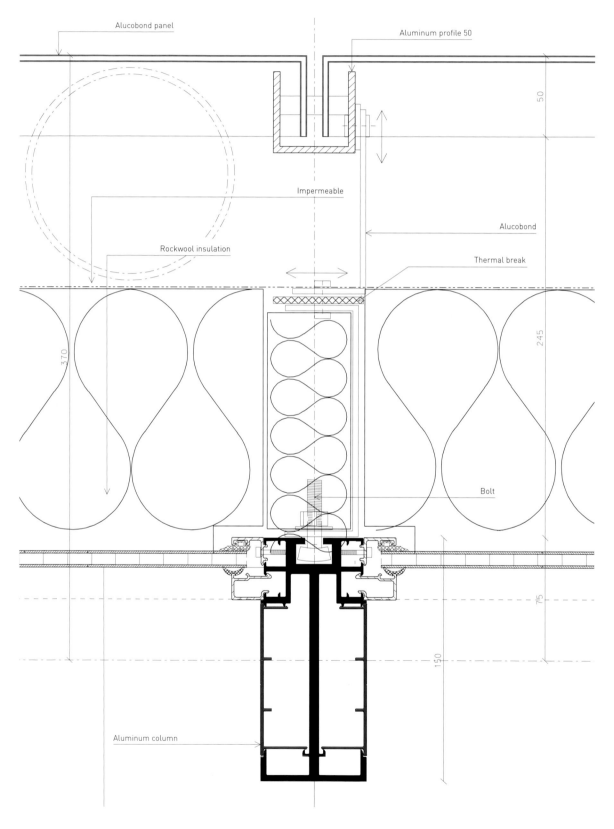

Alucobond panel

Aluminum profile 50

50

Impermeable

Alucobond

Rockwool insulation

Thermal break

370

245

Bolt

75

150

Aluminum column

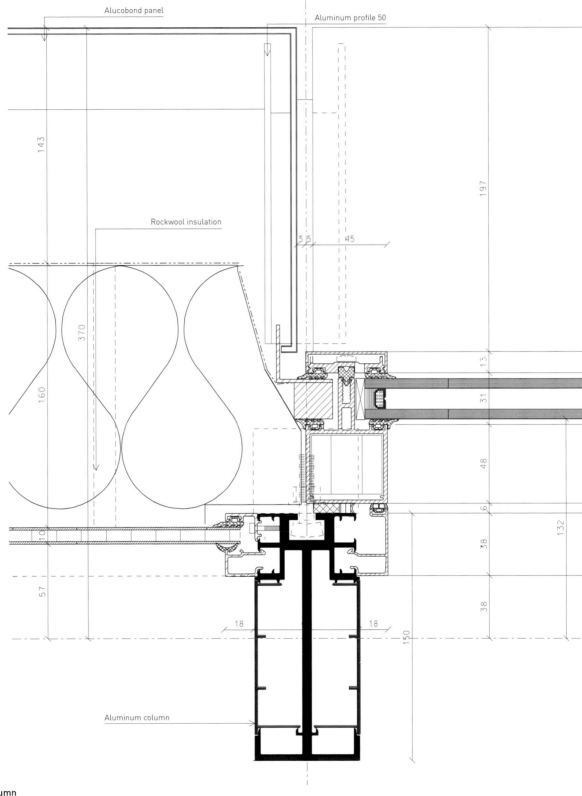

Alucobond panel

Aluminum profile 50

Rockwool insulation

Aluminum column

03 Plan detail at column
04 Plan detail at window

Raum Zita Kern

RAASDORF, AUSTRIA // ARTEC ARCHITECTS
ALUMINUM, MILL-FINISHED AND ANODIZED

DESIGN INTENTION

Within the suburban sprawl surrounding Vienna exists vast rural landscapes, industrialized agriculture, and villages astride large thoroughfares. Adjacent to this but protected by forest and fields is a farm owned by a woman who is both a scholar of literary studies and a farmer. Fruit, vegetables, herbs, chickens, and cats constitute one aspect of her life, while books make up the other. Her original buildings were comprised of spaces for farmwork, cooking, eating, and sleeping, but no interior toilet or study existed.

The architects used aluminum and other materials to give an existing structure a new roof as well as new programmatic space. The juxtaposition of the new and old materials is a metaphor for the owner's dual activities of the time-honored trade of farming and the contemporary profession of literary scholarship. The structure of the existing farm buildings set the framework for the new intervention: the old buildings become the plinth for the new. The existing stockroom with a wood-beam ceiling was transformed into a large, introverted bathroom by removing a few beams and portions of the roof, letting daylight shine in from above. The cowshed below would continue to serve the farm, though the brick vaulted roof was removed because it was in danger of collapse. This project uses materiality to juxtapose not only old and new, but rustic and refined, load-bearing and frame, masonry and metallic, familiar and strange, obvious and obscure. The languages are not only different, but opposite.

MATERIALITY

Aluminum clearly delineates what is new and separate from the life of the existing masonry farm buildings. The new structure presents itself within the farm ensemble as unambiguously new. Its interior form stands in contrast to the old, resembling more a tent than a massive house. The new building becomes abstract, its purpose concealed. The furnishings are simultaneously part of the wall and space-structuring element. Incidence of light and the openings are not in direct relationship to the courtyard. The openings are situated so that the sometimes-drastic storms may be viewed safely from within.

The exterior skin of the building is sheathed with untreated aluminum that was screwed directly onto vertical furring strips, producing a compartmented air space. The semi-reflective surface is articulated only by the precise grid of fasteners and the rhythm of concealed seams. The material takes on the color of the sky, reflecting the mood of the weather and the surroundings. Mill-finished aluminum is bright when new, but over time the surface will dull slightly as it oxidizes, though it will not be susceptible to corrosion or require protective coatings. The sheet format was chosen so that the assembly could be completed by just two people. The height of this format is sufficient to enable installation without requiring horizontal seams.

All exterior aluminum elements—the facade and roof, sheet metal, window profiles, corrugated panels, and metal chimney—were installed in their natural mill finish. To contrast and convey greater refinement, many interior surfaces—shower, the adjoining wall, and all wall-niche surfaces—are finished with anodized aluminum. Where not anodized aluminum, the interior walls are sheathed in poplar plywood sheets, and rubber flooring covers all new areas.

A study for writing is added on the upper floor above the original building. Although it is a part of the courtyard by its location, it is at the same time set apart from it by its materiality and elevated position. The intellectual sphere of the study and the physical sphere of the farm are thus separated in a simple way. Two terraces, accessible by means of sliding and revolving doors, lead out from the study, extending it to the outdoors. The stairs leading up to the new addition are a visibly separate element, and their location on the outside of the existing building connects the new upper volume to the ground.

TECHNICAL

Aluminum is obtained from bauxite, one of the most abundant materials found in the Earth's crust. Its corrosion-resistant properties make aluminum ideal for preventing water penetration and weather-tight connections such as flashing and drip edges. The aluminum cladding is the waterproof barrier in this assembly. The cavity below the cladding provides a channel for condensation to drain and for outside air to circulate.

The aluminum sheets are 4.92 ft. wide by 9.84 ft. tall (150 x 300 cm). Aluminum sheets of this size can be cut, curved, and folded in a factory or on site. At only one-third the density of steel, these sheets were easily manipulated and handled by the small construction crew without mechanical assistance.

The exterior aluminum cladding is .08 in. (2 mm) thick, installed flat with simple butt joints. The sheets are secured using sheet metal screws to wood furring strips oriented vertically. The furring strips are faced with a layer of .08 in. (2 mm) aluminum, which received a bead of silicon caulk around holes and near edges to accommodate thermal movement and prevent moisture intrusion. Concealed vents provide ventilation of the cavity between the plywood sheathing and the aluminum cladding.

The existing clay masonry walls of the former cowshed are capped with a reinforced concrete slab to bear the load of the new upper floor. The timber frame for new wall and roof construction was made in the traditional manner, using subtractive mortise and tennon construction. The frame is sheathed with .31 in. (8 mm) thick plywood sheets.

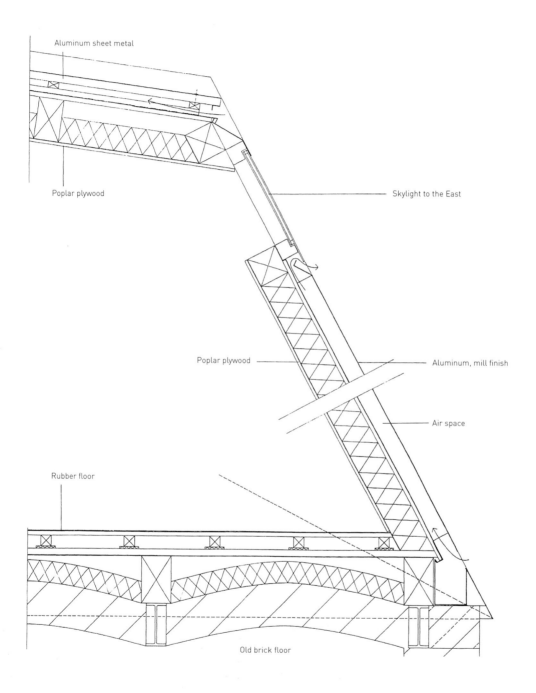

Aluminum sheet metal

Poplar plywood

Skylight to the East

Poplar plywood

Aluminum, mill finish

Air space

Rubber floor

Old brick floor

02

02   Section through upper-level addition
03   Sectional detail at skylight
04   Courtyard facade
05   Courtyard facade, end view

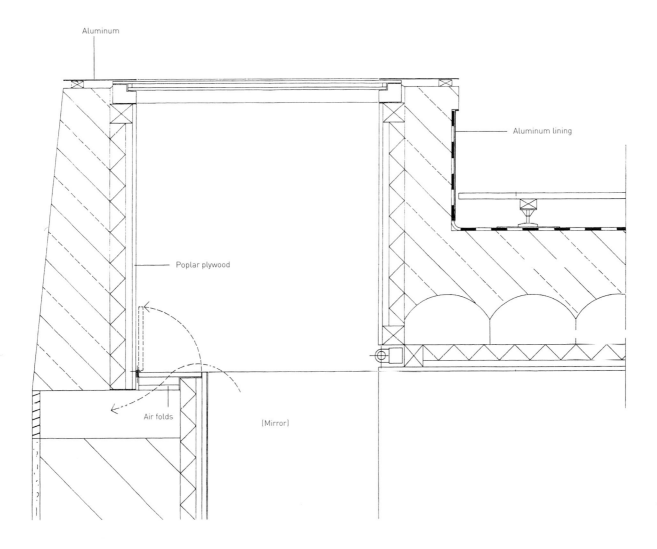

Aluminum

Aluminum lining

Poplar plywood

Air folds

(Mirror)

03

04

05

Max Planck Institute

DRESDEN, GERMANY // HEIKKINEN-KOMONEN ARCHITECTS
POWDER-COATED ALUMINUM, COLOR FINISH

DESIGN INTENTION

This research center for international molecular cell biology and genetics, located along the banks of the Elbe River in historic Dresden, is made up of three buildings consisting of a laboratory block, an animal maintenance unit, and apartments for visiting researchers. A large laboratory building, seminar rooms, a library, and a three-hundred-seat auditorium make up the rest of this scientific campus. Over three hundred scientists from twenty-six countries work here, thus requiring a highly specialized and complex building program. This was realized with a simple, pragmatic geometry combined with contrasting materials that metaphorically represent the sophistication and diversity of the various sciences studied here.

MATERIALITY

This project is a study of different architectural metals and their uses within a complex program of dissimilar components. Deep blue aluminum panels clad the laboratory building, boldly marking it as the heart of the research center. The elongated building has its largest facades facing east and west, the outermost layer of which is a green aluminum lattice, shading the glass and blue aluminum cladding and cutting the solar heat gain during the day. This gives the laboratories an abundance of natural light yet controls the solar heat load. Spaces inside require control over the temperature and light. The latticed facade mitigates the potentially harmful low-angle sunlight while maintaining views.

The contrasting colors create a kinetic visual experience for pedestrians. When viewed head-on, the green grid is hardly visible, but when viewed from even a slight angle—such as while walking alongside the building—the surface takes on an active effect in depth, color, and movement. At approximately 45 degrees vertically and 65 degrees horizontally the green lattice becomes visually solid.

Subdividing the aluminum cladding into panels facilitated fabrication, finishing, and installation of this facade. The module of the metal cladding is carried over to other materials in the building, such as the curtain wall and the formwork for cast-in-place concrete. The concrete primary structural system reveals itself on the interior, standing in contrast to the metal facade elements and interior helical stair. The facades express a spirit of cutting-edge research while also providing needed security.

TECHNICAL

The green of the aluminum screens and the blue of the cladding are achieved through powder coating, a process of applying color to metals using electricity and heat. A powder of thermostatic resins and pigments is applied to a surface through electrostatic bonding, and is then fused to the metal surface as a continuous film by heat.

Powder coating is especially suitable for complex surfaces such as this three-dimensional lattice, because all surfaces will receive the intended coating thickness. Powder coating offers a much broader range of colors and sheens than is possible by anodizing aluminum, and is preferable to solvent-based coatings such as paint because it releases no solvents into the atmosphere.

The lattice is composed of panel segments that are 15 in. tall x 90.5 in. wide (38 x 230 cm). Panels are fixed to a metal frame 22 in. (56 cm) away from the building wall, allowing building maintenance staff to occupy this space when needed. The aluminum lattice divisions are 3.94 in. wide x 1.97 in. tall x 1.97 in. deep (100 x 50 x 50 mm). The aluminum is .16 in. (4 mm) thick. In elevation the lattice is 88 percent void.

The aluminum plate cladding on the building wall is .16 in. (4 mm) thick, fabricated into panels that align with the panels of the lattice. Plate cladding panels are mounted on a corrugated sheet that permits convection vertically through a small cavity between the aluminum plate and the corrugated substrate, reducing heat gain in the wall.

01 Plan
02 Northeast corner

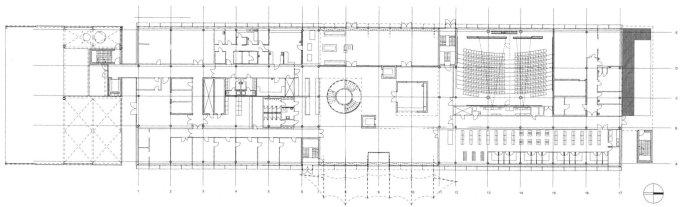

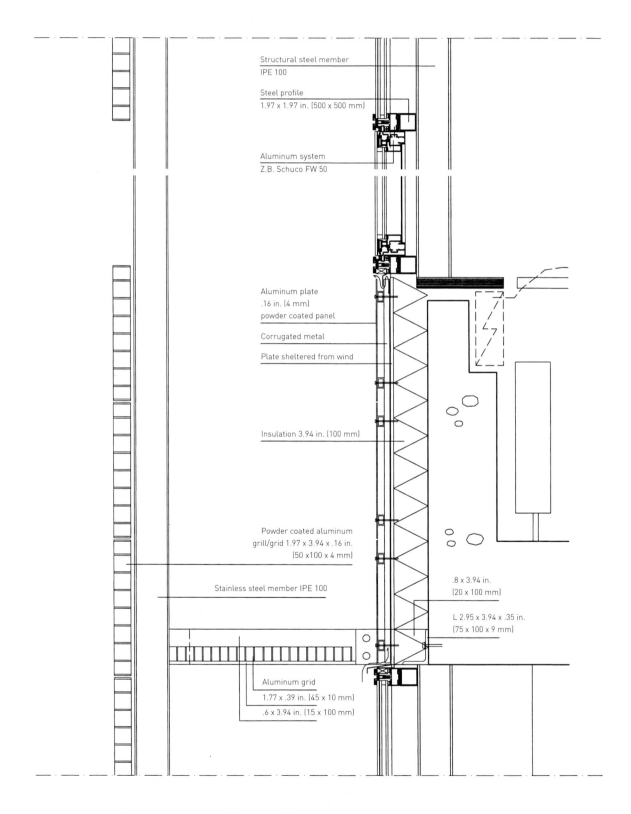

Structural steel member
IPE 100

Steel profile
1.97 x 1.97 in. (500 x 500 mm)

Aluminum system
Z.B. Schuco FW 50

Aluminum plate
.16 in. (4 mm)
powder coated panel

Corrugated metal

Plate sheltered from wind

Insulation 3.94 in. (100 mm)

Powder coated aluminum
grill/grid 1.97 x 3.94 x .16 in.
(50 x100 x 4 mm)

Stainless steel member IPE 100

.8 x 3.94 in.
(20 x 100 mm)

L 2.95 x 3.94 x .35 in.
(75 x 100 x 9 mm)

Aluminum grid
1.77 x .39 in. (45 x 10 mm)
.6 x 3.94 in. (15 x 100 mm)

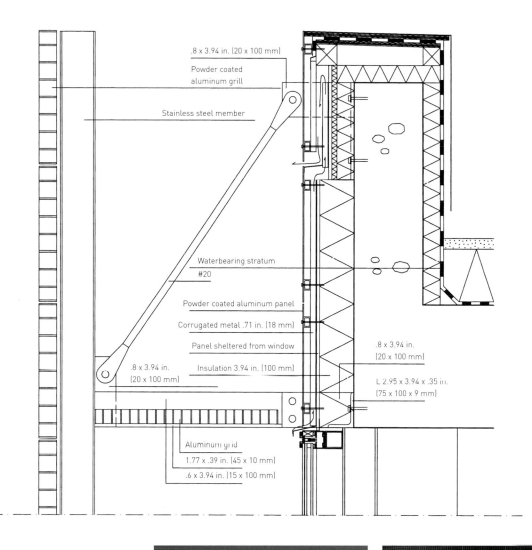

.8 x 3.94 in. (20 x 100 mm)

Powder coated
aluminum grill

Stainless steel member

Waterbearing stratum
#20

Powder coated aluminum panel

Corrugated metal .71 in. (18 mm)

Panel sheltered from window

Insulation 3.94 in. (100 mm)

.8 x 3.94 in.
(20 x 100 mm)

.8 x 3.94 in.
(20 x 100 mm)

L 2.95 x 3.94 x .35 in.
(75 x 100 x 9 mm)

Aluminum grid

1.77 x .39 in. (45 x 10 mm)

.6 x 3.94 in. (15 x 100 mm)

04

05

06

The Embassies of the Nordic Countries in Berlin-Tiergarten

BERLIN, GERMANY // BERGER + PARKKINEN ARCHITEKTEN
COPPER, PRE-PATINATION AND GALVANIC ACTION

DESIGN INTENTION

Six embassy buildings representing the five Scandinavian countries of Denmark, Finland, Iceland, Norway, and Sweden are collected in a parklike setting in a very condensed urban area of Berlin. The sixth structure is a multipurpose building serving as an exhibition hall, restaurant, information exchange, and general gathering place. The free form of this park and its group of buildings is derived from the boundary of the site, the positions of the existing trees, and the location of the adjacent Tiergarten Park. Different Nordic architects were invited to contribute to the final design of each building while a copper wall encompasses all of them, forming a continuous and common element. Wrapping the perimeter of the site, this wall literally and metaphorically unites the five Nordic countries. The large scale gives the group of six buildings the quality of a landmark in the heart of Berlin, while the skin obscures the massing of the embassies and forms a gentle transition to the dimension of the Tiergarten landscape. The particular built elements are thus cut out of a solid whole; the individual building facades define the voids between them. A tension of emptiness is suspended between the buildings like an enduring memory of the whole.

MATERIALITY

The bold character of the enveloping wall is achieved through copper's distinctive oxidized hue, hastened through a pre-patinating chemical process, as well as the manner in which the copper elements were placed in the frame. The louvers permit the quality and quantity of light inside the buildings to be controlled, reducing glare and artificial illumination requirements. The patina on the copper louvers diffuses the sunlight and imparts a subtle hue to the reflected light.

The wall is made up of copper louvers mounted on a stainless steel frame. The position of the louvers controls the light, air, and views available to the occupants. The featured copper band achieves a varied shape in plan, and its louvers are mounted in four different positions, giving designers ample capacity to adjust to varying solar orientations and programmatic needs. This flexibility is efficiently achieved by the mounting detail, permitting the louvers and mullions to be mass produced. The louvers exploit the potential to roll and to cast copper alloys, using both processes in their production. The ductility of copper is demonstrated literally by the curved faces of the louvers, and figuratively by the curving plane of the copper band across the site.

Copper's intrinsic resistance to corrosion makes it a good exterior material. Its natural tendency to oxidize to a distinctive hue is acheived and made uniform in this project by a chemical treatment. Rather than requiring eight to ten years for a coating of copper carbonate or sulfate to form, here a patina was present at the outset.

Several acids may be used to pre-patina copper. The result resembles naturally weathered copper, but is actually not the same chemical compound on the surface. The artificial patina sometimes goes through a transition to the natural patina in the decades that follow construction.

Stainless steel screws and bolts were used to assemble the louvers and the wall, accenting the louvers by using the secondary material of the wall system. However, copper and ferrous metals such as steel are incompatible due to bimetallic corrosion; copper would become the cathode, causing the ferrous metal to corrode. The stainless steel fasteners and mullions were therefore isolated from the copper-based louver materials using nonconductive polymer washers.

TECHNICAL

Each louver is approximately 1.97 ft. (60 cm) wide and varies in length from 2.95–5.91 ft. (90–180 cm). Cast metal armatures at the two ends of each louver produce its convex profile, which is 3.15 in. (80 mm) thick at the center, tapering to 1.34 in. (34 mm) at the two long edges. Copper sheets slip into a curving slot in the armature and become the faces of the louvers.

In some locations the louvers were mounted in the tight-fitting "closed" position by fastening them directly to the vertical mullions. In other locations one of two fittings were used to mount the louvers horizontally or at sloping 45 or 135 degree positions. Frames holding the louvers were mounted to a solid backup wall, or were freestanding in space with a planar glass curtain wall mounted to the inside of the frame.

01 Site plan
02 Copper louvers
03 Copper band facade

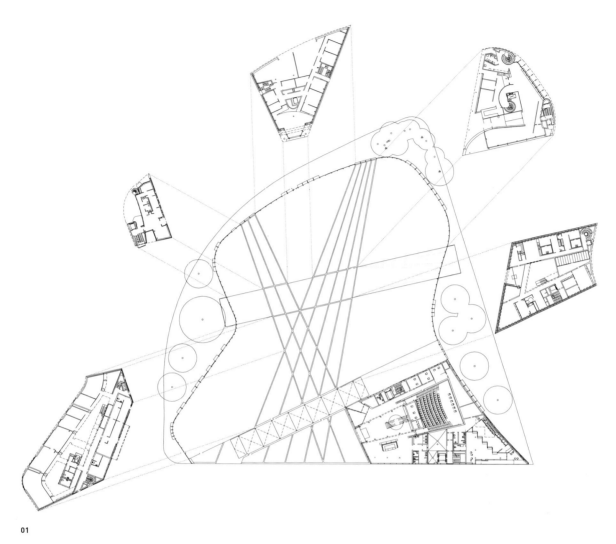

01

02

03

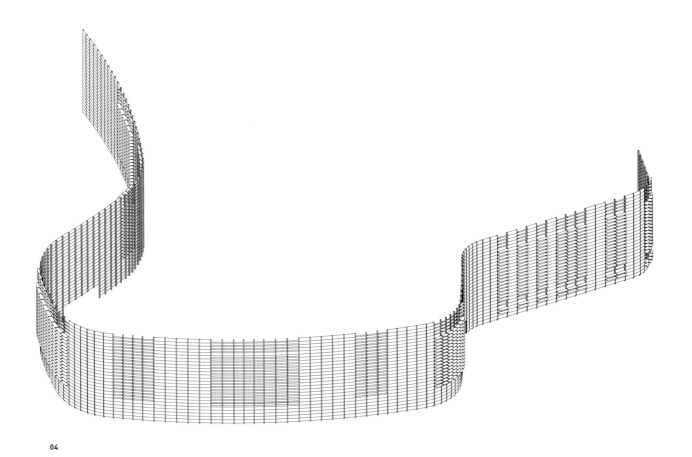

04

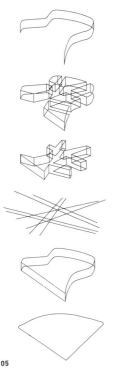

05

06

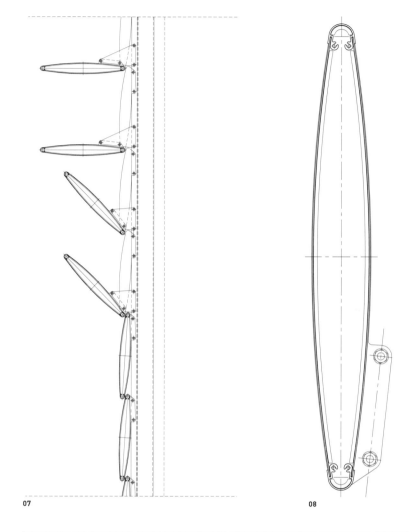

07

08

09

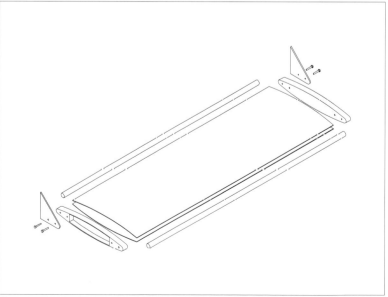

10

Sauna Pavilion

BERKSHIRE MOUNTAINS, MASSACHUSETTS // ARTIFACT DESIGN + CONSTRUCTION
COPPER CLADDING, THERMAL MOVEMENT, MATERIAL COMPATIBILITY

DESIGN INTENTION

This 600 square foot (55.74 sq. m) sauna is located on a small knoll at the end of a meadow, overlooking a pond. The small structure contains a dressing area, closet, outdoor shower, deck, and sauna chamber united under one flat roof plane. The plan spirals out from interior space to exterior space. Four distinct elements of the program are expressed through distinct materials or morphology: a platform that anchors and supports the facility (made of masonry foundation walls and stone pavers); the sauna cube (made of copper-clad wood); the skeletal frame containing transitional spaces (made of heavy frame with red cedar infill); and the folded planes (made of a shiplap screen). Each function of the building is articulated as a separate piece and each are clad appropriately in a material that serves the function.

MATERIALITY

The material palette for this project consists of natural and traditional materials, but with crisp contemporary detailing. Copper sheets, though clearly man-made, have been used for hundreds of years; they offer contemporary performance features without seeming trendy or of the moment. The timber-frame structure is constructed of glue-laminated pine columns and beams upon a slate-paved slab with a concrete block foundation wall. The sauna cube is a well-insulated room that is constructed of light-frame wood construction with copper cladding. Highlighted by its copper finish and surrounded by secondary planes of articulated red cedar boards, this enclosure at the end of the spiral plan becomes the focal building element.

The copper-clad sauna cube resembles a hot ember; it looks hot even when it is literally cold, metaphorically communicating the heat and insulating properties associated with this building, and reminding observers that this material is of mineral origin and was distilled using heat. Copper's conductivity and heat tolerance is well known, thus it seems appropriate cladding for the sauna.

The primary materials in this project will evolve with time, and the change is welcomed. The copper cladding was a light orange color when the building was completed, but will weather to a reddish brown, then dark brown, and eventually may patinate to green. The cedar will also change in color and sheen over time. The design intention was to acknowledge and symbolize changes in the inevitably aging human bodies of sauna users with these changes in the sauna materials.

TECHNICAL

More than any other architectural material, metals expand and contract with changes in temperature. Expansion joints or other types of movement joints are often needed to allow for thermal movement. In this case, the sauna's copper-clad exterior comes in direct contact with a harsh, cold environment, which could cause dramatic expansion and contraction in the metal if not accounted for in the design. Similarly, oil canning, which is the sometimes noisy twisting and warping of a metal surface that is not allowed to freely expand and contract as its temperature changes, may occur if detailing is inadequate.

Thermal movement is a prominent consideration for copper cladding systems because copper's coefficient of thermal expansion is greater than that of many other materials. This is especially so when the cladding application involves broad areas of copper, because the coefficient of expansion of a two-dimensional surface of a given material is twice that of linear expansion. Several features of this project address this potential for thermal movement of copper: the copper sheets are lapped and can move at seams; the wall to which the copper is applied is unusually well-insulated and layered, preventing the sauna's heat from substantially altering the temperature of the cladding even on a cold day; the dimensions of the clad walls are relatively small, the longest wall being just 10 ft. wide x 7.42 ft. tall (3.05 x 2.26 m), allowing accumulated movement to be minimal in such small dimensions. Below the copper are building wrap, .5 in. (13 mm) plywood backing, .75 in. (19 mm) furring strips, .75 in. (19 mm) plywood sheathing, and finally the 2x6 (51 x 152 mm) stud frame and insulation.

In addition to the copper's thermal movement, the designers also had to consider its placement in relation to the other prominent material in this facility, cedar, as the two are chemically incompatible. If in direct contact, or if precipitation crosses from the cedar to copper, the copper may deteriorate prematurely. The cedar is therefore never positioned in the path of water flowing toward the copper. The broad, flat roof even prevents acidic solutions from the overhanging evergreen canopies from harming the copper.

Designers working with metals must also consider the risk of bimetallic corrosion. Copper is among the most cathodic of metals, meaning that such metals as steel, stainless steel, aluminum, zinc, or magnesium would be subject to galvanic or bimetallic corrosion should they come into contact with copper. For this reason, the concealed screws securing the copper sheet to the plywood substrate are copper plated.

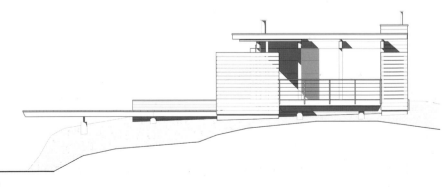

01   East elevation
02   Entry

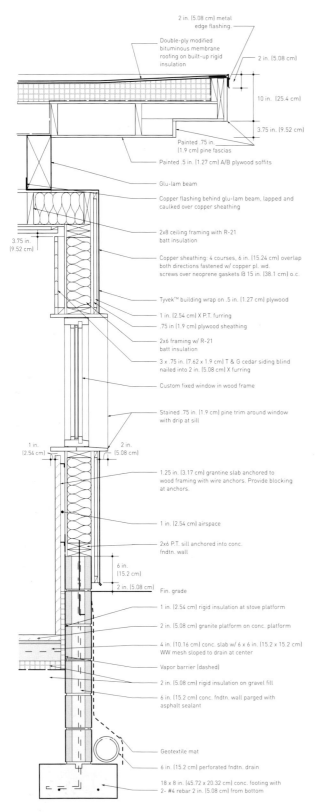

2 in. (5.08 cm) metal edge flashing.

Double-ply modified bituminous membrane roofing on built-up rigid insulation

2 in. (5.08 cm)

10 in. (25.4 cm)

3.75 in. (9.52 cm)

Painted .75 in. (1.9 cm) pine fascias

Painted .5 in. (1.27 cm) A/B plywood soffits

Glu-lam beam

Copper flashing behind glu-lam beam, lapped and caulked over copper sheathing

2x8 ceiling framing with R-21 batt insulation

3.75 in. (9.52 cm)

Copper sheathing: 4 courses, 6 in. (15.24 cm) overlap both directions fastened w/ copper pl. wd. screws over neoprene gaskets @ 15 in. (38.1 cm) o.c.

Tyvek™ building wrap on .5 in. (1.27 cm) plywood

1 in. (2.54 cm) X P.T. furring

.75 in (1.9 cm) plywood sheathing

2x6 framing w/ R-21 batt insulation

3 x .75 in. (7.62 x 1.9 cm) T & G cedar siding blind nailed into 2 in. (5.08 cm) X furring

Custom fixed window in wood frame

Stained .75 in. (1.9 cm) pine trim around window with drip at sill

1 in. (2.54 cm)

2 in. (5.08 cm)

1.25 in. (3.17 cm) granite slab anchored to wood framing with wire anchors. Provide blocking at anchors.

1 in. (2.54 cm) airspace

2x6 P.T. sill anchored into conc. fndtn. wall

6 in. (15.2 cm)

2 in. (5.08 cm)

Fin. grade

1 in. (2.54 cm) rigid insulation at stove platform

2 in. (5.08 cm) granite platform on conc. platform

4 in. (10.16 cm) conc. slab w/ 6 x 6 in. (15.2 x 15.2 cm) WW mesh sloped to drain at center

Vapor barrier (dashed)

2 in. (5.08 cm) rigid insulation on gravel fill

6 in. (15.2 cm) conc. fndtn. wall parged with asphalt sealant

Geotextile mat

6 in. (15.2 cm) perforated fndtn. drain

18 x 8 in. (45.72 x 20.32 cm) conc. footing with 2- #4 rebar 2 in. (5.08 cm) from bottom

03

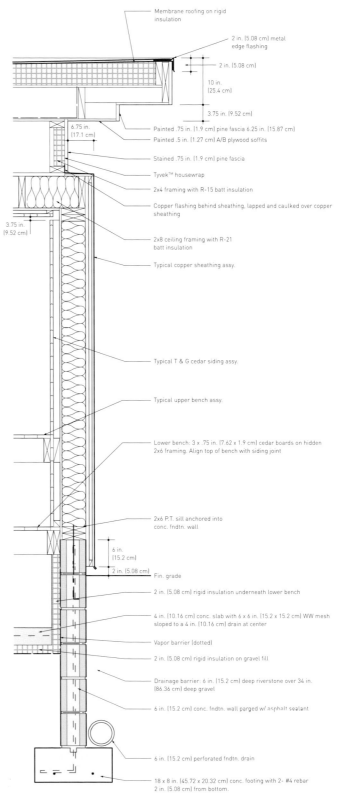

Membrane roofing on rigid insulation

2 in. (5.08 cm) metal edge flashing

2 in. (5.08 cm)

10 in. (25.4 cm)

3.75 in. (9.52 cm)

6.75 in. (17.1 cm)

Painted .75 in. (1.9 cm) pine fascia 6.25 in. (15.87 cm)

Painted .5 in. (1.27 cm) A/B plywood soffits

Stained .75 in. (1.9 cm) pine fascia

Tyvek™ housewrap

2x4 framing with R-15 batt insulation

Copper flashing behind sheathing, lapped and caulked over copper sheathing

2x8 ceiling framing with R-21 batt insulation

3.75 in. (9.52 cm)

Typical copper sheathing assy.

Typical T & G cedar siding assy.

Typical upper bench assy.

Lower bench: 3 x .75 in. (7.62 x 1.9 cm) cedar boards on hidden 2x6 framing. Align top of bench with siding joint

2x6 P.T. sill anchored into conc. fndtn. wall

6 in. (15.2 cm)

2 in. (5.08 cm)

Fin. grade

2 in. (5.08 cm) rigid insulation underneath lower bench

4 in. (10.16 cm) conc. slab with 6 x 6 in. (15.2 x 15.2 cm) WW mesh sloped to a 4 in. (10.16 cm) drain at center

Vapor barrier (dotted)

2 in. (5.08 cm) rigid insulation on gravel fill

Drainage barrier: 6 in. (15.2 cm) deep riverstone over 34 in. (86.36 cm) deep gravel

6 in. (15.2 cm) conc. fndtn. wall parged w/ asphalt sealant

6 in. (15.2 cm) perforated fndtn. drain

18 x 8 in. (45.72 x 20.32 cm) conc. footing with 2- #4 rebar 2 in. (5.08 cm) from bottom.

04

03 Copper wall section through window
04 Copper wall section
05 View from across pond
06 View from deck
07 Interior

05

06

07

Mining Archives

CLAUSTHAL-ZELLERFIELD, GERMANY // VON GERKAN, MARG AND PARTNERS
LEAD CLADDING, REGIONAL RESOURCE

DESIGN INTENTION

This archive building secures the extensive collection of documents on the technological and cultural history of the Harz Mountains in Germany. To protect the archival material from ultraviolet radiation and climatic variations, this portion of the building is a predominately windowless mass. The design inspiration was taken from the form of a book opened at a right angle. The horizontal side of the "book" houses the exhibition and lobby space. The tall vertical side holds the archives and research areas. Indigenous materials from this region are used extensively on the exterior of this building, celebrating the region's material resources.

MATERIALITY

The archive portion of the building is clad in lead panels, referencing the lead ore mining in the region and lending an added level of protection to the valued and vulnerable collection. Lead is associated with density and is known to be a barrier to forces seen and unseen. It is chosen for the archive portion of this building to symbolize security, and to express the beauty and utility of a mineral resource indigenous to this area. The panels are oriented vertically to be consistent with the verticality of this portion of the building. Larch wood, a local timber from the Harz Forest, sheaths the other vertical portion of the building, containing the circulation department and temporary storage for artifacts yet to be archived. Over time, the larch will weather to a light, silver-gray color, complementing the lead, which will weather to a dark gray tone as it ages.

Lead sheets must be cut to manageable weight and size, but most work is done in the field because the material is so easily formed due to its ductility. Though made of sheet metal, the lead cladding on this project demonstrates that it is handcrafted. Its surfaces and seams record the minor variations in its substrate and how it was handled during installation. Lead is protected from corrosion by intrinsic chemical resistance. It will not stain adjoining materials, but it will react with uncured cementitious materials, thus cannot be in direct contact with fresh concrete, mortar, or stucco. Lead cladding in this project is isolated from the concrete structure by a generous cavity and a wood isolating layer.

The thermal movement coefficient for lead is relatively high—approximately twice that of steel. Movement joints should therefore occur at close intervals in lead cladding systems. The largest dimension of lead sheet between expansion joints in this project is only 59 in. (150 cm).

TECHNICAL

The primary structural system in this building is reinforced concrete. All exterior 8 in. (20 cm) load-bearing walls are covered with 5 in. (12 cm) of insulation, which is then covered with a waterproof barrier. A 6 in. (16 cm) cavity separates the wood sheathing and lead cladding from the insulation; through this cavity moisture can condense and drain, and ambient air can naturally convect vertically. Subtle details occur continuously at the bottom and top of this cavity to permit air circulation and water drainage. This enhances the protective quality of the enclosure system and extends the service life of the cladding. Vertical wood furring strips support the sheathing at intervals of 24 in. (60 cm), which also coincides with the raised seams and cleats in the lead cladding.

Metal cladding consists of natural lead sheets measuring 24 x 59 in. (60 x 150 cm), arranged in vertical orientation, with horizontal seams that are staggered a dimension equal to the width of the sheet. The height and width of all building elevations are a multiple of the basic module of these lead sheets, with the columns at the base one module wide. The sheets are held in place with folded seams and cleats, rather than nailed or screwed, as such fasteners would concentrate stress and likely damage the soft metal. Cleats in lead cladding or roofing must be made of a compatible metal, such as lead, copper, or lead-coated copper. Openings in the lead-clad elevations occur at the seams in the cladding, harmonious with the cladding module.

01 Plan
02 West-east section
03 North elevation
04 West façade

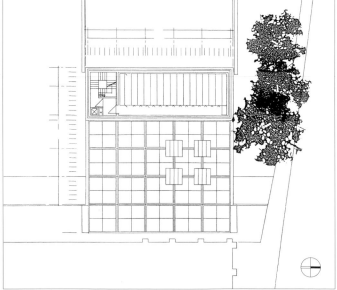

01

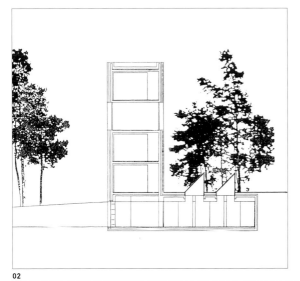

02

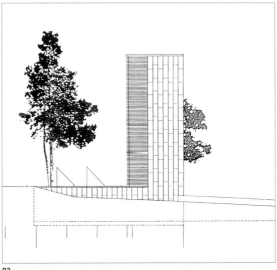

03

04

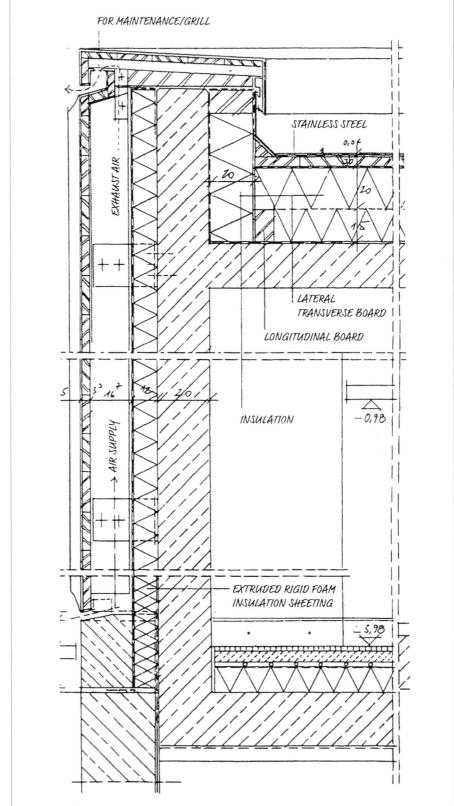

FOR MAINTENANCE/GRILL

STAINLESS STEEL

EXHAUST AIR

LATERAL
TRANSVERSE BOARD

LONGITUDINAL BOARD

AIR SUPPLY

INSULATION

EXTRUDED RIGID FOAM
INSULATION SHEETING

Melbourne Museum

MELBOURNE, AUSTRALIA // DENTON CORKER MARSHALL
PRE-WEATHERED ZINC, COMPOSITE PANELS

DESIGN INTENTION

This museum is a collection of different exhibition spaces that are devoted to collections of natural history and aboriginal cultures. The site is located in a public park adjacent to a neoclassical landmark, the Royal Exhibition Building. The design concept envisions the museum as a small town with two parallel "boulevards" running east-west, dictating the public circulation and the exhibition plan. A variety of cladding colors and textures create a compositional effect and an abstract expression of programmatic pieces.

MATERIALITY

A variety of metals are used to clad the various parts of this museum. The variation in materiality within a metal palette makes the various galleries more readable to visitors without being so dissimilar as to seem chaotic. Several different metal cladding types were used, each contributing a unique color and sheen, as well as a different set of physical properties that are matched to the technical criteria of the specific application. Metals used include zinc, aluminum, and Cor-ten steel; in addition, glass and cellulose fiber-reinforced compressed cement sheet cladding are used in some locations. Fastener strategies also vary in this facility to further distinguish the elements of the program or to address technical criteria. Adjoining panels also vary in how they meet, sometimes abutting and in other applications having either a .20 or .40 in. (5 or 10 mm) reveal. These differences affect the way that the observer reads the material.

Zinc-clad panels were placed on the exterior and interior of the museum. The metal was supplied pre-weathered by its manufacturer; its natural bluish gray color adds to the palette of the building. Zinc is a brittle, relatively low-strength metal that is highly resistant to atmospheric corrosion (though it is vulnerable to acids and alkalis), making it a poor structural choice but excellent for cladding purposes. When exposed to air, a film of zinc carbonate or oxide forms on the surface, protecting it from further oxidation. It has a long life span when left natural and exposed.

Because the strength of zinc is relatively low compared to other metals, composite panels were made using thin zinc sheets attached to a plywood core. These panels were attached to the building using concealed connections in a running bond configuration. Horizontal and vertical overlapping flanges allow for independent movement of the panels as they undergo thermal movement, especially vital on the sunny side of the building. Oxidized zinc is also used for the interior finish surface; etched commissioned artwork was applied to the zinc panels.

Composite panels take advantage of the special properties of each material making up its layered assembly. In this project relatively thin metal sheets are used on exposed surfaces, taking advantage of their attractive appearance and durability. The inexpensive plywood core gives the metal continuous support to avoid buckling, and is readily configured to the appropriate flat or curved shape. If the metals were used without such backing, they would need to be much thicker to have sufficient stiffness, a costly and unwise use of material resources.

Though crisp and refined in finished appearance, this project did not rely on costly or highly specialized means of production. Sheets of the various metals were delivered to the site, as was the plywood backing. Fabrication of the composite panels was carried out at the site using relatively simple means. This allowed fabrication of pieces to be adjusted as needed to meet conditions in the field.

TECHNICAL

Inclined exterior zinc-faced composite panels consist of .03 in. (.8 mm) pre-weathered Rheinzinc panels adhered to .35 in. (9 mm) waterproof plywood, with a synthetic rubber membrane on the inner face. The zinc sheets wrap the corners of the plywood in a proprietary overlap system. Panel sizes are generally 16 ft. wide x 3 ft. tall (4.9 x .9 m). Composite panels were fabricated at the construction site. Composite panels are applied in flat planes, but are also applied in simple curved shapes. Joints between these panels are a .39 in. (10 mm) reveal horizontally and vertically. Panels are secured using proprietary concealed fasteners.

Interior zinc-faced composite panels consist of .08 in. (2 mm) mill-finished zinc panels laminated to .47 in. (12 mm) plywood, with a .02 in. (.6 mm) aluminum backing. These panels are buttjointed to a metal-framed wall using concealed fixing brackets. The composite panels use .12 in. (3 mm) thick oxidized zinc sheets. In some locations, these interior panels are etched with commissioned artwork.

Zinc-clad panels on the exterior and interior of the building are secured using concealed screws to the subframe. This distinguishes the zinc cladding from some others in the facility, which use an expressed stainless steel screw fastener, raised in a .79 in. (20 mm) aluminum custom fitting, a trademark detail used by this architect.

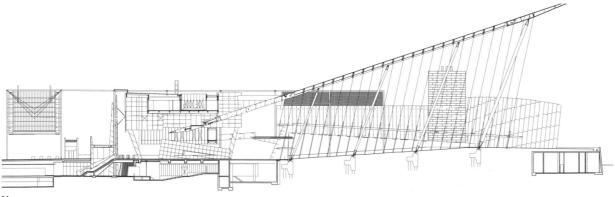

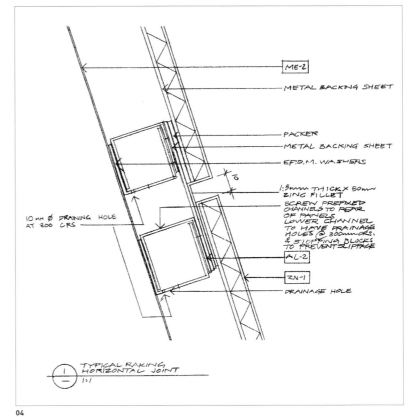

04

02

03

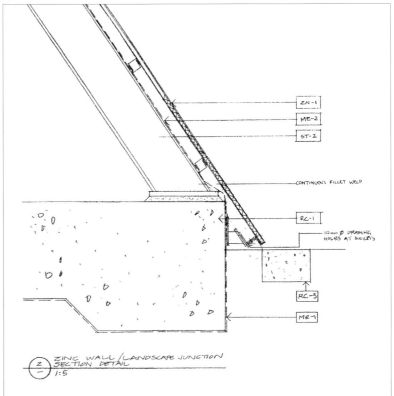

05

PLASTICS

THE BASICS

Plastics are lightweight, resilient, generally resistant to corrosion and moisture, and can be molded and formed into complex shapes. The material is relatively new to the construction industry, although recently there has been extraordinary growth in their use in building construction. Plastics can be generally defined as chainlike molecular structures that are made by either altering natural products or by transforming petroleum, natural gas, or coal products into an object. Most synthetic plastics, however, are made from distilled crude oil, accounting for approximately 8 percent of the world's application of oil resources. All plastics contain carbon, which has the ability to combine with other atoms to form rings or chains at the chemical level. A long chain of molecules is called a *polymer* and a short chain is called a *monomer*. A polymer is a chain of molecules that can be opaque, transparent, or translucent; it is capable of being molded, extruded, cast, or drawn into filaments.

Plastics are more generally defined by two types, *thermoplastics* and *thermosetting* plastics (see page XX), which indicate the way in which heat is involved in their formation. Thermoplastics will deform under heat or pressure and can be reformed into new shapes multiple times. Thermosetting plastics, after being set and formed, will not break down under heat to their constituent chemicals for re-formation; however, these plastics can be used in higher temperature situations.

Materialistically, synthetic polymers, or plastics, have a short history, yet have transformed almost every industry since their invention, including medicine, electronics, aeronautics, fashion, engineering, and construction, to name just a few. In building and construction, plastics were first used as ornament, superficial finish, or as secondary parts for enclosure systems. Only recently have they begun to gain respect and appreciation as a viable primary material, today offering a wider scope of uses such as interior finishes, glazing, plumbing fixtures, and even structural components. Compared to other construction materials, plastics have a lower fire-rating and their use in applications requiring fire resistance are limited. Some of the advantages plastics can offer is that they are lightweight, lower in cost, resistant to corrosion and moisture, can be relatively strong, and are readily shaped. Their reputation as a short-lived fad that is brittle and prone to discolor has recently been revised due to enormous advances in the plastics industry, which has manufactured an unprecedented variety of new products with improved physical properties. Manufacturers are now collaborating with designers to produce higher quality materials and a much broader range of products, particularly for glazing and finishing applications in buildings. Since the material is intrinsically man-made, its characteristics are not limited and will continue to expand. It is highly malleable and changeable, and its depth in color and opacity are equally varied. It has become a design tool of which many architects have taken advantage.

HISTORY

Plastics were first formulated in the nineteenth century, although significant advancements did not occur until well into the twentieth. In 1836 Charles Goodyear processed rubber, which is a natural polymer type of plastic, by treating it chemically with sulfur. The first plastic made from organic material, cellulose, was debuted twenty-eight years later at the Great International Exhibition in London by Alexander Parkes. Parkes's remarkable material, aptly named Pareksine, was moldable under heat and hardened when cooled. It could be transparent or opaque and sculpted into any imaginable shape. It was touted as having all the qualities of rubber yet was less expensive; unfortunately, Parkes's investors ceased funding the product, ironically, due to its high production costs.

The first completely man-made synthetic material was discovered in 1907 by a chemist named Leo Baekeland in New York. He created a thermosetting liquid resin, dubbed Bakelite. It was electrically resistant, chemically stable, heat-resistant, shatterproof, and impervious to cracking or fading. Bakelite came to be used in many applications and is still used today as an electrical insulator or is added to wood to make it more durable. The U.S. military began using it to produce lightweight war machinery and weaponry that was superior to steel, and by World War II was used in many weapons and equipment.

The 1920s was a time of great plastics innovation and invention. Petroleum and natural gas refinement increased, shepherding in a new level of experimentation and discovery of uses for insulation, molded parts, and chemical- and water-resistant products. DuPont was an industry leader, employing chemists who became responsible for the invention of many plastics taken for granted today, such as Nylon and Teflon. Waldo Simon, a chemist at B. F. Goodrich, discovered and developed polyvinyl chloride (PVC), or vinyl, which became an immensely versatile product in the building industry, still commonly used today for components such as pipes, flooring, and siding, among others.

In 1933 two organic chemists stumbled upon perhaps the most significant plastic invention. E. W. Fawcett and R. O. Gibson, working for the Imperial Chemical Industries Research Laboratory, accidentally discovered polyethylene, a product that subsequently came to play a key role in World War II for insulating radar and other military applications. Polyethylene was the first plastic in the U.S. to sell over a billion pounds per year, and continues to be the highest selling plastic in the world today. It is most commonly seen in soda bottles, milk jugs, plastic food storage containers, grocery bags, and many other common objects, but it is also widely used in construction in the form of films and sheets.

Another common plastic, Nylon, became widely used in the 1940s, in everything from women's stockings to military uses. In 1957 a Swiss engineer named George de Maestral invented Velcro, using nylon hooks and loops to revolutionize many common products. The 1950s also brought plastics more commonly to the clothing industry with the use of Lycra and polyester. Laminates such as Formica and molded melamine formaldehyde resin were becoming widely used in furniture and dishware. Tupperware, a polyethylene, was first introduced and quickly became a household name.

In 1956 polyester and fiberglass were used for car and boat body parts. By the 1960s, plastics began to play a critical role in spacecraft parts and computer equipment. The 1970s brought more plastics to the consumer with more selections in housing interiors, clothing, household products, furniture, and electronic products.

As computer technology grew, plastics became even more significant, becoming commonplace as the growth of fiber optic cables and telephone cables were made. Indeed, each decade since the 1950s has brought new and unheralded advances to the plastics industry, making it one of the most ubiquitous materials in the world.

DESIGN CONSIDERATIONS

Plastic is a generic term used to describe several chemical compounds. The most common are polyethylene, polyurethane, polystyrene, polycarbonate, polyvinyl, and polypropylene. As a group, these share many common characteristics, such as their ability to achieve different levels of transparency and color. Plastics typically have a high coefficient of thermal expansion, so construction details must allow for a substantial amount of expansion and contraction due to temperature changes. Plastics are easily cut, formed, and bent, and some are fire-resistant or classified as slow-burning.

The building and construction industry is the second largest consumer of plastics, closely behind the packaging industry. Plastics play an integral role in construction due to their durability, high performance, easy handling, and low cost. They continue to proliferate in the construction of all building types, but most particularly residential buildings. We commonly see plastics in construction today in plumbing fixtures, siding, flooring, insulation, doors, windows, railings, lighting, and glazing, and the list continues to grow. They are also used to modify the properties of other, more traditional construction materials, but recently they have replaced traditional materials altogether in many conditions, largely due to their lower cost, excellent corrosion resistance, and light weight. Additionally, one of the biggest advantages of plastics is their ability to be shaped into limitless forms. Plastics are generally lower density than other building materials, while their strength-to-weight ratio is typically higher. They are usually less affected by water or decay and have a lower thermal and electrical conductivity. Most plastics can be formed and finished to mimic another material, making them popular substitutive options. They can be joined with heat, mechanically with screws or bolts, or by snapping interlocking pieces together with no fasteners. Heat or solvents can be used to soften plastics, allowing two members to harden together and join.

The largest disadvantage to plastics in building applications is that they can be destroyed by fire and may give off toxic gasses. Given the wide range of plastics, all perform differently when subjected to fire. Some plastics burn and create a dense toxic smoke, while others produce combustible vapors, and still others melt. Some plastics are slow burning, such as the acrylics, polystyrene, polyethylene, and cellulose plastics, while others such as the silicones have substantial fire resistance. Rigid PVC is *intumescent*, meaning it burns but becomes self-extinguishing, so the fire is not sustained. Fire ratings depend on the type of plastic, its thickness, and its coating. Many plastics have flame-retardants or resins applied to their surface to increase fire resistance. Ratings exist for flame spread, smoke development, and toxicity of combustion products, all of which should be checked before installation of any plastic, especially for interior applications.

Other disadvantages to plastics include a high level of deformation, expansion, and contraction due to thermal changes, making control joints, expansion joints, and other measures of controlling volume change critical. Compared to other construction materials, plastics are not stiff, and they deflect under heavy load conditions, especially under prolonged loading. Plastics can also be scratched or become brittle if protective films or layers are not added to their surface. Hazing and discoloration can also occur due to age or environmental exposure such as ultraviolet light. This has increasingly become less prevalent with advances in the protective agents that are placed on or in plastics to prevent changes in color or transparency.

TYPES

Plastics fall into two general categories: *thermoplastic* and *thermosetting* plastics. *Thermoplastics*, which include acrylics, nylons, vinyls, polycarbonates, and polystyrenes, are generally linear molecules and will hold their shape at normal temperatures but can be re-formed or re-molded into new shapes when placed under high temperatures. These plastics are recyclable and regain their original properties after being cooled again. They are used for glazing, pipes, vapor barriers, flooring, lighting fixtures, and foam insulation. *Thermosetting* plastics, which include epoxies, melamines, polyurethanes, and silicones, have a more complex molecular structure that is cross-linked in three-dimensions. They can only be formed once and cannot be returned to their basic components through reheating; once they have set or cured, they remain rigid. Thermosetting plastics are generally harder and stronger than thermoplastics. Typical applications of these are for adhesives, laminates, rigid foam insulation, waterproofing membranes, and window frames, among others. Three types of thermoplastics are most often used in building construction:

POLYVINYL CHLORIDE

Polyvinyl chloride, generally called PVC or vinyl, is the most commonly used plastic in building construction. It is resistant to water and some chemicals, is low in cost, and is resistant to tearing. *Rigid* PVC is used most often for hot and cold water pipes, rain gutters, ducts, window frames, tiles, and panels. *Flexible* PVC is used for flexible tubing or hoses, flashing, films, sheets, or floor tiles. Although most rigid PVC is self-extinguishing when exposed to fire, and flexible grades will burn slowly, it cannot be used for purposes with high temperatures, with the highest temperature in some grades being 212 degrees F (100 degrees C).

POLYCARBONATE

Polycarbonate is often used as a substitute for glass. Depending on its color and thickness, different desired levels of light can be achieved, ranging from 35–50 percent light transmission for white sheets and up to 88 percent for clear sheets. It is also half the weight of standard architectural glass. It has one of the highest impact resistances of the thermoplastics; its impact strength over glass is excellent and has over fifteen times greater impact resistance than even high-impact acrylics. It can maintain transparency up to two inches thick, has good dimensional and thermal stability, and is stain resistant. Polycarbonate is commercially available even in remote locations and can easily be installed by unskilled workers using commonly available tools and fasteners such as nails and screws. Polycarbonate panels are also easily cleaned, making them a good choice for an urban environment.

Polycarbonate has a thermal expansion coefficient that is eight times higher than that of glass. This movement must be compensated for in detailing and sheet size selection. If polycarbonate is not treated with a UV protective layer on one or both sides, it will discolor. Polycarbonate panels, such as Lexan and Polygal, come in a wide range of thicknesses, shapes, colors, and specific solar and thermal resistance features. They offer the designer choices because of their varied light transmission, from opaque to translucent to virtually trans-parent. They also provide inexpensive moderate thermal insulation with the use of the multiwalled sheets. They are lightweight, easy to install, and are 100% recyclable. However, they are vulnerable to alkalis and aromatic hydrocarbon. Polycarbonate maintains its properties over a wide range of temperatures, from -40 to 280 degrees F (-40–138 degrees C).

Acrylic, such as plexiglass or acrylite, is a thermoplastic that is most commonly used for skylights, light fixtures, and other glazing applications. Some of the common trade names include Lucite, Perspex, and Plexiglas. Its most valuable characteristic is its transparency, allowing as much as 92 percent overall light transmission. An acrylic sheet is eight to ten times stronger than glass of the same thickness, though acrylics can scratch more easily than glass. Acrylic is easily fabricated and machined and when heated can be formed into different shapes. It has good resistance to weather, heat, and chemicals, however it is combustible. Acrylic sheet is lightweight—usually less than half the weight of a piece of glass—and has moderate resistance to shrinkage and dimensional instability.

Plexiglas was originally a trade name for acrylic plastics (much like Lucite), but today plexiglass has become a common manner of identifying this type of plastic, the chemical name for which is polymethyl methacrylate. At room temperature, plexiglass is solid and glasslike, but at very low temperatures it becomes brittle and is easily shattered. Ultraviolet light-inhibiting coatings can be applied during manufacturing to increase its life-span. Its strength can be enhanced by the use of an additive during its formative chemical reaction, yielding a high-impact acrylic. The unique chemical structure of plexiglass makes its physical properties of clear visibility and hardness an ideal choice for some architectural applications, such as skylights, windows, or signage.

MODIFIERS AND ADDITIVES

More than any other construction material, plastics are formulated to yield specific physical properties. Modifiers and fillers are added to base plastics to produce optimum properties in the finished product.

→ **Plasticizers** are organic compounds that are added to reduce brittleness and provide flexibility and softness.

→ **Stabilizers** are organic compounds added to reduce deterioration from the effects of sunlight, weathering, heat, and other volatile conditions.

→ **Fillers** are non-reacting materials usually added to reduce costs or to improve hardness or resistance to heat or electrical current. Talc and marble dust are two common fillers.

→ **Extenders** are waxes or oils added to give bulk and reduce costs.

→ **Reinforcing fibers**—glass, metal, carbon, or any other material fibers—can be added to increase strength, hardness, stiffness, resistance, and other improvements for a given condition.

→ **Flame retarders** are chemical additives usually added to plastics used in interior spaces or areas near electrical appliances in buildings.

PROCESSING METHODS

There are many ways to process plastics; below are five of the main methods:

→ **Injection molding** allows for a wide range of opportunities in designing and creating any plastic form. Polymer pellets are placed into a hopper and then heated to form a liquid resin, which is then injected into a mold and then cooled. *Co-injection* is when two colors or materials are injected into a mold for a two-color or two-finish product. Although initial production expenses can be high, this process results in a high volume of products at a relatively fast rate, yielding low unit costs. Examples of injection molded products are electrical boxes, exit signs, computer casings, foam plastic, Lego brand toys, and plastic cutlery.

→ **Casting** begins with a liquid form rather than a granule or pellet. It is not normally used in mass production, but rather to produce a higher quality plastic product. It is however one of the simplest and most accessible means of producing a custom designed plastic form. A casting mold is first made from either soft or rigid materials, then the plastic is placed and set. Typical casting plastics include epoxy, polyester, synthetic resins, and acrylics. If a mold can be created, the casting process allows for an almost endless range of shapes to be produced.

→ **Extrusion** is most often used for the production of thermoplastic pipes, sheets, films, and unusual shapes. Their lengths can vary greatly, but extrusions are consistent in cross section. The extrusion process is fairly simple to visualize: granulated polymers, or pellets, which can sometimes be in a powder form, are placed into a hopper, where they are heated and then pushed through a shaped die by a rotating screw. The material is pushed through different temperature zones, where it is cooled by water or air and is condensed, plasticized, and homogenized. A continuous shape is produced and then cut to the desired length. Some examples of extruded plastics include window frames, siding, pipes, and any long shape that has a consistent profile, even if complex. The processing cost is low compared to injection molding, but manufacturers require a minimum order length to justify die fabrication. *Pultrusion* is a variation of the same concept, except the plastic is pulled rather than pushed through the die.

→ **Blow molding** is a variation of the extrusion process, in which large thermoplastic objects can be produced by blowing the plastic through a die against a mold. This process is much like blowing up a balloon made of plastic within a mold, thus creating the shape of the object. Air pressure forces softened vinyl or other plastics into a hollow mold or die to create specific forms, such as plastic bottles.

→ **Calendering** involves taking plastic pellets and feeding them through hot rollers, forming a sheet or film of a desired thickness, then feeding it through cold rollers. The rolling temperature is a primary factor in the plastic's ability to be molded. Embossing the hot rollers allows for any desired textures or patterns to be imprinted on the plastic. Films of polyvinyl chloride (PVC), sheets of polycarbonate, and laminates are created in this manner, for use as flooring, wall covering, and other fabric-like applications.

Shiloh Bus Shelter

ASHEVILLE, NORTH CAROLINA, USA // DESIGN CORPS SUMMER DESIGN/BUILD STUDIO
POLYCARBONATE SHEETS, SAND BLASTING, IMPACT RESISTANCE

DESIGN INTENTION

This project developed when a group of residents in a North Carolina mountain neighborhood called Shiloh requested that architecture students design and build a bus shelter adjacent to their community center and in the local park. The residents helped select the location, at one edge of the park under a Sweet Gum tree and near a stream. They also developed the program with the design students: a bus shelter, a landmark for the community, and a gateway for the park. The community also requested that the materials be durable, despite the limited budget and student skill-levels being pre-professional.

The program had to balance the typical needs of a bus shelter: protection from rain, sun, and wind without creating a hangout for drug dealers or hiding the natural beauty of the site. The two primary sheathing materials, polycarbonate (Lexan) plastic and Alucobond aluminum sandwich panels, were selected to shed water; they are also low mainte-nance and create a rich language of light and reflection. The west-facing screen wall and roof are a compositions of clear plastic, sanded plastic, and aluminum, providing a site-specific arrangement of the opaque, the translucent, and the transparent. In the two-stepped roof, western light reflects off of the aluminum under the sanded plastic.

MATERIALITY

Polycarbonate sheets were used for three main properties: 1) transpar-ency; 2) translucency where shade was needed; and 3) physical flexibility. The transparency of the material met the requirements of the project by allowing "eyes on the street" to see who was in the shelter at all times. The project also required that a person in the shelter would be able to see when a bus was coming and for the bus driver to know if anyone was waiting.

The unique nature of polycarbonate allows for the same material to be easily modified, either left in its natural clear state or sanded to

transmit less light, as in this case, allowing for shade through the roof and walls. All of the details for securing the polycarbonate could be consistent for either condition.

Polycarbonate sheets are flexible, which allowed it to be woven through the steel tube screen. Facing west, this was needed to provide shade while allowing breezes to permeate the structure for cooling. The edge detail was minimal. Polycarbonate is relatively strong, is easily cleaned, and is weather resistant, giving it a relatively long lifespan with little need for maintenance.

TECHNICAL

Lexan is a polycarbonate resin thermoplastic produced by General Electric. It comes in many colors, thicknesses, and profiles, and is a versatile and durable polymer. One of the attributes of polycarbonate sheets that met the community's request for durability is its high impact resistance through a great temperature range, from very cold to very hot temperatures. The manufacturer's product information claims that it is shatter-resistant and virtually unbreakable. With the increased strength of polycarbonate, many walls and roofs can be made with thinner and lighter in weight. In this application, .25 in. (6 mm) thickness was selected. Additionally it is resistant to exposure from the ultraviolet rays of the sun.

Polycarbonate can be fabricated with common carpentry tools. For this project, a "rabbet" detail was developed that allowed the use of smaller, less-expensive sheets and that could allow for expansion and contraction. This detail was also used for the aluminum composite panels, fulfilling the design objective for both surfaces to appear seamless. The over-lapping joint was milled on a router, with two edges of each sheet milled to interlock. Several sandblasting techniques were attempted before a process was selected to "frost" the surface to the desired level of translucence.

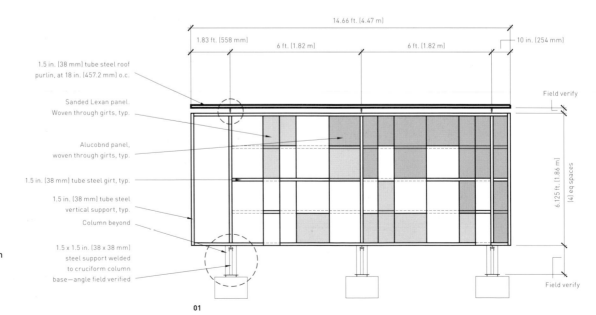

1.5 in. (38 mm) tube steel roof purlin, at 18 in. (457.2 mm) o.c.

Sanded Lexan panel. Woven through girts, typ.

Alucobnd panel, woven through girts, typ.

1.5 in. (38 mm) tube steel girt, typ.

1.5 in. (38 mm) tube steel vertical support, typ.

Column beyond

1.5 x 1.5 in. (38 x 38 mm) steel support welded to cruciform column base—angle field verified

14.66 ft. (4.47 m)
1.83 ft. (558 mm)
6 ft. (1.82 m)
6 ft. (1.82 m)
10 in. (254 mm)
Field verify
6.125 ft. (1.86 m)
(4) eq spaces
Field verify

01 North-south section
02 East elevation
03 West elevation
04 Lexan detail

01

02

03

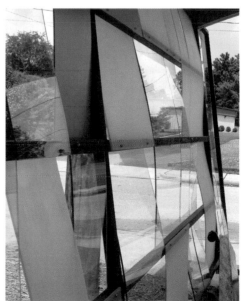

04

05 Alucobond lower-roof plan
06 Lexan upper-roof plan
07 Wall with different transparencies
08 Roof shadows
09 North (street) elevation
10 West elevation
11 Rabbet-detail section
12 Rabbet-detail section

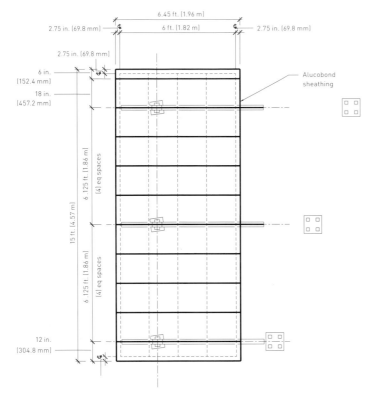

6.45 ft. [1.96 m]

2.75 in. [69.8 mm]   6 ft. [1.82 m]   2.75 in. [69.8 mm]

2.75 in. [69.8 mm]

6 in. [152.4 mm]

18 in. [457.2 mm]

Alucobond sheathing

6.125 ft. [1.86 m] (4) eq spaces

15 ft. [4.57 m]

6.125 ft. [1.86 m] (4) eq spaces

12 in. [304.8 mm]

05

07

10.89 ft [3.32 m]

2.75 in. [69.8 mm]   6.23 ft. [1.89 m]   4.66 ft. [1.42 m]

6 in. [152.4 mm]

18 in. [457.2 mm]

72°

6.125 ft [1.86 m] (4) eq spaces

15 ft. [4.57 m]

2 ft. [609.6 mm]

15.81 ft [4.81 m]

6.125 ft [1.86 m] (4) eq spaces

108°

1 in. [25.4 mm]

Lexan sheathing

5.89 [1.79 m]

06

08

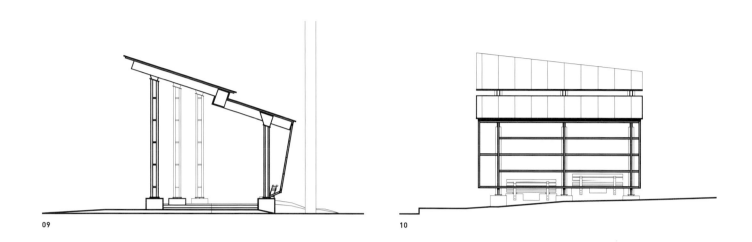

09

10

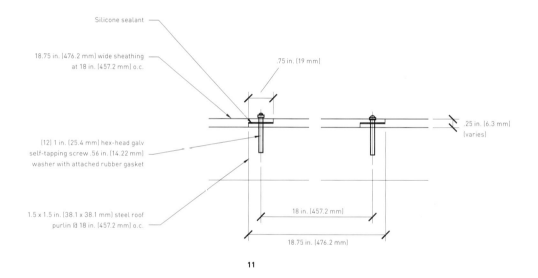

Silicone sealant

18.75 in. (476.2 mm) wide sheathing
at 18 in. (457.2 mm) o.c.

.75 in. (19 mm)

[12] 1 in. (25.4 mm) hex-head galv
self-tapping screw .56 in. (14.22 mm)
washer with attached rubber gasket

.25 in. (6.3 mm)
(varies)

1.5 x 1.5 in. (38.1 x 38.1 mm) steel roof
purlin @ 18 in. (457.2 mm) o.c.

18 in. (457.2 mm)

18.75 in. (476.2 mm)

11

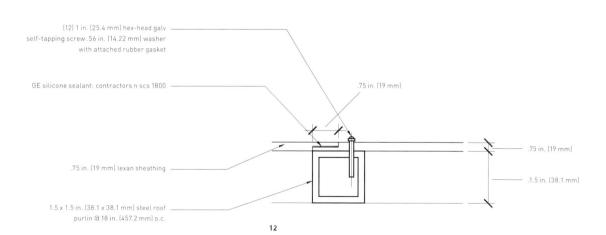

[12] 1 in. (25.4 mm) hex-head galv
self-tapping screw .56 in. (14.22 mm) washer
with attached rubber gasket

.75 in. (19 mm)

GE silicone sealant: contractors n scs 1800

.75 in. (19 mm)

.75 in. (19 mm) lexan sheathing

1.5 x 1.5 in. (38.1 x 38.1 mm) steel roof
purlin @ 18 in. (457.2 mm) o.c.

1.5 in. (38.1 mm)

12

Church in Urubo

URUBO, BOLIVIA // LIGHT: JAE CHA
EXTRUDED POLYCARBONATE CLADDING, LIGHT TRANSMITTANCE

DESIGN INTENTION

This 1,250-square-foot (113-sq. m) church is located a short distance from Santa Cruz, Bolivia, in a rural village where most of the people live in traditional mud huts. Most of the men in this economically challenged village travel to their work in the city and are sometimes gone for weeks. The community did not have any spaces for public meetings or any other type of large gathering. This structure was therefore designed to be used mainly by women and children as a kindergarten, a marketplace, and a church. Due to its remoteness and modest economic means, this region has a limited selection of building materials available to it, requiring that materials selected be few and conventional. The design concept was to create a circular plan that is equally open on all sides to symbolize the acceptance of anyone to participate freely in the space, regardless of background, lifestyle, attitude, or religion. The plan allows for stools and benches to be moved and placed anywhere, unlike the prescribed, fixed seating in conventional church design. The design and planning of this structure took eight months, but the church was built in only ten days by congregation members, local skilled workers, and volunteers recruited by the architect from the U.S.

MATERIALITY

Using two simple locally available and affordable materials—pressure-treated timber as structure and translucent polycarbonate sheeting—this building creates a feeling of transience through its use of light and space. Polycarbonate sheets were positioned on site to determine the best patterns of light and shade as the sun moves over the building. Using different layering techniques and by varying the pattern of open and closed panels, views were framed and the level of light within was coordinated with the structure's position on the site. With the simplest materials, construction methods, and detailing, this building becomes a sculpture of light using the lightweight translucent panels.

This project is an elemental, tentlike assembly of frame and skin. Loads are carried only by the wood frame; the polycarbonate cladding does not contribute to the structural stability, and furthermore is incomplete, implying an envelope more than actually functioning as one. Rigid moment connections are used to provide lateral stability to the frame, allowing the wall cladding to be free of structural sheathing or diagonal bracing. This freedom from structural obligation, combined with an interest in an open skin, led to this unusual solution. The simple palette of materials and ease of assembly made construction by an unskilled workforce possible.

TECHNICAL

The polycarbonate sheets are extruded with a corrugated profile, increasing the longitudinal stiffness of the sheets but leaving lateral stiffness unchanged. The design exploits this by installing the cladding with its stiff axis oriented vertically to span 2.75 ft. (84 cm) without backing, but curving the panel in its weak horizontal axis. The sheets clad approximately 50 percent of the area of the inner and outer cylinder surfaces. Cumulatively, approximately 85 percent of the wall area is clad with at least one layer of polycarbonate.

Wood framing that supports the cladding is located at intervals of 4.75 ft. (1.45 m) on-center horizontally, and 2.75 ft. (.84 m) on-center vertically. Polycarbonate panels are cut to match these dimensions, with a small overlap if meeting another panel. If lapped vertically, the upper panel overlaps the lower panel.

A *moment frame* is a skeletal but rigid assembly of columns and beams in the superstructure, and is intrinsic to such construction processes as cast-in-place concrete frames and some welded steel frames. A *moment connection*, or *rigid connection*, is one in which two structural members are highly resistant to rotation between the members. Rigidity can be achieved in a frame by imbedding continuous vertical members in stable geological materials. More often it is achieved by using shear walls, bracing, or by creating moment connections in the superstructure. A stiff sheathing material can stabilize the frame, but in this case it does not. Instead, the frame is made stable by using rigid joints that prevent rotation between horizontal and vertical members.

01 Elevation
02 Plan
03 View from the south
04 Interior circulation
05 View from the interior

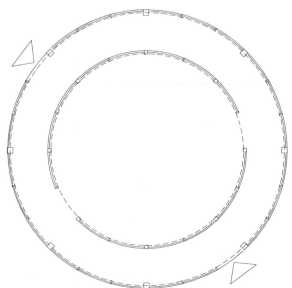

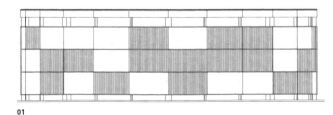

01

02

03

04

05

Colmenarejo Municipal Hall

COLMENAREJO, SPAIN // ABALOS + HERREROS
CORRUGATED POLYCARBONATE CLADDING

DESIGN INTENTION

This municipal hall is located in a small community within metropolitan Madrid. In danger of being subsumed by the sprawling city, this civic building is intended to give an identity to this once fragmented small town. The main goal was to strengthen civic pride by creating a meeting facility as an extension of the public square. The inclusion of natural and man-made materials creates a provocative juxtaposition, through which the designers hoped to create a representation of the organic and the artificial, or the old and the new, symbolizing the state of this small village that is struggling to resolve the traditions of its past with the immediacy of its future.

MATERIALITY

White corrugated polycarbonate is used to sheath the exterior of the building facing the public square, creating a minimal, simple face, yet also giving the public square a fresh new facade. Woven plant materials sheath the interior of the wall cladding, referencing the natural and old. The designers strongly advocate using a material palette that is recyclable, biodegradable, or otherwise environmentally appropriate. Here, the twig mats are biodegradable and the steel and polycarbonate are recyclable. Thermoplastics such as polycarbonate are very slow to biodegrade, but they can be returned to the production process for reuse.

Polycarbonate cladding is technically appropriate for this project because it is a precipitation barrier, protecting the organic plant screens, while its translucency provides needed illumination to the interior. It is symbolically appropriate because it embodies the contemporary spirit of the village, and associates the public square with the interior of the municipal building.

TECHNICAL

The primary facade of this small municipal building adjoins the public square. It uses luminous materials and a series of pivoting panels to achieve a high degree of spatial continuity between the village square and the building interior. Pivoting doors are framed with steel tube sections, and are clad identically on inner and outer faces with matching polycarbonate panels. Each door is 8.73 ft. (2.66 m) tall and 6.56 ft. (2 m) wide. The corrugated polycarbonate panels are 3.28 ft. (1 m) tall and the full width of the facade. They have a corrugation profile of 1.96 in. (50 mm) and a cycle of 7.48 in. (190 mm), making it stiff enough to span more than 6.56 ft. (2 m) between studs.

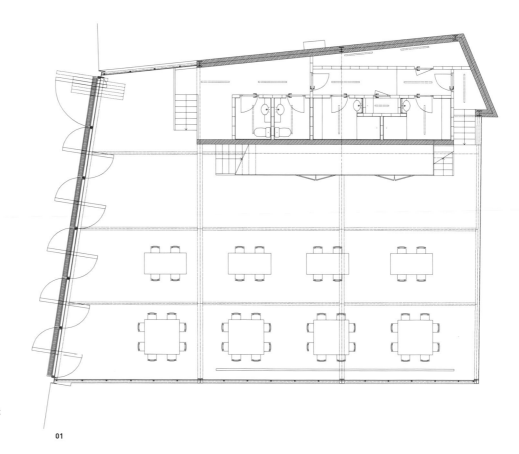

01   Ground-floor plan
02   Interior view of entry facade
03   Exterior view of entry facade, night
04   Interior view of meeting space

01

02

03

04

05

06

07

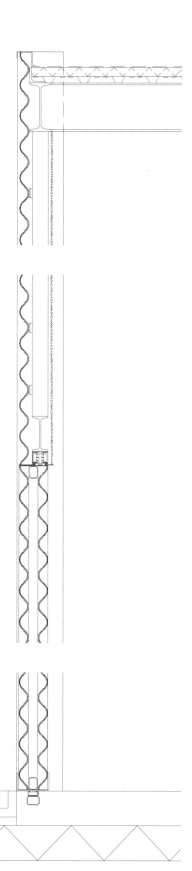

08

09

Ma Atelier and Gallery

FUKUOKA PREFECTURE, KYUSHU, JAPAN // HIROYUKI ARIMA + URBAN FOURTH
CORRUGATED POLYCARBONATE CLADDING, TRANSLUCENCY

DESIGN INTENTION

This artist's gallery and workshop is located on a rocky hillside of the southern-most island of the Japanese archipelago. Five box-shaped volumes are linked together on a sloped site to create interconnected spaces framing views to the surrounding landscape. The gallery spaces are usually used for exhibitions but also host different functions such as concerts and readings. The roof serves as both an exhibit space and a scenic outlook where one can see distant views of the Genkal Sea and outlying rice paddies. The goal was to create a series of exhibition spaces that are diverse in character as well as to create a private workzone for the artist. Varied special conditions were achieved by controlling the qualities of light, primarily through the use of luminous polycarbonate cladding.

MATERIALITY

All of the finished materials—cedar, cementitious panels, sheet metal, and corrugated plastic sheet—are readymade products that can be purchased at building materials retail suppliers without need for customization or special orders. The theme of interconnected space is achieved by controlling the transparency, translucency, and opacity of the five volumes. Polycarbonate is used as the translucent material, which is ideal as a diffused light filter for viewing artwork. Transparency is achieved with glass and opacity with cementitious panels.

The luminous exterior wall is made using light-transmitting cladding over a simple frame. No other materials are present, thus thermal insulation is low, and all building services are distributed elsewhere. Because so much is observable, the designer can reassess conventional features such as stud spacing to subtly affect the reading of space and to filter natural light.

The quality and quantity of daytime lighting in the gallery is excellent due to light-transmitting cladding and reflective interior finishes, resulting in a significant reduction in artificial lighting needs. Profiled polymer products optically distort light, thus even clear material such as used in this project offer an unfocused view to the surroundings. This was a desirable quality in this project, in order to focus one's attention on the installations within the space.

TECHNICAL

The primary structural system is a steel frame, while the secondary structural system is a light cedar stud frame. The east and west elevations of the gallery level are clad with clear corrugated polycarbonate, installed on both sides of the painted cedar stud frame. This material is also used as interior partition cladding in some locations.

The polycarbonate sheets are 22.7 in. (576 mm) high and are lapped 3.1 in. (80 mm) at horizontal seams. The corrugation profile is .35 in. (9 mm) deep; metal extrusions and gaskets receive the polycarbonate at all corners and edges. Fasteners securing the polycarbonate are 7.6 in. (192 mm) on center, vertically. Studs supporting the cladding vary in their spacing; they are 10.5 in. (268 mm) on center on the west elevation, 21.2 in. (538 mm) on center on the east elevation, and 27.8 in. (705 mm) on center on an interior partition framing the stair.

01 Site plan
02 West elevation
03 Interior view toward
    polycarbonate wall
04 Stair

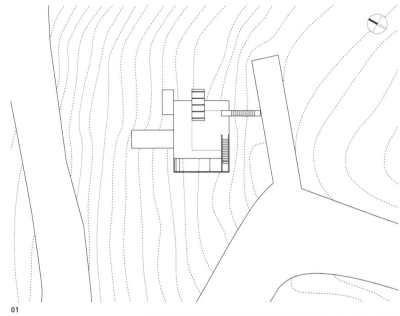

01

02

03

04

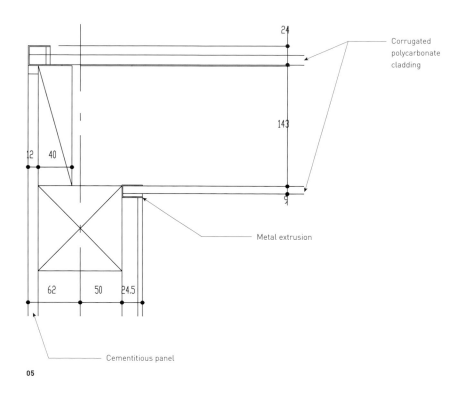

Corrugated polycarbonate cladding

Metal extrusion

Cementitious panel

05

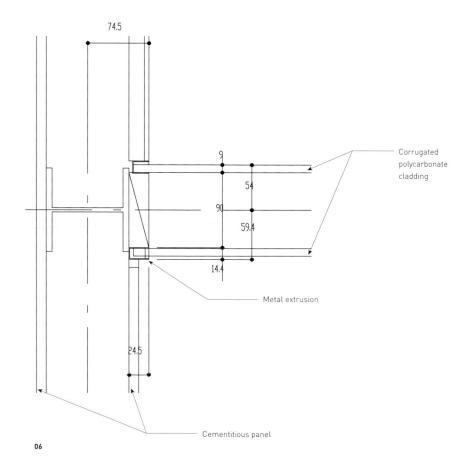

Corrugated polycarbonate cladding

Metal extrusion

Cementitious panel

06

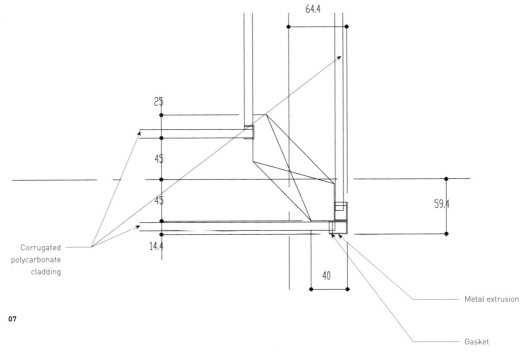

Corrugated
polycarbonate
cladding

Metal extrusion

Gasket

07

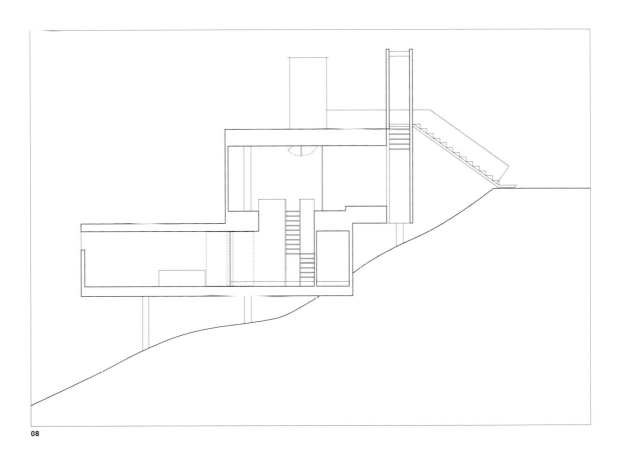

08

50 Argo Street

SOUTH YARRA, AUSTRALIA // O'CONNER + HOULE ARCHITECTURE
POLYCARBONATE VENEER, VISUAL SCREEN

DESIGN INTENTION

This house for a family of five is located in a suburban neighborhood with mixed uses and styles. It is sited on a small corner lot that is just 623 square feet (190 sq. m), approximately 22 percent the size of a tennis court. The small site forced great emphasis to be placed on prioritizing the spatial goals of the family and using the entire site. The design intention was to challenge preconceived ideas of what a new house represents in this diverse neighborhood. Rather than the typical suburban house ideals such as a manicured front yard and driveway, this house attempts to address urban issues such as its two street frontages and its relationship to the overall neighborhood scale. Changing the amount of transparency and visual engagement with the neighborhood on the two street fronts allowed the volume to respond to the context through its scale, by breaking down the material planes through a play of translucency. The challenge was to engage the neighborhood with their day-to-day living while retaining privacy. The wall system is composed of four common materials: translucent plastic, transparent glass, opaque timber frame, and concrete masonry units. This project utilizes the layering of these four planes, creating a rich range from transparent to opaque.

MATERIALITY

The typical wall structure for this house is a concrete block cavity wall with insulation and gypsum board on the interior and corrugated plastic sheeting on the exterior. The use of this plastic cladding on the exterior as a veneer provides for the desired range of translucency. Window openings in the concrete block allow light into the interior while still remaining private behind the polycarbonate. In areas where total transparency was desired, steel-framed windows were inserted into the plane of the plastic wrapping. The different levels of transparency allowed others to see into the house to partially narrate the lives of the family, while still providing for areas of privacy elsewhere. Through the use of plastic this house was able to animate the neighborhood and contribute to the existing architectural context.

Polycarbonate cladding is an outer veneer over the masonry walls of this building. It allows the domestic program of the house to occupy the public edge yet maintain necessary privacy. The polycarbonate cladding gives continuity, almost homogeneity, to all elements on the east elevation, including movable and fixed elements as well as opaque and luminous elements. Few materials are so versatile.

The polycarbonate veneer gives the architect freedom to arrange the apertures on this elevation in unexpected ways because they are seldom seen as one composition, concealed as they are behind the polycarbonate veil. Differences between underlying conditions are made ambiguous by the detailing, in which the veneer edge does not align in all cases with the underlying forms. For instance, the polycarbonate sheets are able to cantilever up to 5.9 in. (150 mm) beyond their support, concealing the mullion or doorframe behind.

TECHNICAL

Polycarbonate diffuses light, is relatively easy to install, and is a resilient siding material. One of its advantages is that gaskets may not be required to achieve a watertight seal, except where moisture is under pressure. Gaskets in a glazing system can shrink, resulting in water leakage. Polycarbonate can be installed in direct contact with wood, concrete, or other materials, perhaps eliminating gaskets or glazing tape below the sheet.

On the primary elevation of this building, translucent corrugated polycarbonate cladding is applied vertically over a masonry or wood-framed wall. The cladding is held off of the outer face of the masonry by 1.97 in. (50 mm) galvanized steel top hat furring strips at 23.62 in. (600 mm) on center at ground level, and at approximately twice that interval on upper levels. In other locations this material is applied to a solid core door, overhead garage door, and over fixed sash, maintaining a unified appearance in the elevation.

The corrugated polycarbonate profile is 1.97 in. (50 mm) deep and has a cycle of 5.9 in. (150 mm). It is secured with hex socket screws with domed neoprene washers. Aluminum angles terminate the polycarbonate cladding at the parapet, corners, and some apertures. In other locations the polycarbonate extends slightly beyond the edge of the masonry substrate. Both of these edge details accommodate minor thermal movement of the polycarbonate cladding.

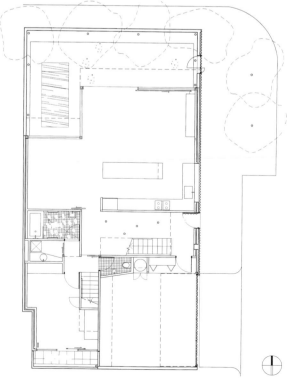

01 Ground-floor plan
02 Major street facade
03 South facade

01

02

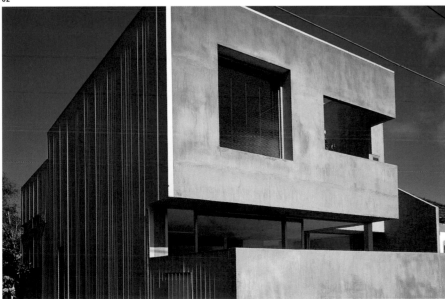

03

04 Wall section detail of south wall
05 Exterior, day
06 Exterior, night
07 Plan detail
08 Plan detail at window

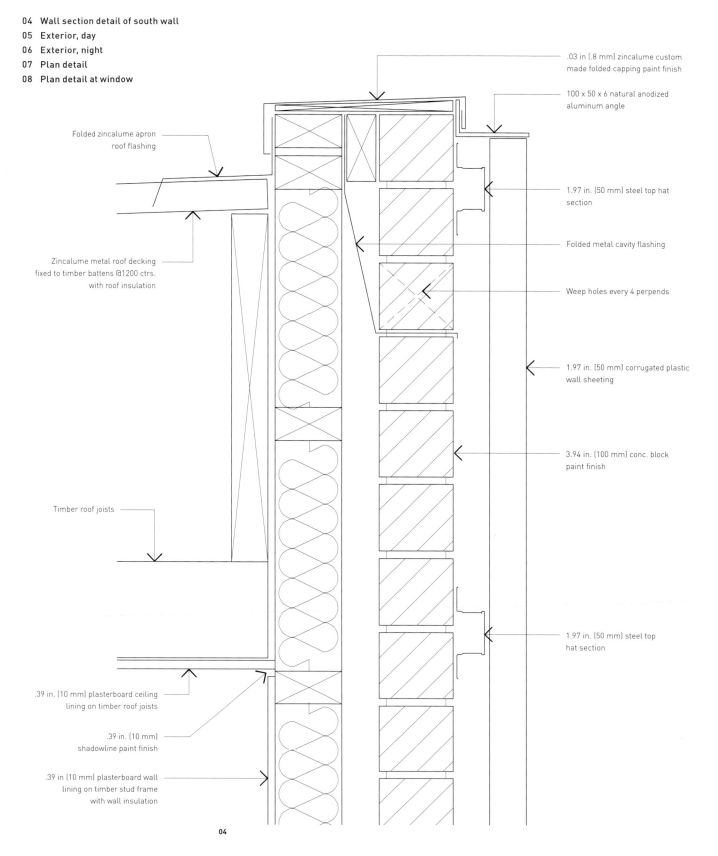

.03 in (.8 mm) zincalume custom
made folded capping paint finish

100 x 50 x 6 natural anodized
aluminum angle

Folded zincalume apron
roof flashing

1.97 in. (50 mm) steel top hat
section

Folded metal cavity flashing

Zincalume metal roof decking
fixed to timber battens @1200 ctrs.
with roof insulation

Weep holes every 4 perpends

1.97 in. (50 mm) corrugated plastic
wall sheeting

3.94 in. (100 mm) conc. block
paint finish

Timber roof joists

1.97 in. (50 mm) steel top
hat section

.39 in. (10 mm) plasterboard ceiling
lining on timber roof joists

.39 in. (10 mm)
shadowline paint finish

.39 in (10 mm) plasterboard wall
lining on timber stud frame
with wall insulation

04

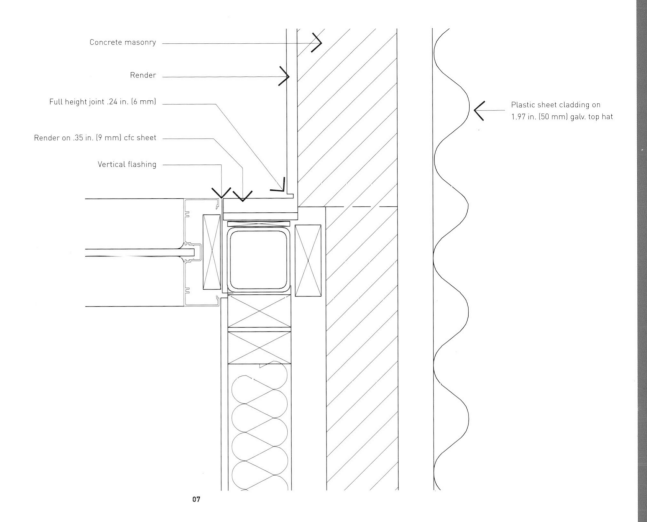

Concrete masonry

Render

Full height joint .24 in. (6 mm)

Render on .35 in. (9 mm) cfc sheet

Vertical flashing

Plastic sheet cladding on
1.97 in. (50 mm) galv. top hat

07

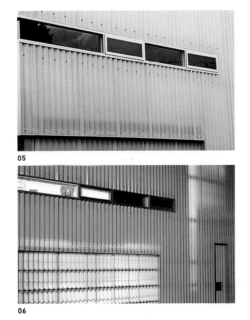

05

06

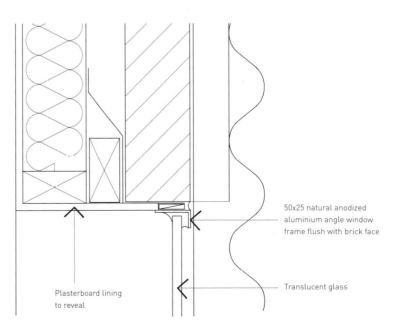

50x25 natural anodized
aluminium angle window
frame flush with brick face

Translucent glass

Plasterboard lining
to reveal

08

House in Imazato

IMAZATO, TAKAMATSU KAGAWA, JAPAN // KATSUYASU KISHIGAMI
CORRUGATED POLYCARBONATE, FILTERED LIGHT AND SOUND

DESIGN INTENTION

This house is located on a small site in the suburbs of a city that is becoming increasingly urbanized and developed. The design concept is to use a courtyard within the residence to organize the interior spaces of the house, allowing for differing levels of privacy. Every room in the house faces in toward the courtyard rather than out to the street. The courtyard internalizes the residence but at the same time allows light to pass through its walls, preventing any feeling of being closed in. The courtyard wall allows for interaction with the outside environment through light, shadow, and sound, all of which are constantly filtering into the space.

MATERIALITY

The traditional theme in Japanese architecture of translucent material over a frame is crafted here using contemporary materials and methods of assembly. Using a translucent polycarbonate sheet for the walls optimally controls the levels of privacy, light, and interaction with the surrounding neighborhood. The courtyard ensures privacy for the residence, but through the use of this translucent material allows for an ever-changing experience within, through the variances of light, shadow, and sound. The courtyard walls are made of corrugated polycarbonate sheets, echoing the characteristic material choice used in the agricultural facilities and greenhouses of this once rural, agricultural area.

The cladding consists of two materials that share many morphological features—corrugated galvarium (thermal spray-coated steel), used to clad climate-controlled private spaces, and corrugated polycarbonate, used to clad the open courtyard. They have identical profiles and are cut to identical modular panel sizes, thus mullion and corner details are consistent, highlighting the convergence by diverse industries to make products that are compatible in their physical characteristics.

TECHNICAL

Polycarbonate is one of the hardest plastics made and can have many times greater impact resistance than glass, which is why it is often used for glazing. The sheets used here transmit 82–89 percent of the incident light, and are approximately 50 percent the weight of glass.

Panels are installed on the inner and outer faces of a steel frame that consists of tube section columns at intervals of 6.89 ft. (210 cm) and light gauge steel sections at 1.38 ft. (42 cm) on center. The corrugated sheets are lapped one cycle at horizontal seams. Screws secure sheets to the steel frame at approximately 5.9 in. (15 cm) intervals vertically.

01 Ground-floor plan
02 Upper-floor plan
03 East-west section
04 North-south section
05 Polycarbonate street facade

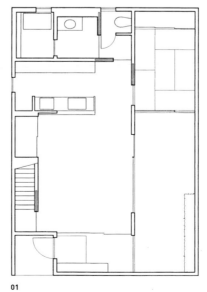

01

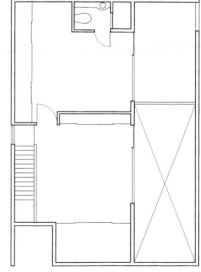

02

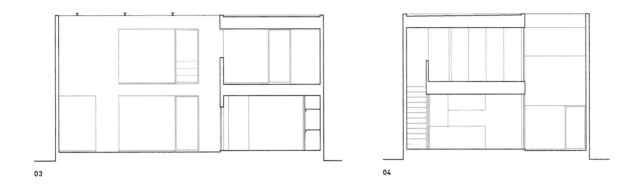

03   04

05

06 Interior courtyard
07 Exterior view at night
08 Plan detail
09 Section detail at top of polycarbonate wall

07

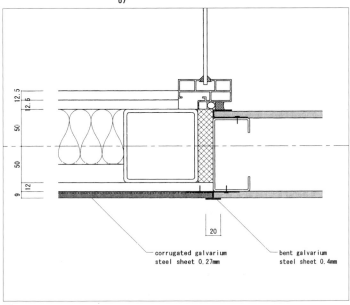

12.5
12.5
50
50
9 | 12

20

corrugated galvarium
steel sheet 0.27mm

bent galvarium
steel sheet 0.4mm

08

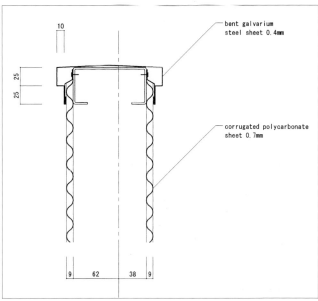

10

25 | 25

25

bent galvarium
steel sheet 0.4mm

corrugated polycarbonate
sheet 0.7mm

9 | 62 | 38 | 9

09

Arauco Express

SANTIAGO, CHILE // FELIPE ASSADI
MULTIWALL POLYCARBONATE SHEET, TRANSPARENCY

DESIGN INTENTION

This building is a pick-up facility for merchandise that was ordered online or through the mail. The simple program consists of a lobby/pick-up area, storage space, and restrooms. The linear floor plan allows for three customers in automobiles to simultaneously be served by the three functions: purchasing, payment, and pick-up. The procedure accommodates people who don't want to leave their vehicle or whose parcel is burdensome. The building is an object in an open retail parking lot and is seen from all sides. It was designed to appear as more than a storage facility, which is the majority of its program. It is a bold, luminous sign advertising its services.

MATERIALITY

The unusual reflectance and transmittance characteristics of multiwalled polycarbonate are demonstrated in this project. The structure is long and narrow—13.12 ft. wide x 49.21 ft. long x 27.89 ft. high (4 x 15 x 8.5 m)—in order to accommodate the drive-by traffic patterns. It is a simple steel structure with a double skin of wood panels, over which is a multilayered polycarbonate skin, giving the building a luminous presence through its translucent layer.

Compared to glass, polycarbonate cladding is lighter, less expensive, and is easier to install using simple details. The building's appearance changes constantly due to varying daylight conditions, and the reflections of passing vehicles. The skin appears translucent during daytime and transparent at night. Between the wood and polycarbonate are 150 blue-hued fluorescent lights to illuminate the building after sundown, when most people pick up their merchandise on their way home from work. The blue light is in contrast to the orange glow of the surrounding street and parking lot lighting, enhancing the building's unique presence. It is a cool, radiant beacon set in the middle of an otherwise nondescript parking lot.

Despite the translucent cladding, the interior spatial conditions are not revealed to the exterior; the translucent skin limits visual access to the shallow layer outside of the programmed spaces.

TECHNICAL

Multiwalled or cellular plastic is an efficient structural shape that provides strength yet is lightweight. Layered thermoplastic elements with complex profiles, such as this double-walled shape, can be easily produced by extrusion. The profiles typically consist of two or more "walls" separated by partitions perpendicular to the faces such as polygal. The plastic product gains rigidity through its multiwalled profile, which also enhances its acoustical and thermal protection and its impact resistance. A variety of specialized chemical treatments can be integrated into the polymer or applied to the surfaces to further enhance thermal and light-transmitting properties of these products.

The polycarbonate skin in this project is made up of sheets that are 3.28 ft. wide x 27.89 ft. long x .39 in. thick (1 m x 8.5 m x 10 mm). The exterior wall height of this building is set by the available length of these sheets, not by the height of the interior space. The length and width of the building also match the module of the cladding panels. The panels are secured in a metal mullion system that is held off of the substrate using steel tube sections at 5.84 ft. (1.78 m) vertically and 3.28 ft. (1 m) horizontally, cantilevered 1.31 ft. (40 cm) off of the primary steel frame. The interstitial space lends visual complexity to the elevation and is sufficient to allow access for maintenance of the skin and lighting fixtures.

The panels have planar surfaces with a series of .39 in. (10 mm) wide cells longitudinally. The webs between cells stiffen the faces and compartmentalize the cavity to improve insulation. The webs also alter light optically, thus the product is considered translucent rather than transparent.

01 Exterior at night
02 Detail

01

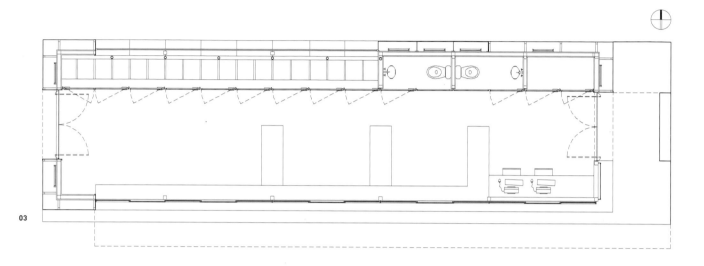

03

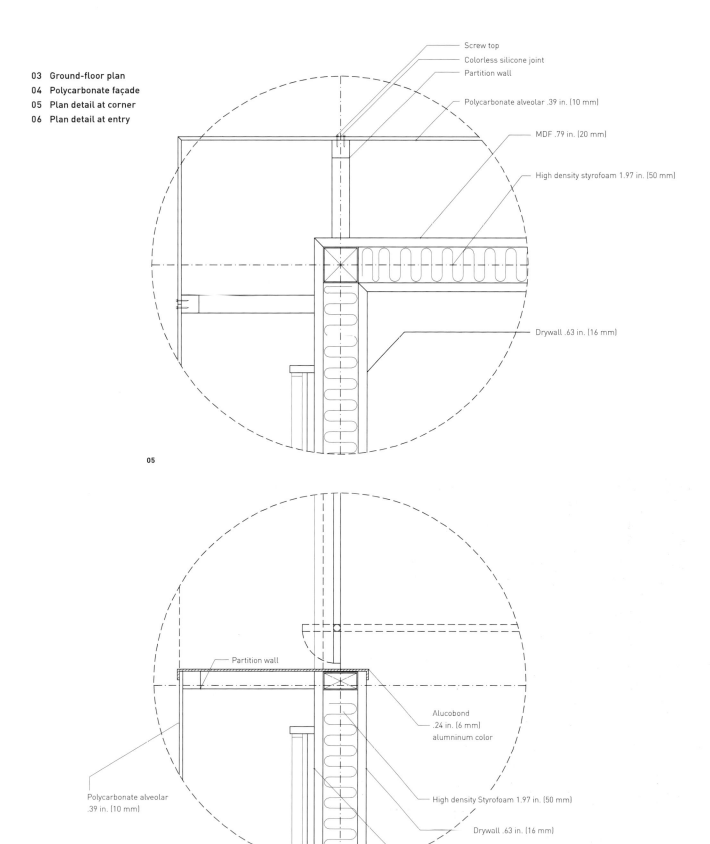

Screw top
Colorless silicone joint
Partition wall
Polycarbonate alveolar .39 in. (10 mm)
MDF .79 in. (20 mm)
High density styrofoam 1.97 in. (50 mm)
Drywall .63 in. (16 mm)

05

Partition wall
Alucobond .24 in. (6 mm) aluminum color
Polycarbonate alveolar .39 in. (10 mm)
High density Styrofoam 1.97 in. (50 mm)
Drywall .63 in. (16 mm)
MDF .79 in. (20 mm)

06

EKO Park Expo Pavilion

WARSAW, POLAND // APA KURYLOWICZ & ASSOCIATES
MULTIWALL POLYCARBONATE SHEET, TRANSLUCENCY

DESIGN INTENTION

This 3,337-square-foot (310 sq. m) rectangular building was originally constructed as a temporary marketing office for a new development of luxury residential buildings in downtown Warsaw. It was built economically with the intention of being disassembled after its initial purpose was fulfilled. Unexpectedly, the building has been kept as an art and architecture exhibition space, becoming a vital resource for the adjacent urban park as a cultural and public building.

The designer's goal was to construct a transparent building from "non-material" elements to allow for the free movement of light, information, and traffic within and around the building. This space changes depending on the time of day and year, weather, and the form of activity within the building. The transparency of the building is further enhanced by the opening of one corner that connects to the park.

MATERIALITY

The goal of "non-materiality," or obscuring the material identities within the building, was accomplished through the application of transparency and translucency. Using this strategy, the cladding material's presence is diminished in favor of other materials and artifacts inside. The building materials do not terminate the visual field; they are not the emphasis. White polycarbonate panels sheath the walls and ceiling to create a simple yet ever-changing interior space, as the dynamic condition of natural light changes constantly over the course of the day and the seasons. The giant yellow typography that screens the polycarbonate facade brands the building as a place of significance within the park. Using white polycarbonate permits plenty of light in the space but also controls unwanted glare.

Multiwall polycarbonate panels are the only moisture barrier or thermal barrier in the public facades of this building. This profile is stiff enough to span the more than 6.56 ft. (2 m) vertically between supports. They are also to a large extent the source of illumination for the gallery during daylight hours. Few materials offer these structural and enclosure capabilities in a single product. The result is an exterior wall that is minimal in its material mass but which offers high performance in terms of the desired features.

These polycarbonate panels are also impact resistant and are easily cleaned, making them a good choice for an urban environment. In this design, damaged panels can be replaced from the exterior with little difficulty.

TECHNICAL

The luminous wall is created by a slender galvanized steel frame and multiwall polycarbonate panels. The panels are 1.69 ft. wide x 28.87 ft. tall x 1.57 in. thick (51.5 x 880 x 4 cm). Polycarbonate panels of this sort are extruded in one axis. In this project the panels were fabricated in building-height dimensions, eliminating the need for intermediate horizontal joints in the elevation, except where the cladding type changes. This eases installation and reduces potential for moisture intrusion at the joints. Aluminum extrusions receive the polycarbonate on all horizontal edges except at the parapet, where the metal coping does so.

The panels are white translucent in most locations, but clear panels are used in one portion of the primary elevation. Near the base of the primary elevation, operable awning sash are clad with coplanar translucent polycarbonate panels. The sash are each 3.28 ft. (100 cm) tall and 5.77 ft. (176 cm) wide, and have an insect screen fixed to the inside of the frame.

Polycarbonate is expected to undergo significant thermal movement, which accumulates in this design chiefly at the top of the building-height panels. The metal coping has a flange, which laps the upper edge of the polycarbonate panels sufficiently to accommodate anticipated movement. The primary structural steel frame has vertical steel trusses bracing the facade at intervals of 11.58 ft. (353 cm). Vertical 3.15 in. (8 cm) steel tube section mullions occur at 5.79 ft. (176.5 cm) intervals. The polycarbonate cladding is braced at intervals of 3.28, 4.92, or 6.56 ft. (1, 1.5, or 2 m) vertically, using horizontal 3.15 in. (8 cm) steel tube sections.

On the primary facade, florescent lighting is mounted vertically at 5.08 ft. (155 cm) intervals in four staggered rows, backlighting the cladding brightly from the interior.

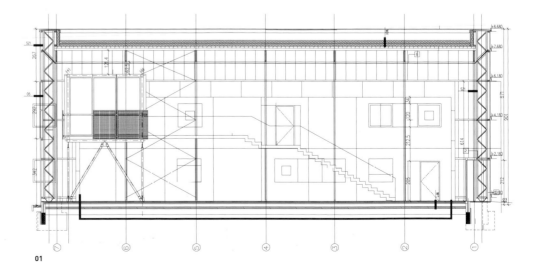

01 Section
02 Ground-floor plan
03 Illuminated exterior view

01

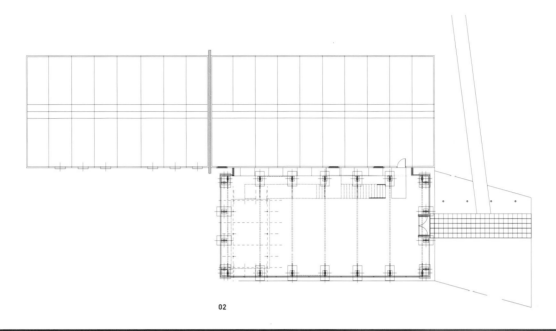

02

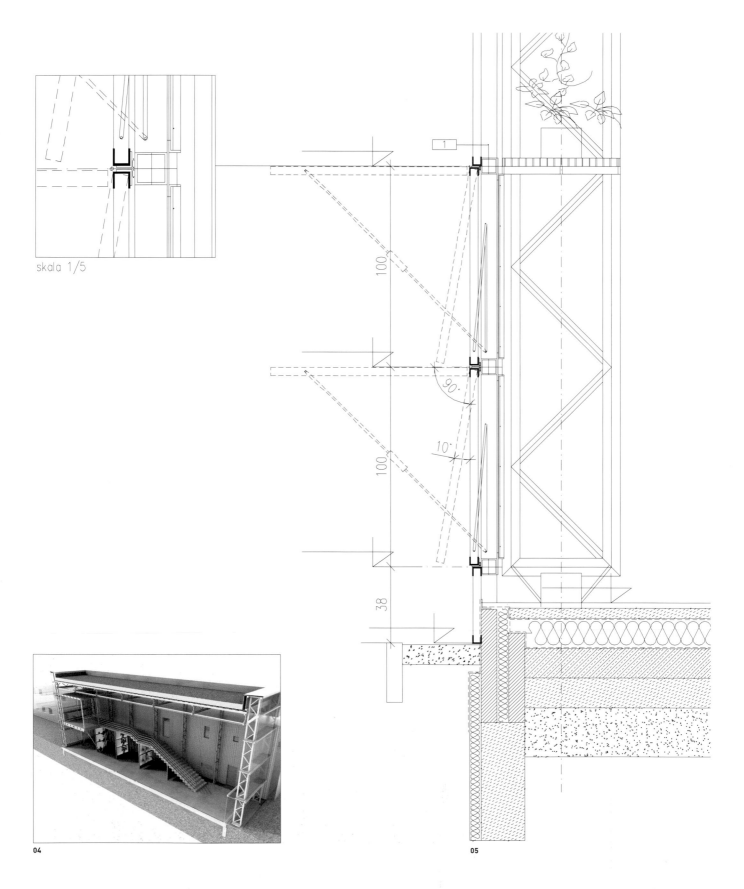

skala 1/5

1

100

90°

10°

100

38

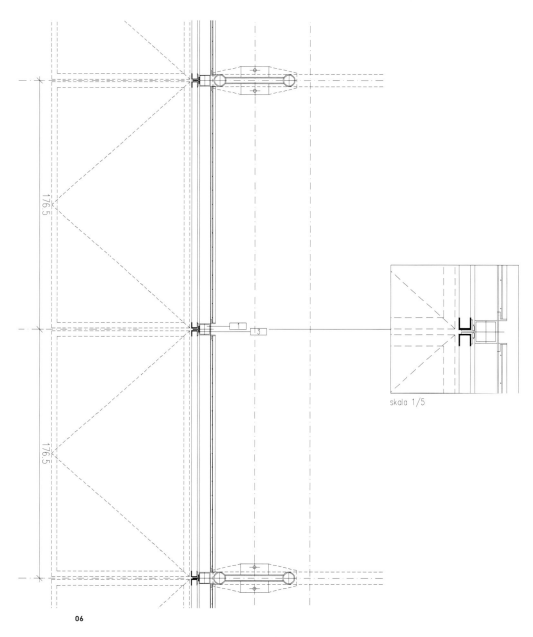

skala 1/5

176.5

176.5

06

07

08

Polymer Engineering Centre

BROADMEADOWS, VICTORIA, AUSTRALIA // COX SANDERSON NESS
FIBERGLASS EXTRUDED CUSTOM PROFILES, THERMAL BRIDGING, GEL-COATING

DESIGN INTENTION

The Polymer Engineering Centre is a 23,680-square-foot (2,200 sq. m) microcosm of a plastics manufacturing plant, replete with laboratories, meeting rooms, offices, and teaching spaces. The design attempts to shape a collaborative role between the public community in the area and private users of the building, as well as a shared link between the plastics industry and the education community. The building is seen as a working model that prepares vocational students for a career in the progressive plastics industry. It is intended to be a showcase for and exemplar of material possibilities. The familiar process of creating plastic by extrusion is the seed of the design concept for the building. The linear form references the extrusion of a material through a die, as is commonly used in plastics manufacturing. This is magnified to the scale of the building's section and repeated along its 262 ft. (80 m) length. In both this building design and in plastics manufacturing, this technique is shown to be an efficient means to produce complex profiles. The building not only advocates for the formal beauty and adaptability of plastic, but also for its environmental qualities.

MATERIALITY

In this project, the wall material is also the roof material; the exterior moisture barrier is also a light-transmitting skin; the insulating system is also a convection system: few materials or assemblies can perform all of these functions. The building is a steel skeleton clad in a double layer of translucent corrugated fiberglass. The plastic skin provides a lightweight solution for thermal bridging and direct heat transmittance while allowing natural lighting throughout most of the building. The translucency of the plastic lights up at night like a lantern and attractively presents the use of plastics in construction to observers. The steel structure is custom made to receive this plastic cladding.

Located in a hot, dry climate, and oriented with its long face toward the hot afternoon sun, this building uses the wall not as a barrier but as a channel for air movement to passively exhaust unwanted heat, simultaneously bringing in optimal daylight and reducing the need for artificial cooling of the interior space.

TECHNICAL

The primary structural system is a steel frame, composed of tube section columns and custom-fabricated trusses to form the curved roof and north wall. Custom-fabricated parallel chord trusses span horizontally between vertical trusses located at gridlines. These trusses occur at intervals varying from 32.1 to 47.9 in. (81.5 to 121.6 cm) on-center vertically to support the inner and outer cladding. They hold the layers of cladding apart to permit air to circulate vertically in the cavity.

The corrugated profile of the cladding stiffens the material in its longitudinal axis but offers inherent flexibility to be curved in the lateral axis, provided the radius of curvature is not too short. Post-tensioning the skin into a curved profile reduces the chance that it will flutter or buckle due to lateral loading. The minimum radius of curvature of the cladding in this project is 15.7 ft. (4.8 m).

The corrugated fiberglass cladding is an Australian-made product called Cool-lite GC, which provides diffused light and only 23.5 percent total heat transmission due to gel-coat technology. Gel-coat is a factory-applied film that has a nominal thickness of .004 in. (100 microns), which is chemically cross-linked to the fiberglass sheet, and therefore unable to delaminate. Tests found it to be the most weather-resistant polymer coating system available. It is expected to significantly improve on the historic tendency of fiberglass to suffer poor translucency, yellowing, and surface erosion over time. Special care was taken to avoid damage to the surface coating during installation.

Corrugated sheeting profiles were installed using the fastening screws together with 1.26 in. (32 mm) weathertight washers for a secure and waterproof finish. The screws were not overtightened, to avoid causing the sheet to buckle, which would allow water penetration at the seal or sheet overlap. Fasteners were installed at every crest at both ends of the sheet and at every second crest at intermediate purlins. Cladding sheets were installed by pre-drilling oversized holes to allow for expansion and contraction. Fiberglass panels undergo thermal movement at less than half the rate of polycarbonate sheets, making them more compatible with steel and aluminum frames and trim.

Where end lapping was required, a minimum 11.81 in. (300 mm) overlap was provided. Foam end closure strips were installed at the ends of the sheets to exclude dirt, birds, and vermin.

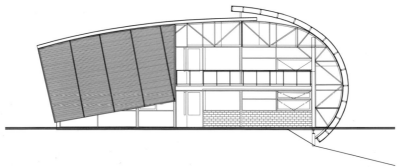

01 North elevation
02 South façade
03 West elevation at night

02

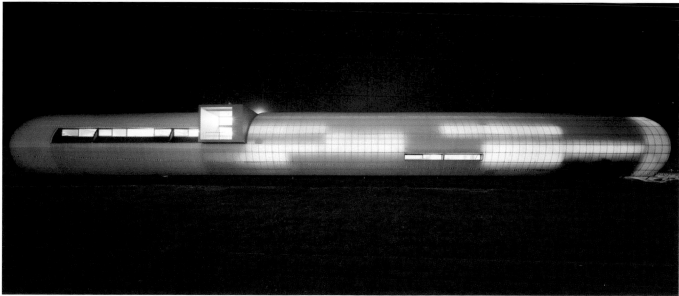

03

04   Structural frame produces building profile
05   Digital model of skin and structure
06   Interior truss supports

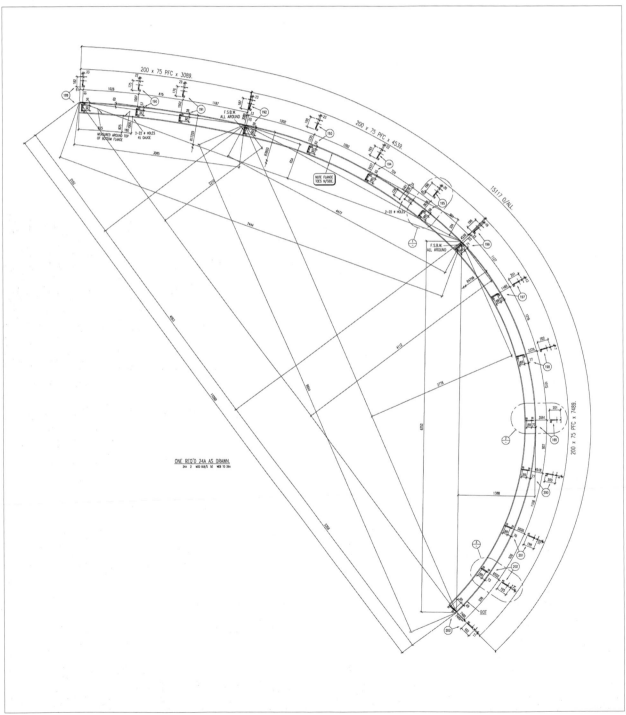

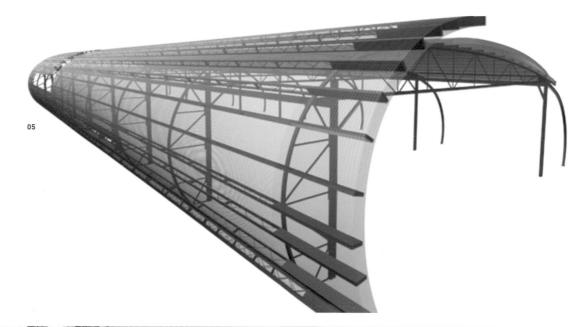

05

06

Montreux Parking Garage

MONTREUX, SWITZERLAND // LUSCHER ARCHITECTS
SILICONE-COATED FIBERGLASS MEMBRANE, TENSILE STRUCTURE

DESIGN INTENTION

The city of Montreux, Switzerland, invited entries for a design competition in 2003 for designing a park and rail garage that would represent "a utility objet d'art" (utilitarian object of art), and using the latest technology in construction. The competition also called for the structure to have a definition and presence at night. This parking garage is located in a dense urban area with close proximity to the rail station Montreux-Oberland Bernois, Golden Pass, and Glion-Naye. The carpark adds seventy parking spaces on top of the existing 219-space facility, and is intended to encourage riding the rail. The concept of the roof is that it is made up of "beams of air" under pressure using a system the designers call "tensairity" (tension + air + integrity), held at each end by metal posts. The color of lighting is modified according to different events happening in the city.

MATERIALITY

A membrane roof was used to create a stark contrast of materials between the heaviness of the solid forms surrounding the station at the edge of Lake Geneva. The lightness and translucency of the membrane gives the roof a fluid and transforming quality. The material allows for a diffusion of daylight into the garage during the day, while at night is lit by different colors creating a distinct landmark in the city.

TECHNICAL

A column-free canopy span of over 90 ft. (28 m) was achieved using an innovative hybrid of conventional steel bowstring truss with a compressed air chamber in place of conventional steel struts. The extraordinarily slender steel tube sections that serve as the compression arch at the top chord of the truss would normally buckle under loads, but is prevented from doing so by the pneumatic chamber that prestresses the steel and stabilizes it laterally. The architects, engineers, and fabricators collaborated in an exemplary fashion, carefully refining and testing a full-scale prototype of the beam to verify its capabilities. The resulting patented truss design is less deep and has half the weight of conventional forms of construction.

The hybrid beam is a truss containing a tapered cylinder that is repeated twelve times at intervals of 19 ft. (5.8 m), resulting in a covering that is 207 ft. (63 m) long, open at both ends to permit vehicular and pedestrian movement. Once the "tensairity" beams were in place, they were draped with a fabric cover to provide weather closure between beams. This fabric is a tensile membrane that is anchored continuously to the steel arch at the top of each beam; at the eaves the canopy is anchored at frequent intervals to the steel tube section that spans in the form of an inverted arch between the top of each column. Precipitation follows the curved roof shapes to leave the roof at mid-points between columns.

Overall beam depth is 4.83 ft. (1,465 mm), spanning 90 ft. (28 m) for a span of approximately nineteen times the depth. Top and bottom chords of the truss are tube sections that are 7.9 in. wide x 3.9 in. deep x 3/16 in. thick (200 x 100 x 5 mm). Gusset plates join them as they converge to bear on the columns. Three lines of steel tubes act as lateral bridging, connecting top chords at every fourth point along their spans.

The fabric used to make the tension membrane is a silicone coated glass fiber fabric; it is fire retardant, somewhat elastic, and has a life expectancy of at least twenty-five years. The air pressure inside the beam is only 2 psi (.0125 MPa). Any drop in pressure is immediately corrected by a compressor that receives a signal by internet from sensors in each beam. At 4 ft. (1,200 mm) intervals along the length of each beam .28 in. (7 mm) threaded tension rods link the arching top chord and horizontal lower chord to keep the compressed air tubes centered in the truss and to prevent them from deforming the steel members.

Naturally luminous by day, the canopy and beams become sources of diffused artificial light at night. Fixtures incorporated into the tapered ends of the air-inflated volumes can be adjusted to introduce white or colored light into the space. The shroud of the light fixture is also the compression ring to which the inflated tubes are anchored using custom fabricated hardware.

The long edges of the facility are screened with a continuous fine stainless steel mesh that is pulled taut vertically between the tops of the 8 degree inclined columns and cast-in-place concrete walls below. The mesh permits plenty of ventilation for the parking facility and offers security to pedestrians and autos in this busy location.

The project was completed eleven months after winning the competition. The unusually long beams were fabricated off site by their developer and delivered to the construction site by rail. Limited staging area near the site made such strategies necessary.

01 Site plan
02 Canopy at dusk
03 Canopy in context of railyard

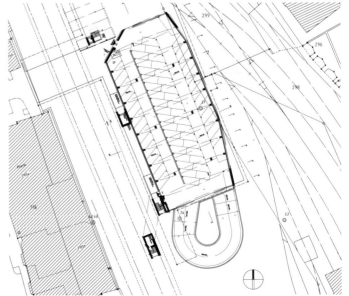

02

03

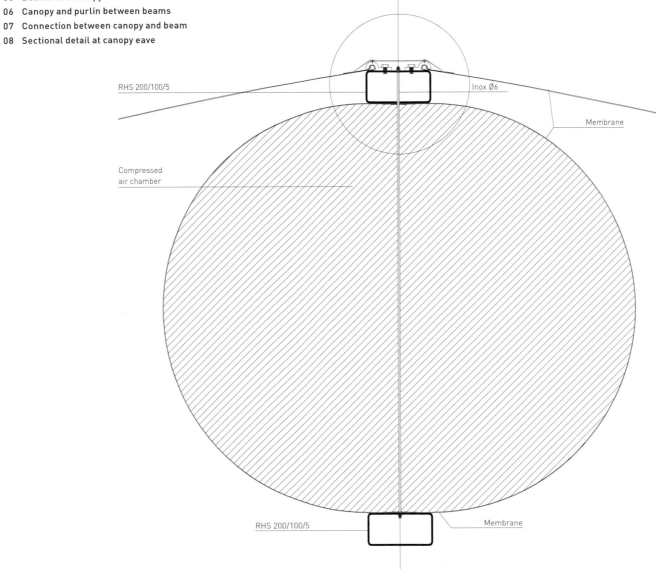

RHS 200/100/5

Inox Ø6

Membrane

Compressed
air chamber

RHS 200/100/5

Membrane

04

05

06

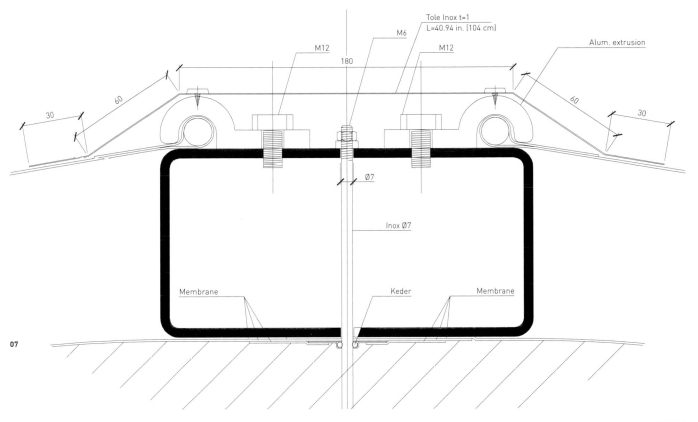

07

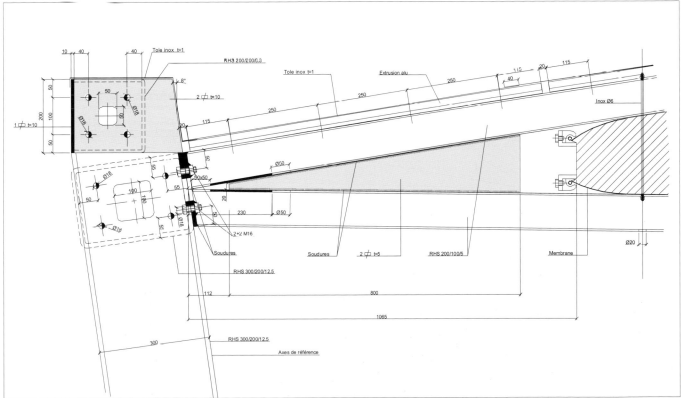

The Olympic Amenities Building

SYDNEY, AUSTRALIA // DURBACH BLOCK MURCUTT ARCHITECTS
TEFLON-COATED FIBERGLASS MEMBRANE

DESIGN INTENTION

This series of identical structures was built for the Sydney 2000 Olympics in a flat, nondescript parking area to act as landmarks or beacons for people arriving by bus and cars. The six ribbed-tension buildings hold restroom facilities, water fountains, and telephones, among other services. One of the primary intentions was that the buildings act as orientation points for visitors via their identifying colors and lights. But most successfully these buildings create a unique presence within the vastness in scale of this setting through the use of form and material. The buildings are efficiently produced using a repetitive plan and a common palette of materials. Each is made recognizably different by varying their color.

MATERIALITY

Several common plastic membranes were considered for the project, which had strict time and budget constraints, as well as an interest in serving as an exemplar regarding sustainable design. The plastic membrane has both a high level of translucency and strength; the curved membrane roof and the varying levels of light throughout the day create a sense of activity and energy. These undulating forms use the fabric membrane as an effective natural illumination by day which then becomes a glowing feature by night.

TECHNICAL

The plastic membrane product used is Flontex, a German-made Teflon sandwich laminate over a woven glass fiber core material. Advantages offered by Teflon-coated fiberglass in this application included its favorably low off-gassing of volatile organic compounds, its resistance to soiling in the environment, and its ability to conform to the shapes called for in the design.

The stitched fabric sheet is simply stretched tautly over the rigid steel frame and pulled down the faces, where its hem was secured using steel plates and screws to the steel members. The fabric is relatively simple in its pattern. Though made of the most durable plastic membrane, the skin was held above floor level to make the passage of people easy and to protect it from the actively curious.

About 2,670 square feet (250 sq. m) of Teflon-coated fiberglass were used to make the roof and upper walls of each building. This project demonstrates the versatility of this material to make a seamless transition from wall to roof, and to be a light-transmitting water barrier.

01 Exterior view, night
02 Interior canopy detail
03 Section
04 Section details

01

02

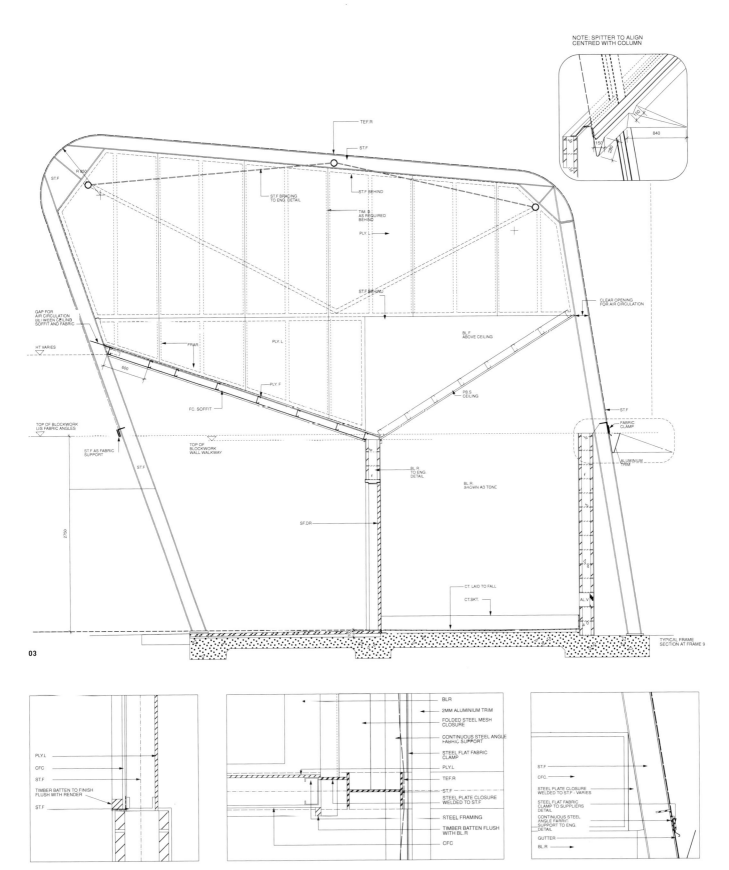

NOTE: SPITTER TO ALIGN
CENTRED WITH COLUMN

150

840

150

280

TEF.R

ST.F

ST.F

R 850

ST.F BEHIND

ST.F BRACING
TO ENG. DETAIL

TIM. D.
AS REQUIRED
BEHIND

PLY. L

ST.F BEHIND

CLEAR OPENING
FOR AIR CIRCULATION

GAP FOR
AIR CIRCULATION
BETWEEN CEILING
SOFFIT AND FABRIC

BL.F
ABOVE CEILING

HT VARIES

600

PLY. L

FRAR

FABRIC
CLAMP

ST.F

PLY. F

PB.S
CEILING

ALUMINIUM
TRIM

FC. SOFFIT

TOP OF BLOCKWORK
U/S FABRIC ANGLES

TOP OF
BLOCKWORK
WALL WALKWAY

ST.F AS FABRIC
SUPPORT

BL.R
TO ENG.
DETAIL

ST.F

BL.R
SHOWN AS TONE

SF.DR

2750

CT. LAID TO FALL

CT.SKT.

AL.V.

TYPICAL FRAME
SECTION AT FRAME 9

03

PLY.L

CFC

ST.F

TIMBER BATTEN TO FINISH
FLUSH WITH RENDER

ST.F

BLR

2MM ALUMINIUM TRIM

FOLDED STEEL MESH
CLOSURE

CONTINUOUS STEEL ANGLE
FABRIC SUPPORT

STEEL FLAT FABRIC
CLAMP

PLY.L

TEF.R

ST.F

STEEL PLATE CLOSURE
WELDED TO ST.F

STEEL FRAMING

TIMBER BATTEN FLUSH
WITH BL.R

CFC

ST.F

CFC.

STEEL PLATE CLOSURE
WELDED TO ST.F - VARIES

STEEL FLAT FABRIC
CLAMP TO SUPPLIERS
DETAIL

CONTINUOUS STEEL
ANGLE FABRIC
SUPPORT TO ENG.
DETAIL

GUTTER

BL.R

04

Index

Bibliography

Allen, Edward. *Fundamentals of Building Construction: Materials and Methods*. New York: John Wiley and Sons, 2004.

Brock, Linda. *Designing the Exterior Wall: An Architectural Guide to the Vertical Envelope*. New York: John Wiley and Sons, 2005.

Cerver, Francisco. *The Architecture of Glass: Shaping Light*. New York: Hearts Books, 1997.

———. *House Details*. New York Whitney Library of Design, 1998.

Ching, Francis D. K., and Cassandra Adams. *Building Construction Illustrated*. New York: John Wiley and Sons, 2001.

Compagno, Andrea . *Intelligent Glass Facades: Material, Practice, Design*. Basel: Birkhauser, 1999.

Cowan, Henry J., and Peter R. Smith, *The Science and Technology of Building Materials*. New York: Van Nostrand Reinhold Company, 1988.

Donzel, Catherine. *New Museums*. Paris: Telleri, 1998.

Ford, Edward. *The Details of Modern Architecture* vols. 1 and 2. Cambridge, Mass.: MIT Press, 1990 (vol. 1) and 1996 (vol. 2).

Frisch, David, and Susan Frisch. *Metal: Design and Fabrication*. New York: Whitney Library of Design, 1998.

Heikkinen, Mikko, and Markku Komonen, "Light Cutting Green Grid," *The Finnish Architectural Review*. 2/2002; p. 36

Hornbostel, Caleb. *Construction Materials: Types, Uses and Applications*, 2nd ed. New York: John Wiley & Sons, 1991.

Hughues, Theodor, Ludwig Steiger, and Johann Weber, *Timber Construction, Details, Products, Case Studies*. Basel: Birkhauser, 2004.

Juracek, Judy A. *Surfaces*. New York: W.W. Norton, 1996.

Kaltenbach, Frank, ed. *Translucent Materials*, Basel: Birkhauser, 2004.

Knapp, Stephen. *The Art of Glass*. Gloucester, MA: Rockport Publishers, 1998.

Krewinkel, Heinz W. *Glass Buildings*. Basel: Birkhauser, 1998.

The Material Connexion Resource Library, New York, NY.

Niesewand, Nonie. *Contemporary Details*. New York: Simon & Schuster, 1992.

Rosen, Harold J., and Tom Heineman. *Architectural Materials for Construction* New York: McGraw-Hill, 1996.

Ruske, Wolfgang. *Timber Construction for Trade, Industry, Administration*. Basel: Birkhauser, 2004.

Schittich, Christian, et al. *Glass Construction Manual*. Birkhauser, 1999.

Stungo, Naomi. *Wood: New Directions in Design and Architecture*. San Francisco: Chronicle Books, 1998.

Wiggington, Michael. *Glass in Architecture*. London: Phaidon, 1996.

Zahner, L. William. *Architectural Metals: A Guide to Selection, Specification, and Performance*. New York: John Wiley and Sons, 1995.

Illustration Credits

The drawings that appear in this volume were provided by the architects, using the graphic symbols and drafting conventions common in their practices. Minor alterations to these drawings have been made to translate notes and convert some dimensions to make the information more broadly useful to readers.

Page 12 James Carpenter Associates
Page 52 Ulrich Schwartz
Page 106, 115 Herrn Eduard Hueber
Page 144 Willem Franken Fotographie
Page 218 Tohru Waki

Glass
440 House
01–08 Fougeron Architecture

Architecture Pavilion of Braunschweig Technical University
01, 04–06 Von Gerkan, Marg and Partners; 02, 03, 07, 08 Klemens Ortmeyer

Church of the Sacred Heart
01, 02, 04 Florian Holzherr; 03, 05, 06 Allmann Sattler Wappner Architekten; 07 Jens Passoth

Crystal Unit III
01, 05 Kubota Architect Atelier; 02–04 Nobuaki Nakagawa

The German Foreign Ministry, Lichthof facade and roof
01–08 James Carpenter Design Associates

Glass Stair
01, 04, 05 Paul Warchol; 02, 03 Architecture Research Office (ARO) with Guy Nordenson, engineer

Laminata Glass House
01, 03 Kruunenberg Van der Erve Architecten; 02, 04–06 Luuk Kramer Fotographie

Masons Bend Community Center
01–05 Bryan Bell

New 42 Studios
01, 04 Platt Byard Dovell White Architects; 02, 03 Elliott Kaufman

R128
01, 03, 05, 06 Werner Sobek; 02, 04, 08, Roland Halbe

Concrete
Burley Barling House
01, 03, 05, 08 Ward Carter Art & Architecture; 02, 04, 06, 07 Derek Swalwell

Crematorium
01 Werner Huthmacher; 02 Axel Schultes Architekten; 03 Ulrich Schwartz

De Blas House
01–06 Alberto Campo Baeza
Falmouth Recreation Center
01–08 Galante Architecture Studio

Hafengebaude Rohner
01, 05 Herrn Eduard Hueber; 02–04 Baumschlager & Eberle

Harrison Residence
01, 02, 06, 07, 09 Ward Carter Art & Architecture; 03–05, 08 Derek Swalwell

LOOK UP Office
01, 06–08 Anin Jeromin Fitilidis & Partner; 02–05 Holger Knauf

Maryhill Museum of Art Overlook
01–07 Allied Works

Price O'Reilly House
01, 02, 05 Engelen Moore; 03, 04 Ross Honeycutt

Retirement Home
01, 02, 04, 09 Steinmann & Schmid Architekten; 03, 05–08 Ruedi Walti Fotograf

Signal Box Switching Station
01, 02, 05 Gigon/Guyer Architekten; 03, 06 Harald F. Müller; 04, 07 Heinrincht Helfenstein

Valdemaqueda Town Hall
01, 04–06 Paredes Pedrosa Arquitectos; 02, 03 Sánchez & Baltanás

Yamaguchi Prefecture Pavilion
01, 04, 07, 08 Kubota Architect Atelier; 02, 03, 05, 06 Mitsuo Matsuoka

Wood
Bamboo Canopy
01, 04, 06 nArchitects; 02, 03 Frank Oudeman; 05, 07, 08 Jorge Pereira

BTV Commercial and Residential Building
01, 04, 05 Baumschlager & Eberle; 02, 03, 06 Herrn Eduard Hueber

GucklHupf
01, 02 Paul Ott and Hans Peter Wörndl; 03, 04 Hans Peter Wörndl
House in Kromeriz
01, 02, 05, 07 ARCHTEAM; 03, 04, 06 Ester Havlova

ILMASI School
01, 06–08 Despang Architekten; 02–05 Olaf Baumann

Messenger House II
01, 02, 08–13 MacKay-Lyons Sweetapple Architects; 03, 05, 07 Steven Evans; 04, 06 James Steeves

Sirch Woodworking Manufacturing
01, 04, 06, 08 Baumschlager & Eberle; 02, 03, 05, 07 Herrn Eduard Hueber

Think Tank
01–03 Gumuchdjian Architects

Metal
Aluminum Forest
01, 02 Willem Franken Fotographie; 03, 04 Architectenbureau Micha de Haas

Christ Pavilion, Expo 2000
01, 04–06, 09 Von Gerkan, Marg and Partners; 02, 03, 07, 08, 10, 11 Klaus Frahm and Jürgen Schmidt

Embassies of the Nordic Countries in Berlin-Tiergarten
01, 03, 04, 07, 10 Christian Richters; 02, 05, 06, 08, 09, 11 Berger & Parkkinen

Future Shack
01–07 Sean Godsell

Kavel 37
01, 02, 07–09 Heren 5 Architecten; 03–06 Kees Hummel

Kew House
01–06 Sean Godsell

Liner Museum
01, 04 Gigon/Guyer Architekten; 02, 03, 05 Heinright Helfenstein

Max Planck Institute
01, 03, 04 Heikkinen-Komonen Architects; 02, 05, 06 Jussi Tiainen

Melbourne Museum
01, 04, 05 Denton Corker Marshall; 02, 03
John Gollings

Mining Archives
01–03, 07 Von Gerkan, Marg and Partners; 04,
05 Jürgen Schmidt; 06 Klaus Frahm

Modular VII Chiller Plant
01, 02, 04 Esto Photographics; 03, 05, 06 Leers
Weinzapfel Associates

Power Station North
01 Eduard Hueber; 02–05 Bétrix &
Consolascio Architekten

Raum Zita Kern
01, 04, 05 Margherita Spiluttini; 02, 03 Artec

Sauna Pavilion
01, 03, 04 Artifact Design & Construction; 02,
05–07 David Joseph

Schemata XI
01–09 Studio 804, University of Kansas

Springtecture H
01, 02, 05 Yoshiharu Matsumura; 03, 04
Shuhei Endo

Südwestmetall Reutlingen
01, 03–05 Allmann Sattler Wappner
Architekten; 02, 06, 07 Jens Passoth

Tram Stations
01–12 Despang Architekten

Plastic
50 Argo Street
01–07 O'Connor & Houle Architecture

Arauco Express
01, 02, 04 Juan Purcell; 03, 05, 06
Felipe Assadi

Church in Urubo
01, 02 Jae Cha; 03–05 Daniel Lama

Colmenarejo Municipal Hall and Main Square
01, 05, 09 Abalos & Herreros; 02–04 Marie
Bleda and Jose Marie Rosa

Eko Park Expo Pavilion
01, 02, 05, 06 APA Kurylowicz & Associates;
03, 04, 07, 08 Wojciech Krynski

House in Imazato
01–04, 08, 09 Katsuyasu Kishigami; 05–07
Tohru Waki

Ma Atalier and Gallery, Fukuoka Prefecture
01, 05–08 Hiroyuki Arima & Urban Fourth;
02–04 Kouji Okamoto

Montreaux Parking Garage
01–08 Luscher Architects

The Olympic Amenities Building
01, 02 John Gollings and Patrick Bingham
Hall; 03, 04 Durbach Block Associates

Polymer Engineering Center
01, 04, 05 Cox Sanderson Ness; 02, 03, 06
Diana Snape, Gollings Studio

Shiloh Bus Shelter
01–02 Bryan Bell